TEACHING COMPREHENSION

A Systematic and Practical Framework With Lessons and Strategies

Eileen Carr, Ph.D.,
Loviah Aldinger, Ph.D.,
Judythe Patberg, Ph.D.

from THINKING**WORKS**

New York • Toronto • London • Auckland • Sydney
Mexico City • New Delhi • Hong Kong • Buenos Aires

Teaching *Resources*

Author Dedications

EILEEN CARR: *For my husband, our children, and their families, thank you for your love and support.*

LOVIAH ALDINGER: *To my husband, Dick, and our Louie. Thank you for always being there.*

JUDYTHE PATBERG: *To my husband, Bill, and my sons— Will, Zach, and Jon—who show me the joy of living every day.*

Acknowledgments

We wish to thank all ThinkingWorks teachers and students. Their support and enthusiasm is greatly appreciated. A special thanks to the following teachers who shared their work and their students' work for this book:

Diana Baden	Jeffrey Eccleston	Karen Mitchell
Verdell Battle	Kristine Edler	Betty Newton
Marilyn Baugh	Rose Gadus	Carolyn Nusbaum
Dawn Becker	Yvonne Gayle	Linda Pratt
Andrea Bennett	Robin	Tracy Preuss
Kristi Bettinger	Gerkensmeyer	Ann Randolph
Julie Boice	Holly Glassford	Desi Ruiz
Christine Brewer	Donna Hester	Nancy Schroeder
Sheryl Brown	Judy Hirsch	Andrea Snyder
Deborah Carlisle	Karen Kerekes	Ann Stvartak
Barbara Cook	Shauna Klausner	Claudia Trombla
Pat Daniel	Helen Lazette	Tara Urbanyi
Jessica Daoust	Rebecca Levison	Katherine Wait
Mattie DeWeese	Jamie Lyell	Julie Wallace
Matt Dombi	Kathleen Mattimoe	Cheryl Wozniak
Lorraine Doner	Anita Mauter	Ronnell Zeisler
Susan Drabek	Jim McMorgan	
Andrew Dugan	Denise Melter	

Cover design by Josué Castilleja
Interior design by Maria Lilja
Photo credits: James Levin/Studio 10/SODA, pages 7, 37, 67, 113, 175, 221;
Tom Hurst/SODA, pages 89, 139, 203

1 2 3 4 5 6 7 8 9 10   40   10 09 08 07 06 05 04

Table of Contents

CHAPTER 8: Assessment of ThinkingWorks Strategies . .203

CHAPTER 9: Putting It All Together .221

APPENDIX A: Alignment of ThinkingWorks Strategies With Cognitive Processes . . .262

APPENDIX B: ThinkingWorks Strategies Aligned to Standards .266

REFERENCES 275

Introduction

As university teacher educators, we have long believed in the efficacy and worth of strategies instruction as a vehicle for helping students understand both narrative and expository text. Because school districts often ask us to work with their teachers on improving students' comprehension of text and application of learning, we decided to address in our courses and institutes on teaching comprehension what we saw as several major problems associated with strategies instruction. Teachers had little information about the kinds of thinking the strategies encouraged students to engage in when reading text and why strategies instruction could be so effective in helping students both learn from text and transform what they learn to express their own ideas and create new knowledge. Another problem that we saw was that there were numerous strategies that research had proven to be effective and teachers were wondering how to integrate those strategies into their instruction in a practical, feasible way. We developed the ThinkingWorks framework and this book as a response to those problems.

We've taught the ThinkingWorks framework to over 5,000 teachers in urban, suburban and rural school districts. Often, teachers from the same school have participated in the program so that they could use the framework and strategies across content areas and grade levels. In the past few years, we have reviewed and refined the framework, even developing a few new strategies or adapting some existing ones. We hope that you will find this book valuable and use it to implement comprehension instruction in your classroom.

Eileen Carr

Toviah Aldinger

Judythe Patberg

CHAPTER 1

Comprehension
Strategies
Instruction

KINDERGARTEN TEACHER: *Isn't a lot of comprehension instruction too difficult for my students? They can't read and their attention span is so short. Aren't we pushing them too much?*

GRADE ONE TEACHER: *My students are just beginning to read. They need a lot of practice with word recognition. That's where most of our time is spent.*

GRADE TWO TEACHER: *Word recognition and fluency are still top priority so that my students will be ready to "read to learn."*

GRADE THREE TEACHER: *I don't know where to begin. How can I differentiate comprehension instruction to meet the diverse needs of my students?*

GRADE FOUR TEACHER: *I have so much content to cover and all the state and national standards to consider. How can I do all that and spend time teaching comprehension?*

GRADE FIVE TEACHER: *My students have difficulty inferring meaning and analyzing text. Are there strategies to help them?*

GRADE SIX TEACHER: *Extending meaning is our problem. How can I encourage my students to transfer what they have learned to new situations?*

We hear comments like these in every school we visit, both here in Ohio and across the country. Clearly, teachers want their students to read and understand text, but too often when it comes to teaching, they don't know where to start or how to fit reading instruction into their already busy schedules. We believe that giving students the tools to comprehend is at the core of all student learning. As such, comprehension instruction should be woven into everyday teaching. Just how to do this is a challenge we all face, as evidenced in the teacher comments above. In response to this need for a practical, meaningful way of teaching reading comprehension, we have developed the ThinkingWorks framework. The lesson planning guide and strategies instruction described in this book offer a complete model of teaching for comprehension so that all students can succeed as readers. See Figure 1A for a graphic overview of the ThinkingWorks framework.

The purpose of this book is to provide you with a way of selecting and implementing research-based strategies that will help students in grades K–6 comprehend text and apply what they have learned. In this chapter, we begin by discussing research on the comprehension process and on comprehension instruction. We then describe cognitive processes that research shows are essential for understanding text and applying what we've learned. We introduce the ThinkingWorks Lesson Planning

Guide, which is a systematic, practical way to plan lessons with strategies that will help your students use the cognitive processes necessary for comprehension and higher level thinking (see Figure 1B on page 12). Using the framework, you plan a lesson that consists of four strategy components: background knowledge, vocabulary, comprehension, and application/extension. After describing those components, we present sample lessons using the framework. We then describe and give examples of the Direct Explanation Model, an effective teaching model on which our strategies instruction is based. We end the chapter with a description of how the book is organized.

FIGURE 1A

WHAT IS IT?

An easy-to-use lesson planning guide that facilitates reading strategies instruction

WHY IS IT EFFECTIVE?

- Develops cognitive processes
- Organizes reading strategies into four manageable, meaningful categories
- Links to state learning standards

ThinkingWorks Framework

HOW DOES IT WORK?

Teachers prepare a lesson by selecting four strategies to meet the needs of their students. They record on the lesson planning guide the cognitive and language processes that the lesson encourages students to use.

	STRATEGIES			
	Background Knowledge	Vocabulary	Comprehension	Application/Extension
COGNITIVE PROCESSES	Structured Overview	Personal Clues	Frames/Summaries	Discussion Web/Summary or Editorial
Develop Background Knowledge	✔			
Expand Vocabulary Knowledge	✔	✔		
Use Text Structure	✔		✔	
Set a Purpose for Learning	✔		✔	
Infer/Select Information			✔	
Create Images			✔	
Relate/Connect Ideas			✔	
Clarify/Monitor Understanding			✔	
Analyze			✔	✔/✔
Synthesize				✔/✔
Evaluate/Justify				✔/✔
Create/Invent				
LANGUAGE PROCESSES				
Read			✔	/✔
Write			/✔	✔
Listen/View	✔	✔	✔/✔	✔
Communicate Orally	✔	✔	✔/✔	✔/

What are cognitive processes?

Cognitive processes are thinking skills that readers use to comprehend text and apply what they've learned. Examples are inferring, relating and connecting ideas, and monitoring comprehension. Cognitive processes are not used discretely, but are interconnected. Mature readers use a network or group of processes that work together when they read and think critically.

What are comprehension strategies?

Comprehension strategies are protocols or procedures we can teach students that will lead them to use the cognitive processes that are critical to comprehension and application of learning. Examples are summarization strategies (e.g., Four-Step Summary, About Point Writing Response), questioning strategies (e.g., Question Answer Relationship, Questions for Quality Thinking) and prediction strategies (e.g., Prediction, Prediction Chart). Comprehension strategies are not to be taught or used as rote procedures. Rather, accompanied by think-alouds or cognitive modeling, first by the teacher and then by both the teacher and students, these strategies help make students aware of the types of thinking they are doing when comprehending text and applying learning. By using comprehension strategies, students practice using cognitive processes and eventually learn to use the processes independently and automatically.

Research About Comprehension and Comprehension Instruction

Research has given us a lot of information about the cognitive processes that skilled readers must use as they read in order to comprehend and apply information. Comprehension itself involves more than thirty such cognitive processes, including activating background knowledge, monitoring comprehension, drawing inferences, creating mental imagery, and bringing to bear a knowledge of text structure (Block & Pressley, 2002). Students who are not able to use these cognitive processes profitably and automatically by grade three may fall so far below their peers that they will not catch up, even if their decoding skills are at grade level (Block, 2000).

Experienced readers employ these processes automatically. In fact, these processes seem so natural that we may not even be aware we are using them. In that sense, they are hidden. For example, a critical cognitive process is *inferring*. Yet many of us wonder how we learn to infer and, by extension, how we can actually teach students to infer. Here's where the research comes in: studies have identified both cognitive processes and the strategies that students can use to initiate these processes. These strategies include overt steps or procedures that act like a road map of how to think.

Since the late 1970s, researchers have validated a number of individual strategies consisting of routines or procedures that students can follow to improve their comprehension of text—strategies that can be applied before, during, and after reading (Pressley et al., 1992). For example, prediction and summarization strategies encourage readers to use a number of cognitive processes and therefore think in particular ways. Prediction is a powerful strategy that requires students to use the cognitive processes of inferring and setting a purpose for learning. Summarization strategies require students to use the cognitive processes of inferring, selecting and relating important ideas, and monitoring comprehension.

Recent research has focused on the development of flexible approaches to the teaching of comprehension strategies. Since not all strategies work equally well in all situations (or for all learners), researchers suggest that students benefit from instruction in the use of a repertoire of reading comprehension strategies (Duke & Pearson, 2002; Pressley, 2002). The strategies that we introduce in this book are in essence "thinking tools" that students can use flexibly to help them comprehend text and apply what they have learned. Through instruction over a period of time—a process that includes teacher explanation, cognitive modeling, and student practice—students learn how to use strategies that involve the coordination and use of multiple cognitive processes.

As we mentioned earlier, comprehension strategies consist of specific steps or procedures. However, our goal is not to teach students to use a set of rote procedures for a particular strategy and leave it at that. Quite often students are asked to complete comprehension strategies without being made aware of the cognitive processes they are using. We believe a different approach is needed. We suggest that, when teaching students to use a strategy, you use cognitive modeling, or think-alouds, to show students your own thinking processes. You can also encourage students to model out loud their thinking as they complete a strategy. By discussing the cognitive processes we use when we complete a strategy, we help students become conscious of how they are thinking. Eventually, with repeated use of a strategy, students will learn to use cognitive processes independently and automatically.

Cognitive Processes Used in the ThinkingWorks Framework

The ThinkingWorks framework is a lesson planning guide (see Figure 1B) that utilizes twelve cognitive processes essential for the comprehension of text and the application of learning. Our aim, in limiting the processes to twelve, is to take the many processes that have been identified in the research and reduce them to a smaller set of descriptors (Ennis, 1985). We consider the processes that we use in the framework to be super-ordinate in nature, meaning they encompass other cognitive processes. For example, inferring is the foundation of processes such as pausing to reflect, drawing conclusions, and interpreting an author's perspective. We believe that using our set of processes will make your comprehension instruction both manageable and reflective of what happens when students read and think effectively. In addition to cognitive processes, the framework also includes the four language processes of reading, writing, listening/viewing, and oral communication. In planning a lesson, you will want to consider which language processes your students will be using. Some lessons may focus on students' use of oral language skills, others may require students to do writing connected to reading, while still others may involve students in using all four language processes.

Following is an explanation of the cognitive processes that appear in the framework (Carr & Aldinger, 1994; Carr, Aldinger, & Patberg, 2000).

ACTIVATE/BUILD BACKGROUND KNOWLEDGE Students' background knowledge acts as a data bank from which to draw experiences that will help them understand and reflect on new information (Johnson & Pearson, 1984). Teachers should assess and help students build, extend, and activate their relevant background knowledge. The activation and building of background knowledge is critical and underlies all of the other cognitive processes in our framework, each of which has been identified as essential for learning.

EXPAND VOCABULARY KNOWLEDGE Many words students encounter are labels for unfamiliar concepts. If learners do not know key vocabulary in a text, they will have difficulty understanding new information (Biemiller, 2001). Students should be actively involved in learning definitions of words by elaborating

---

FIGURE 1B

ThinkingWorks Lesson Planning Guide

	STRATEGIES			
	Background Knowledge	Vocabulary	Comprehension	Application/ Extension
COGNITIVE PROCESSES				
Develop Background Knowledge				
Expand Vocabulary Knowledge				
Use Text Structure				
Set a Purpose for Learning				
Infer/Select Information				
Create Images				
Relate/Connect Ideas				
Clarify/Monitor Understanding				
Analyze				
Synthesize				
Evaluate/Justify				
Create/Invent				
LANGUAGE PROCESSES				
Read				
Write				
Listen/View				
Communicate Orally				

on their meaning and linking new words and meanings to their own background knowledge (Carr & Wixson, 1986). Through effective vocabulary instruction and wide reading, students are able to expand their vocabulary and learn word meanings independently (Graves & Watts-Taffe, 2002).

USE TEXT STRUCTURE Knowledge of how a text is organized helps readers understand and apply information (Pearson & Gallagher, 1983). Text structure also provides an outline for writing and summarizing information. In addition to identifying and using the author's structure in narrative and expository text, students need to learn how to impose their own structure on unorganized information.

SET A PURPOSE FOR LEARNING Setting a purpose for learning helps students to focus on information while reading and to recall certain aspects of the text (Prichert & Anderson, 1977). It is important for students to be able to set their own purpose for learning, independent of teacher input.

INFER/SELECT INFORMATION Information about concepts that students must understand is not usually stated explicitly in the text but must be constructed by the reader. The reader selects relevant information for inferring by discerning a variety of clues in the text and by connecting that information to his or her background knowledge (Carr, Dewitz, & Patberg, 1989). Inferring is a critical cognitive process because it allows readers to construct main ideas, predict and hypothesize, draw conclusions, recognize and interpret authors' perspectives, generate and answer questions, compare and contrast information, and paraphrase information.

CREATE MENTAL IMAGES Mental images add depth and breadth to learning (Gambrell & Bales, 1986; Trabasso & Bouchard, 2002). They help readers comprehend by linking text information and background knowledge. Constructing meaningful images helps students integrate, retrieve, and retain information.

RELATE/CONNECT IDEAS Relating information within, across, and beyond the text helps the reader make sense of the text and remember and synthesize information (Carr, Dewitz, & Patberg, 1989). Relating ideas involves summarizing, generalizing, questioning, organizing, and reorganizing information.

CLARIFY/MONITOR UNDERSTANDING In order for skilled readers to actively construct meaning from text, they must monitor their comprehension so that they are aware when their understanding falters. They can then call on strategies to help themselves make sense of the text. In other words, skilled readers are metacognitive or strategic readers; they are aware of and in control of using reading strategies to support comprehension (Paris, Lipson, & Wixson, 1983).

ANALYZE Analysis engages students in critical thinking. In analyzing the text, they examine and break information into parts so that they can identify causes or motives, infer information, and find evidence to support generalizations (Bloom, 1956; Perkins, 1990). Analysis helps students process information deeply and critically.

SYNTHESIZE Synthesis extends students' learning by enabling them to think about information in a new way (Bloom, 1956). Students create a "fresh view" of the information by integrating elements in a different format or constructing alternative solutions (Perkins, 1990; Zull, 2002).

EVALUATE/JUSTIFY Evaluation and justification encourage readers to present and defend their opinions about the information presented in a text (Block & Pressley, 2002; Perkins, 1991). Using a set of criteria, they make judgments about the validity and quality of an author's work (Bloom, 1956). This form of critical thinking helps students extend their learning.

CREATE/INVENT Creation and invention require readers to be engaged in inventive and divergent thinking (Costa & Kallick, 2000; Perkins, 1991). Students can use a number of strategies to help them apply learning in new and unique ways.

Remember, as mentioned earlier, cognitive processes are not used individually or separately when we read. They are interconnected. We use them in a group or cluster when we read and think. Encouraging students to use cognitive processes is the goal of all educators because, as they use them, students become better thinkers, readers, and writers in all content areas and across all grade levels.

In the next section, we discuss the strategies section of our framework, or lesson planning guide (Figure 1B). We explain why a ThinkingWorks lesson has four strategy components and what those components are.

The ThinkingWorks Lesson: Four Strategy Components

Research shows that, in addition to a strategy that focuses students' attention on comprehension (e.g., relating, organizing, visualizing, and inferring information in a text), an effective comprehension lesson should include a strategy for helping students activate their background knowledge and a strategy to help them understand important vocabulary (Pressley, 2002). When students link new information to their background knowledge and develop an understanding of key vocabulary in a text, their compre-hension of that text is enhanced. In addition, we recommend that your lesson also include an application/extension strategy, because students need to be able to manipulate and transform information into new understandings and ideas that they express in their own words (Zull, 2002). Applying what they have learned helps students develop new and deeper understandings of information and become independent producers of knowledge (Bloom, 1956; Perkins, 1990; Zull, 2002). We believe that an effective comprehension lesson for either narrative or expository text must contain these four strategy components: background knowledge, vocabulary, comprehension, and application/extension (Carr & Aldinger, 1994; Carr, Aldinger, & Patberg, 2000).

All four strategy components involve students in active thinking and use of the four language processes (e.g., reading, writing, listening/viewing, and oral communication). Many of the strategies incorporate large- and or small-group discussion and thus students have many opportunities to use and develop their listening/viewing and oral communication skills. In addition, we believe that writing in response to reading is a powerful way of understanding and learning content. We show how students can do writing in connection with most of the strategies that we describe in the book. Also, in each of the narrative and expository text chapters, we present specific writing strategies that require students to do different kinds of writing in response to their reading (e.g., summaries, editorials, letters, compare/contrast essays). A key writing strategy that we reference frequently is the About Point Writing Response. We present that strategy in full on page 16; it is a component of many comprehension strategies and writing extensions.

Due to the four-part nature of a ThinkingWorks lesson, you will usually teach the lesson over several class periods and several days. The background knowledge and the vocabulary strategy may be taught on one day, while the comprehension strategy may extend over a two-to-three-day period. You may introduce the application/extension strategy as the culminating part of the lesson on yet another day. The strategy components in a lesson will usually be introduced in a linear fashion, that is, background knowledge and vocabulary strategies before reading, the comprehension strategy next, followed by an application/extension strategy to help students use what they have learned in a new way. However, students may use the strategies in a recursive fashion when they have to activate background knowledge or deal with difficult vocabulary at several points during the lesson. In most cases, the strategies presented in this book can be used with both narrative and expository text. There are a few exceptions, such as Story Grammar and its variations, which are used only with narrative text, and the Exploration Frame, which is used only with science content.

Following is an explanation of each strategy component in the ThinkingWorks framework, including supporting research and examples of strategies.

About Point

Many of the strategies described in this book make use of About Point (Martin, Lorton, Blanc, & Evans, 1977). About Point is a fundamental strategy that helps students determine the main idea of a text. It is extremely effective because it provides students with a simple but powerful way of understanding the main ideas in expository text. Students work their way through a text by examining each paragraph and asking themselves what it's about and what point it makes. They then combine these two pieces of information to construct a statement that reflects the main idea of the paragraph.

For instance, Sarah Murray's fourth graders had read a paragraph about immigration. She decided to use About Point to help her students grasp the main idea of the piece. Her lesson went something like this.

Ms. Murray: We're learning about immigrants to our country. There's so much information to read and remember. We're going to practice a strategy that will help us remember the important points from our reading. It's called About Point, and it will work with anything you read. Let's practice it on this paragraph we just finished. Here's a little organizer we can use to record our thoughts. [Draws About Point outline on board, as shown in Figure 1C.] The first thing we do is ask ourselves, What is this paragraph about? Any thoughts?

Students: Immigrants.

Ms. Murray: Very good. That's the first step. It seems easy, but we need to always keep in mind the topic that we're reading about. We don't want to get distracted by details; we've got to keep the big picture in our heads. Let's write it down [writes *immigrants* in the About section of the organizer]. All right, now that we know what this paragraph is about, we need to determine what point the author is making. We'll ask ourselves, What important point is the author making about the topic, immigrants?

Student 1: Well, it says that immigrants came from Germany.

Ms. Murray: Yes, that's true.

Student 2: It also says that immigrants came from Ireland.

Ms. Murray: That's also true. Is that the main point the writer is making, that immigrants came from Ireland and Germany?

Student 3: It also lists other countries. They came from all over.

Ms. Murray: You're right. Why do you think the author listed all those countries?

Student 2: Maybe she wants us to know that immigrants came from lots of places.

FIGURE 1C

About: Immigrants
Point: came from all over the world to live here

Statement: Immigrants came from all over the world to live here.

Sarah Murray models the use of About Point with this simple organizer.

Ms. Murray:	I think you're on to something. It is important for us to know that people came to our country from all over the world. Do you think that is the main point of this paragraph we just read?
Students:	Yes.
Ms. Murray:	I agree. We'll write, people came from all over the world [writes on organizer under Point]. Now, let's summarize this information by creating a sentence to help us remember it. We're going to keep reading about immigration, but we want to remember this important point. We write an About Point statement by combining the two ideas we just discussed. We will write, Immigrants came from all over the world to live here. Excellent. We will practice this About Point strategy frequently. As you read, I'd like you to remember to ask yourself those questions: What is this about? What important point is the writer making about the topic? You can record your answers in your journal or on a piece of paper; if you write them down, it will be easier to remember them. Then when you want to review your reading, you'll have a good starting point. Also, if I ask you to write a summary or do some other sort of writing, you'll have completed an important step. Okay, let's continue our reading about immigration.

After much modeling and guided practice, students become adept at using this strategy independently to determine the main idea of a paragraph. The strategy can also be applied to longer pieces of text and can serve as the foundation for all sorts of writing.

About Point Writing Response

About Point Writing Response (Carr, 2000) is an adaptation of About Point that provides a structure for writing in response to narrative and expository text. With this strategy, students use the process of identifying a point and determining what they want to say about it to construct the main idea for their own writing in response to a text. First, students ask themselves, What do I want to write about? (the About). Then, they ask themselves, What point do I want to make? (the Point). They jot down their thoughts in brief phrases (we call them kernels of information) on the Outline portion of the About Point Writing Response Planning Guide (see template at right and on the CD). Students then write at least three details to support their About Point. Next, students complete the Outline by writing a phrase for a closing. Finally, students use the Outline as a guide to flesh out their thoughts and write them in sentences on the Summary portion of the guide.

ABOUT POINT WRITING RESPONSE PLANNING GUIDE

Outline	Summary
About:	
Point:	
1.	
2.	
3.	
Closing:	

BACKGROUND KNOWLEDGE

When reading, we link new information in a text to what we already know—that is, our background knowledge. Building or increasing our background knowledge about a topic enhances our understanding of a text written on that topic. More importantly, however, we must find ways to activate our current background knowledge and relate it to what we're reading. While a great deal of research done in the 1970s and 1980s established a link between background knowledge and comprehension (Anderson & Pearson, 1984), recent research focuses on methods to encourage readers to apply their background knowledge appropriately so they can make the necessary inferences and elaborations for sophisticated comprehension to take place (Pearson & Duke, 2002).

Our framework shows you how to teach strategies that activate and build students' background knowledge, helping them use what they know to understand the texts they read. For example, the strategy Experience Text Relationship or ETR (Au, 1979; see page 91) encourages students to quickly activate their personal knowledge about a topic and to build their knowledge by sharing what they know with each other. Second-grade teacher Olivia Hearst reflects on why she chose to use ETR in a lesson on the story, *Two Bad Ants* (Van Allsburg, 1988): "I chose Experience Text Relationship because I wanted my students to think about text-to-self connections. I thought that if they knew ahead of time that they were going to read about a situation similar to something they may have experienced, it would spark their interest in reading and help them with comprehension."

Following is an excerpt from Olivia's lesson on ETR.

Ms. Hearst:	Have you ever had to give something you wanted for yourself to someone else?
Mario:	Yes, my baby brother and I went on an Easter egg hunt and I had to give half of my eggs and candy to him because he didn't find any.
Justin:	I gave a little girl some of my candy at a parade once. She was crying because all the big kids were running in front of her and taking the candy.
Mario:	I won three stuffed animals at a fair and I had to give one to my little sister so she'd stop crying.
Shanequa:	My mom gave my brother and me a milkshake to share in the car. Even though I wanted to drink it all, I gave some to my brother.

Ms. Hearst: Sometimes it is hard to ignore what we want and do the right thing. We may get so carried away thinking about ourselves that we forget to follow the rules, be sensible, or think of others. When this happens, we usually run into trouble. We are going to read a book called *Two Bad Ants*. In this book two ants are in a similar situation. We are going to read to find out what happens to them.

VOCABULARY

There has been a great deal of work in recent decades documenting that students' active involvement in learning the meanings of words is critical to comprehension. We know that good readers have more extensive vocabularies than poor readers (Freebody & Anderson, 1983) and that readers improve their comprehension when they improve their vocabulary (Beck, Perfetti, & McKeown, 1982). Despite the finding that comprehension depends on vocabulary, however, there is very little good vocabulary instruction taking place in many classrooms (Watts, 1995; Biemiller, 2001). Furthermore, there is a paucity of research on vocabulary in informational reading; this research is especially needed because of the recent explosion of technical vocabulary and the increase in the number of students for whom English is a second language (Ogle & Blachowicz, 2002).

Good vocabulary instruction encourages students to become actively involved in defining words by elaborating on definitions and relating words and definitions to their personal experiences. As they learn to use such strategies, students become independent learners (Carr & Wixson, 1986). They develop a curiosity about the world and are motivated to learn new words. With the Personal Clues (Carr, 1985; see page 144) strategy, students understand and retain new vocabulary by linking word meanings to their own background knowledge. Personal Clues is also a useful strategy for ESL learners who can write clues in their first language or use pictures to enhance their retention of a word's meaning. Here's how Jim Pike, a sixth-grade teacher, introduced the Personal Clues strategy to his students.

Mr. Pike: We are going to read a story that has some words in it that you might not know. So, before we begin, I'd like to go over some of these vocabulary words with you. The vocabulary words are listed on your paper. We'll do the Personal Clues strategy to help you remember the definitions of the words. The first word on your paper is *disdainfully*. Does anyone know what *disdainfully* means? I might say, "I looked at you disdainfully." Steven, do you know what it means?

Steven:	Like you look at someone in a mean way, with a mean face.
Mr. Pike:	Yes, you look at someone like you don't want anything to do with them. You look at them scornfully, like you are rejecting them and they are not worth your time. If I say to Dwayne: "Dwayne, you're a great kid, thanks for helping me take my books to the car," am I speaking disdainfully to him?
Savannah:	No.
Mr. Pike:	Josh, if one of your friends said, "What do *you* know anyway?" is he speaking disdainfully?
Josh:	Yes.
Mr. Pike:	Okay. Good. You have the meaning. Everybody put down *scornfully* or *rejecting* on the line under disdainfully where it says *definition*. Now let's complete the line that says *clue*. I want everyone to think for a minute of a person or an event in your life when you saw someone act disdainfully. Think of someone in your neighborhood or on TV who acted *disdainfully*. Choose an example that makes the meaning of disdainfully clear to you and that will help you recall the meaning at a later time. Can anyone think of such an example?
Shane:	I'm thinking of our neighbor, Mr. Lensky, who looks mad when a car goes by with teenagers who are playing the music too loud.
Angel:	I'm going to use "mad at mom" because sometimes I look at my mom that way, I mean, disdainfully, when she grounds me.
Mr. Pike:	Now if Angel used Shane's clue of Mr. Lensky, she wouldn't be able to remember the definition of disdainfully because that clue has nothing to do with her personal experience. So each one of you has to have your own clue to remember the definition. Each of you go ahead and write a personal clue in the box under disdainfully. When you want to study your definitions, use a paper to cover your clue and the definition. If you can't remember the definition of the word, uncover your clue. The clue will help you recall the meaning of the vocabulary word.

See Figure 1D for an example of Personal Clues created in this lesson.

Personal Clues

Word:	disdainfully
Clue:	Mr. Lensky
Definition:	scornful, rejecting

Word:	disdainfully
Clue:	mad at mom
Definition:	scornful, rejecting

Sixth graders developed these personal clues to help them remember the word *disdainfully*, which appears in their upcoming reading.

COMPREHENSION

After twenty-five years of research on comprehension strategies instruction, it is clear that many students need to be taught well-validated comprehension strategies to construct meaning from text (Pressley & Block, 2002). Comprehension strategies are specific, learned procedures that can foster active, competent, self-regulated, intentional reading. These strategies help students seamlessly coordinate and integrate different cognitive processes as they are reading text (Williams, 2002). By learning and using a number of strategies to help them comprehend and remember text, students eventually come to know how to use the strategies on their own in many different ways.

Like many teachers, you may use KWL (Know, Want to Know, Learned; Ogle, 1986; see page 120) often in your classroom. It is such a good strategy because when students do KWL, they are using a number of cognitive processes, such as activating background knowledge, setting a purpose for learning, relating and connecting ideas, and monitoring comprehension. Third-grade teacher Kim Baker says, "Many of my students have difficulty with comprehension. Their growth in understanding and higher-level thinking has been tremendous when using KWL to guide their thinking. However, a number of my students have difficulty selecting important information and tend to list numerous details from the text when they are writing down what they have learned in the L column. So I often ask my students to use the About Point strategy when they are completing the L column (see page 16 for a description of About Point). With About Point, students examine each paragraph and identify the topic or the 'about.' They then decide what 'point' the author is making in the paragraph. Putting an 'about' with a 'point' is a simple way for my students to identify the main idea in a section or a paragraph of text. They can turn their 'about points' for each paragraph into statements that can be the basis for a summary." Figure 1E shows how Kim's third graders used the About Point strategy to complete the L column of their KWL chart on polar bears. Kim contends that using the two strategies together greatly enhanced their comprehension.

About Point Strategy Used with KWL

ABOUT POINTS	STATEMENTS FOR L COLUMN OF KWL
About: polar bears' adaptations **Point:** help them survive in the Arctic	Polar bears' adaptations help them survive in the arctic.
About: clear, hollow fur **Point:** acts as a greenhouse to collect sunshine and warm their black skin	Their clear, hollow fur acts as a greenhouse to collect sunshine and warm their black skin.
About: broad, clawed paws **Point:** help them travel over ice and hunt for seals	Broad, clawed paws help them travel over ice and hunt for seals.
About: polar bears' size **Point:** provides the strength to travel distances for food	The polar bear's size helps provide the strength to travel distances to find food.
About: walking hibernation **Point:** allows the bears to conserve energy when food is scarce	A system of walking hibernation allows the bears to conserve energy when food is scarce.
About: hibernation **Point:** is not seasonal and can change quickly if food becomes available	Polar bears' hibernation status is not seasonal and can change quickly if food becomes available.

Third graders recorded what they learned from their reading on polar bears in the L column of their KWL chart. To develop their statements, they completed the About Point strategy, shown in the first column.

APPLICATION/EXTENSION

Along with strategies for helping students activate/build background knowledge, understand difficult vocabulary, and comprehend the text, the ThinkingWorks framework includes strategies to help students accomplish the goal of applying or extending their learning. Frequently, we hear teachers say that their students have difficulty extending the meaning of a text. Having so much content or material to cover, teachers think that they can't spend time on extension activities. In addition, most of the curriculum and most texts focus on comprehension. We believe that it is not enough to understand text. We want students to be able to apply and extend what they understand to new situations. Students can only become advanced thinkers by applying what they have learned.

Recent research suggests that students can and must use a wide range of strategies to help them interpret, evaluate, analyze, synthesize, acquire a new perspective, consider diverse points of view, and use information in a new situation (de Bono, 1991; Costa & Kallick, 2000; Perkins, 1991). Therefore, the application strategy component is as important a part of your lesson as the other three. Fortunately, research has identified a wide variety of application/extension strategies for both narrative and expository text.

The RAFT (Santa, 1988; see page 122) strategy encourages students to apply and extend their knowledge by presenting their viewpoint to others through discussion and writing. When they are using RAFT, students may be using the cognitive processes of analysis, synthesis, evaluation/justification, and creation/invention, depending on the assignment. Students can use the RAFT outline as the basis for writing a letter, an essay, or a report presenting their viewpoint to another person. The four letters in the RAFT outline represent the following:

R: role of the writer (e.g., a scientist or a character in a story)

A: audience to whom the response is addressed (e.g., a friend, a newspaper, or a government official)

F: format of the writing (e.g., a friendly letter, a business letter, an editorial, a brochure, or a report)

T: topic or "About Point" (e.g., persuade a legislator to vote on an issue, tell a group of friends about a party, or invite a character in a book to dinner)

Once Kim Baker and her students finished the About Point and KWL strategies, as described in the previous section, she asked students to use the RAFT technique to extend their learning by using it in a new situation. Kim gave students the following assignment:

> Take the role of a scientist who studies polar bears in their habitat. Write a letter to friends at a zoo to inform them of an environment that would be suitable for a polar bear. Be sure your letter contains the five necessary parts (heading, greeting, body, closing, and signature). When writing your letter, use the information that you read about to inform zoo personnel. You can write that information in the Details section of the RAFT outline.

Kim brainstormed with students to come up with ideas for their letter. The class discussed the following points:

> To design a "zoo space" for polar bears, think of how they live in the arctic and how their needs can be met in a zoo. Think about factors such as temperatures in the arctic, the types of food that polar bears eat and how they catch food, their need for a stimulating environment and the range of their habitat.

Figure 1F shows how Jared, one of Kim's students, completed the assignment, using the RAFT strategy to outline his letter.

When the four strategy components are taught as a group in a lesson, your students will be using the cognitive processes necessary for comprehending text and applying learning. Using our framework and lesson planning guide will help you select strategies to include in your instruction. In addition, using the framework encourages you to analyze and reflect on the strategies you choose so that you know which cognitive processes and which language processes—reading, writing,

FIGURE 1F

RAFT Outline

R: Scientist
A: Zoo personnel
F: Friendly letter
T: About: polar bears
Point: need a special habitat in the zoo to thrive
Details:
- used to arctic cold
- they're large and need space to explore
- need water hole to catch seals for food and stimulation

Letter

Dear Zoo Personnel,

I have studied about polar bears and have learned that they need a special habitat in the zoo to thrive. A perfect habitat would include several things. Polar bears are used to the arctic cold, so they would need ways to cool off in warm weather, such as water for swimming and air-conditioned space. They are over seven feet tall and can weigh a half a ton. They need space to roam. They are used to hunting seal, so seals should be in nearby waterways to provide stimulation for the polar bears. These are some things that would improve their habitat.

Sincerely,
Jared

A third grader's RAFT Outline and letter

listening/viewing, and oral communication—those strategies encourage students to use. To help you plan your lessons, we have aligned the strategies that we introduce in this book with the twelve cognitive processes that appear in the lesson planning guide (see Appendix A). The alignment covers both narrative and expository text.

Two Lessons Using the ThinkingWorks Framework

Research has identified a number of strategies for each of the four components (background knowledge, vocabulary, comprehension, and application/extension) of instruction in the ThinkingWorks framework. In this book, you will revisit some familiar strategies and learn many new ones. Our goal is to provide you with a wide range of strategies so that you will have a diverse repertoire from which to choose when planning your lessons. The strategies you choose for a particular lesson will be determined by your assessment of your students' needs and your instructional goals and materials. Following are examples of a narrative and an expository lesson based on the ThinkingWorks framework. We have provided a brief rationale for the strategies that are used in the lessons and, for each lesson, we have suggested an alternative strategy based on a consideration of particular student needs.

NARRATIVE LESSON

In this lesson, Andrea Snyder is developing an integrated language arts and science lesson for her third graders who are reading *Verdi* (Cannon, 1997), a story about a python who doesn't want to change color and become boring like the older snakes. Andrea's lesson has a dual purpose. First, she wants her students to develop their literacy skills. Therefore, they will be examining the author's use of characterization and the ways in which a character's beliefs and the story events are interrelated. Students will also be practicing their writing skills. Second, Andrea wants students to build their knowledge about reptiles, which is one of their science topics. Reading about snakes in a narrative text will pique students' interest and increase their conceptual understanding of the topic.

Andrea discusses why she chose the following four strategies for her lesson: Semantic Map for activating background knowledge; Possible Sentences for building vocabulary; Action Belief Chart for developing comprehension; and Literary Report Card and Character Sketch for extending learning. Samples of student work appear next to her descriptions.

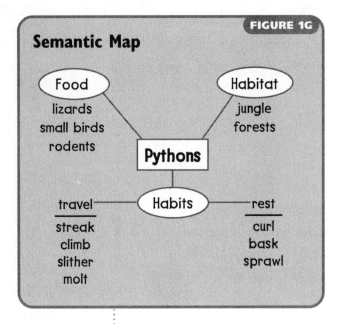

FIGURE 1G

Semantic Map

Food: lizards, small birds, rodents

Habitat: jungle, forests

Pythons

Habits

travel: streak, climb, slither, molt

rest: curl, bask, sprawl

BACKGROUND KNOWLEDGE: SEMANTIC MAP

(Johnson & Pearson, 1984; see page 39)

The Semantic Map gives my students the opportunity to recall prior knowledge about a topic and organize the information by categories. They often know quite a lot about the topic, but as they engage in collective brainstorming, they motivate each other to mentally "rummage around" for more information. During discussions, misconceptions are uncovered and vocabulary is introduced. After reading, we revisit the Semantic Map so students can add information to it that they have learned. (See Figure 1G.)

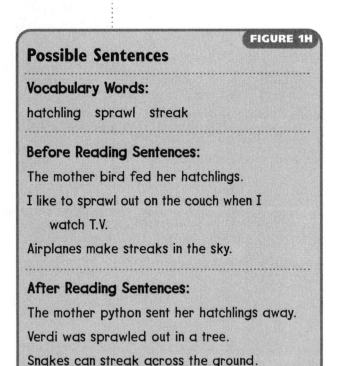

FIGURE 1H

Possible Sentences

Vocabulary Words:

hatchling   sprawl   streak

Before Reading Sentences:

The mother bird fed her hatchlings.

I like to sprawl out on the couch when I watch T.V.

Airplanes make streaks in the sky.

After Reading Sentences:

The mother python sent her hatchlings away.

Verdi was sprawled out in a tree.

Snakes can streak across the ground.

VOCABULARY STRATEGY: POSSIBLE SENTENCES

(Moore & Moore, 1992; see page 94)

This is a strategy that helps my students practice using the vocabulary words both before and after reading. Before reading, we discuss the meaning of key words and students write sentences using those words. When they are reading, they look for the words to see how they are used in the context of the story. Then, after reading, they reinforce their understanding of the vocabulary by writing new sentences. This time, their use of the words reflects the story content. (See Figure 1H.)

COMPREHENSION STRATEGY: ACTION BELIEF CHART

(Beach & Marshall, 1991; see page 82)

The Action Belief Chart encourages my students to think about the characters in the story and their contributions to the plot. I want them to practice inferring and to understand how the characters relate to one another in the context of the story. (See Figure 1I.)

FIGURE 1I

Action Belief Chart

Title: Verdi

Character:	Action:	Belief:
Dozer	growled at Verdi.	He thinks Verdi should be quiet and not disturb him.
Verdi	tried to scrub off the green	Verdi wants to stay yellow and not become a boring green snake.

APPLICATION/EXTENSION STRATEGY: LITERARY REPORT CARD

(Johnson & Louis, 1987; see page 49) and

CHARACTER SKETCH

(Carr, Aldinger, & Patberg, 2000; see page 51)

I thought that having my students complete a Literary Report Card and Character Sketch would extend their understanding of the characters in the book. This strategy encourages students to focus on a specific character. They have to analyze how his or her personality traits are reflected in story events. The Character Sketch provides students with an opportunity for writing in response to the text. (See Figures 1J and 1K.)

FIGURE 1J

Literary Report Card

Character: Verdi

Subject	Grade	Comments
pride	A	Verdi was very proud of his bright yellow skin and black stripes.
friendliness	A	Verdi tried to be friends with the greens. Verdi made friends with the new yellow hatchlings even though they were rude.
politeness	B	Verdi was rude when he interrupted the greens. He was polite by talking to the yellow hatchlings.
maturity	F	Verdi was very childish, he didn't want to grow up to be a green.

Character Sketch

Outline:

About: Verdi

Point: Was an unusual python who was proud of his yellow skin and did not want to grow into a boring green python.

Details:

1. Verdi wondered why he should grow up big and green and tried to ask the green snakes, but all they did was lie around and complain.
2. Verdi tried to jump, climb, and keep moving so he could stay yellow and not become boring and lazy like the greens.
3. Verdi got upset when he started to turn green and tried to scrub it off.

Closing: Verdi turned green and learned to enjoy quiet and still be active.

Summary:

Verdi was an unusual python who was proud of his yellow skin and did not want to grow into a boring green python. Verdi wondered why he should grow up big and green and tried to ask the greens himself. All they did was lay around and complain. Verdi decided to jump, climb, and keep moving so he could stay yellow and not become lazy and boring like the greens. Verdi was very upset when he realized he was turning green and tried to scrub the green off. Verdi turned green and learned to enjoy quiet and still be active.

SELECTING AN ALTERNATIVE STRATEGY

Andrea knows that some of her students may have difficulty completing the Action Belief Chart. She decides to ask students who need extra support to complete a Plot Relationships Chart (Schmidt & Buckley, 1991; see page 29) before trying the Action Belief Chart. With a Plot Relationships Chart, students identify and review important parts of the story including the goal, problem, and resolution. They focus on four words or prompts that lead them through the story. They identify the main characters (Somebody), the goal (Wanted), the problem (But) and the resolution (So). Figure 1L shows how a student completed this strategy. Once students do a Plot Relationships Chart, they can then proceed to analyze specific actions of characters and the relationship of those actions to the character's beliefs as required in the Action Belief Chart strategy.

Alternative Strategy:
Plot Relationships Chart

Somebody	Wanted	But	So
Verdi	to keep his yellow skin and not become a boring green python	even though he kept moving and tried to be different from the other snakes, he changed colors.	he turned green and learned to enjoy quiet and activity

EXPOSITORY LESSON

Dawn Becker is planning a lesson for sixth-grade students who are studying Thurgood Marshall as part of a celebration of civil rights leaders. She wants her students to understand the historical period in which Marshall lived and the significant contributions he made to the legal profession and to society. In addition, Dawn wants her students to develop research skills and extend what they have learned by writing a report. She describes the ThinkingWorks lesson she developed to meet these goals below.

BACKGROUND KNOWLEDGE: SEMANTIC MAP

(Johnson & Pearson, 1984; see page 39)

A Semantic Map prompts my students to discuss information about Thurgood Marshall. Class members have limited knowledge about him, but, through a teacher-led discussion, they get an idea of what they will be learning and what concepts they will want to research. (See Figure 1M.)

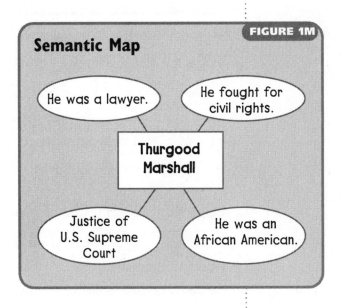

FIGURE 1M

Semantic Map

He was a lawyer.

He fought for civil rights.

Thurgood Marshall

Justice of U.S. Supreme Court

He was an African American.

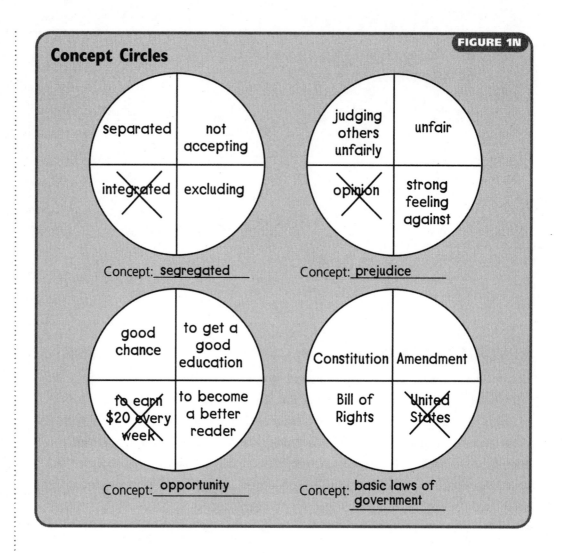

Concept Circles

FIGURE 1N

Concept: segregated

Concept: prejudice

Concept: opportunity

Concept: basic laws of government

VOCABULARY: CONCEPT CIRCLES (Vacca & Vacca, 1999; see page 41)

The vocabulary in this lesson is difficult. With the version of Concept Circles that we are using, my students will study and discuss examples, synonyms, and antonyms for key concepts related to the life and era of Marshall. I know that they will develop a broad understanding of those key concepts. (See Figure 1N.)

COMPREHENSION: I-CHART (Hoffman, 1992; see page 131)

This strategy provides students with a visual structure for carrying out the various aspects of a research project, such as selecting a research topic, developing research questions, locating resources to answer them, and writing a report.

I use the I-Chart as a guide for modeling how students can develop questions and relate information from different sources to answer the questions. (See Figure 1O.)

I-Chart

Topic: Thurgood Marshall	Q1: What has Marshall done for schools?	Q2: What important jobs has Marshall had?	Q3: What has Marshall done for civil rights?	Q4: Why was Marshall important to our country?
Source 1: Thurgood Marshall and Equal Rights	Segregation in public schools was outlawed by U.S. Supreme Court	He was a judge on the U.S. Court of Appeals.	Marshall worked for NAACP, the largest civil rights organization.	He was very good and nice to us.
Source 2: FunkandWagnalls.com	Court decision banning racial segregation in public schools.	He was a U.S. Solicitor General from 1965 to 1967.	He was a stalwart defender of civil rights.	He did so many things to help our country.
Source 3: ThurgoodMarshall.com	He ended the legal separation of black and white children in public schools.	The first African American Supreme Court Justice.	He led a civil rights revolution.	He helped integrate our country.
Summaries:	Marshall ended the separation in public schools.	Marshall was the first African American Supreme Court Justice, a U.S. General, and a Judge.	Marshall worked for NAACP, and was a stalwart defender of civil rights, and led the civil rights revolution.	Marshall is important to our country because he helped integrate us and bring us together.

APPLICATION/EXTENSION: JOURNAL RESPONSE (Fulweiler, 1982; see page 102)

By using a journal, my students have the opportunity to express what they think and how the material is of value to them. Students' journal entries also help me assess the effectiveness of the lesson. (See Figure 1P.)

Journal Entry

March 9, 2001

I enjoyed this project this week because it was about someone that not very many people know about, and we can teach them about Marshall. I would like to learn more about other people using this method.

Studying Marshall was interesting because I knew nothing about Thurgood Marshall before I started studying him. I would like to study more about integration and fighting for civil rights. Thank you Mrs. Becker for sharing this with us.

Jenni

SELECTING AN ALTERNATIVE STRATEGY

Several students in Dawn's class become overwhelmed when reading a lot of text. They find it difficult to sort through text to select information for the I-Chart. She has those students use an alternative strategy, About Point Notetaking (Carr, Aldinger, & Patberg, 2000; see page 16). It helps them pick out and organize important information as they are reading the research for their report. The strategy provides students with a simple structure for identifying the main ideas in each

---

FIGURE 1Q

Alternative Strategy: About Point Notetaking

About:
Thurgood Marshall

Point: was a leader in the fight for civil rights.

Details:
1. Marshall became head of the NAACP.
2. He took on Malcolm X.
3. African Americans should be treated equally.

About: Marshall

Point: was a lawyer in Brown vs. Board of Education suit (in 1960s).

Details:
1. Believed in ending segregation.
2. Won integration for all schools.
3. Tried to put an end to prejudice against race.

About: Thurgood

Point: was also a judge for the United States Supreme Court.

Details:
1. Appointed by John F. Kennedy (J.F.K.) to the Federal Court of Appeals.
2. Nominated by Lyndon Johnson to the Supreme Court.
3. First African American to ever hold that position.

Summary: Report on Thurgood Marshall and Civil Rights

Who is Thurgood Marshall? Well, if you don't know, read this report and find out.

Thurgood Marshall was a leader in the fight for civil rights. He became head of the NAACP and took on Malcolm X. He said that African Americans should be treated equally.

Marshall was a lawyer in the Brown vs. Board of Education suit in the 1960s. He believed in ending segregation. Marshall tried to put an end to prejudice and won integration for all schools.

Thurgood was also a judge for the U.S. Supreme Court. He was appointed by John F. Kennedy to the Federal Court of Appeals. He was then nominated by Lyndon Johnson to the Supreme Court. He was the first African American to ever hold that position.

section of the text and then selecting supporting details. They use the information to write a summary, which can be their report. Figure 1Q shows how a student completed the About Point Notetaking strategy.

The ThinkingWorks framework can be an effective aid for planning and evaluating your instruction. When Dawn planned her lesson, she thought about the skills that her students would need to achieve the lesson goals. She then selected strategies that would help her students develop those skills. Since Dawn has a repertoire of strategies to call upon, she had the flexibility of choosing an alternative strategy for those students who needed additional support understanding information from text.

Using the Direct Explanation Model to Teach Strategies

Students ultimately become independent, strategic learners by automatically and routinely using cognitive and language processes. We have shown how strategies instruction encourages students to use those processes effectively. Students learn strategies over time through the instruction and practice that teachers provide, beginning in the primary grades. The Direct Explanation Model (Duffy & Roehler, 1982) is an effective way of teaching strategies to students. Throughout this book, the teaching procedures that we recommend for introducing these strategies to your students are based on the elements of direct explanation.

According to the Direct Explanation Model, you begin by explaining the strategy clearly to your students. You describe what the strategy is, why it is important, how to use the strategy, when and where the strategy should be used, and how to evaluate its effectiveness. Direct explanation also includes a stage of cognitive modeling in which you use explicit instructional talk or a think-aloud to describe the thought processes employed while performing the task. Cognitive modeling provides a clear picture of how accomplished readers think.

For example, Sara Kingsley models for her first graders how to answer an inferential question based on the story *Nessa's Fish* (Luenn, 1997), a book that is part of the social studies curriculum. Nessa is an Eskimo girl who goes on a fishing trip with her grandmother. When her grandmother becomes ill, Nessa must take charge and protect her grandmother, as well as the fish they have caught, from various dangers.

Sara uses a strategy called Question Answer Relationship or QAR (Raphael, 1982; see page 182). With this strategy, students answer three different types of questions: "right there" (literal), "think and search" (inferential), and "on your own" (information to construct answers is not found in the text, but in students' experiences and beliefs). Sara models the thinking she does to answer the "think and search" question: *In what ways did Nessa demonstrate the character trait of bravery?* She says, "First, I would think about what I know about the meaning of *bravery*. To me, *bravery* means being responsible and following through with a task even if you are scared. Now that I know what bravery involves, I'll act like a detective and think of clues in the story that will help me decide how Nessa is brave. I remember that she scared off wild animals several times to protect her grandmother and the fish. Since she is young girl and alone, I bet she was frightened. I would say that Nessa was very brave because she acted responsibly by protecting her grandmother from the wild animals, even though she was scared."

After modeling the strategy, it is important to provide opportunities for students to practice it on their own (Tharpe & Gallimore, 1989). After thinking aloud about *bravery*, Sara asks her students to answer the question, *How was Nessa clever?* To do so, students have to draw on their background knowledge and search for clues in the text. Initially, Sara guides the students in accessing their background knowledge by asking them to discuss the meaning of clever. She reminds them that they have used that word to describe Miss Nelson, a character in a story that they read earlier in the year, *Miss Nelson Is Missing* (Allard & Marshall, 1977). Sara then prompts her students to think of actions that Nessa took that demonstrate intelligent decision making. In this way, she scaffolds their learning of the strategy.

Sara knows that her students often achieve more when they work in groups rather than working alone, so she uses a small-group instructional strategy, Think-Pair-Share (McTigue & Lyman, 1988) to support her students as they practice answering an inferential question. Once she has posed the question about whether Nessa is clever and has provided prompts, individual students reflect on what they know and draw on information from their reading to arrive at possible answers (Think). They then pair up in teams to discuss and synthesize their ideas (Pair). Finally, each pair relates its thoughts to the class (Share). After discussion, the students reach the consensus that Nessa was very clever. They identify two examples of intelligent decision making on Nessa's part: she decided to remain with her grandmother in one place so her family could find them and she was able to think of different ways to scare off the wild animals.

Over time, as students become proficient with comprehension and application/ extension strategies, you will be able to gradually release responsibility to them so they can complete them independently (Pearson & Gallagher, 1983). Students will learn that using these strategies can help them comprehend and think in particular ways. They can then call up that thinking when needed and apply it flexibly whenever they encounter new text and other types of learning material.

How to Use This Book

The ThinkingWorks framework is used as an organizing structure for the main body of this book. In Chapters 2 through 7, ThinkingWorks lessons varying in grade level and content are presented for teaching both narrative and expository text. Figure 1R is an overview of the strategies presented in the book. Each chapter suggests a particular group of strategies for a lesson and includes a full explanation of each strategy, its purpose, how to teach it using the Direct Explanation Model, and examples of student work with the strategy. Many of the examples are of work done by students in a large, urban district who were learning to use comprehension strategies. Also included in each chapter are several alternative strategies that you may want to consider using, based on an evaluation of your students' needs and the content material for your lesson. Chapter 8 shows how you can use performance-based assessment measures with strategies instruction. Chapter 9 provides a number of ThinkingWorks lessons taught by teachers who have used the ThinkingWorks framework. Included are teachers' reflections regarding their lessons and their selection and implementation of particular strategies. Two appendices conclude this book. The first is the Alignment of ThinkingWorks Strategies with Cognitive Processes. The second is Strategies Aligned to Language Arts Standards. We have included this latter appendix because it is important for teachers to align their lessons with state or national standards. Because so many of the ThinkingWorks strategies have visual organizers, blackline masters for them are included on a CD-ROM disk in a pocket in the back of the book. We have also provided brief overviews of the strategies on strategy explanation sheets included on the CD-ROM.

In summary, the goal of comprehension instruction must be conceived as helping students develop the strategies they need to understand and apply what they read. At the center of this idea is an informed, reflective teacher who can make decisions about the best practices for developing her students' understanding of a given topic, as well as helping them become independent and thoughtful problem solvers. With this acknowledged, we encourage you to learn the strategies presented in this book and use the ThinkingWorks framework to plan your instruction. In doing so, you will be able to see how the various strategies fit with your goals and materials and how the choice of strategies engages readers in using different cognitive processes. We also encourage you to talk with your colleagues about the ThinkingWorks framework, because strategy instruction is most effective when it is embedded in the school curriculum and coordinated across grade levels and subjects.

ThinkingWorks Strategies

NARRATIVE TEXT

	Background Knowledge	Vocabulary	Comprehension	Application/Extension
CHAPTER 2	Semantic Map	Concept Circles	Story Grammar Circle Story Story Pyramid Plot Relationships Chart	Literary Report Card Character Rating Scale Emotions Chart

CHAPTER 3	Problem/Solution Guide	Concept of a Definition	Story Map from
			    Characters' Perspectives
			Probable Passage
			Action Belief Chart
				Compare/Contrast
				    Venn Diagram
				SCAMPER

CHAPTER 4	Experience Text
	Relationship (ETR)
		Possible Sentences	Personal Response/
			    Literary Analysis
			Prediction/Prediction
			    Chart
				Journal Response
				Literary Poster
				Pictorial Outline

NOTES: Some of the strategies can be used with expository text. Many of the strategies have a writing component.

EXPOSITORY TEXT

	Background Knowledge	Vocabulary	Comprehension	Application/Extension
CHAPTER 5	Anticipation Guide	Concept of a Definition/Technical	KWL KWL Plus I-Chart About Point About Point Notetaking	RAFT SCAMPER (Expository)
CHAPTER 6	Structured Overview	Personal Clues	Frames Description Sequence/Time Order Compare/Contrast Cause/Effect Problem/Solution Exploration/Science	Discussion Web Proposition/ Support Outline Editorial
CHAPTER 7	Quickwriting/Knowledge Rating Scale	Semantic Feature Analysis	Question Answer Relationship (QAR) Question, Clues, Response Questions for Quality Thinking Thinking Minds Reciprocal Teaching	Four-Step Summary Learning Logs

NOTES: Some of the strategies can be used with narrative text. Many of the strategies have a writing component.

CHAPTER 2

Understanding
Narrative
Text Structure

In This Chapter:

Most texts belong to one of two broad categories: narrative or expository. These two text types are organized quite differently. Narrative text tells a story and generally uses a single, underlying organizational structure. Narratives generally present a sequence of events involving characters who have a problem to solve; they end with a resolution to the problem. This structure is consistent and recognizable throughout most forms of fiction and is thus familiar to and easily remembered by readers.

Narrative texts are the main type of text used in the primary grades and include various literary genres such as fiction, biography, fairy tales, fables, and folk tales. Many of the genres have been read to children outside of school, so most children enter school with a relatively well-developed, although tacit, understanding of narratives (Graves et al., 1998). Nevertheless, children still have a great deal to learn about narratives in school, such as how narratives differ from exposition and how to recognize the theme in a story.

While most children have a basic schema for narrative text structure, their understanding of a particular story is often incomplete and reflects the recall of isolated facts. They need a way to integrate the information they read to truly understand a text. This brings us to the rationale for the lesson sequence presented in this chapter: we teach these particular strategies not only to help students grasp the content of a specific story but also to help them understand more generally how the structure of a story contributes to its meaning. Students can learn to use these strategies to process and integrate information as they read and write, thereby improving their comprehension and writing ability (Carr, Dewitz, & Ogle, 1988).

ThinkingWorks Lesson Plan Sequence for Understanding Narrative Text Structure

To help students understand narrative text structure, we have designed the following lesson sequence:

BACKGROUND KNOWLEDGE: . . . . Semantic Map

VOCABULARY: . . . . Concept Circles

COMPREHENSION: . . . . Story Grammar

APPLICATION/EXTENSION: . . . . Literary Report Card

While the Semantic Map and Concept Circle strategies can be used to activate background knowledge and build vocabulary for any text, Story Grammar and Literary Report Card work specifically with narrative texts. In addition, we present several alternative comprehension and application/extension strategies that work particularly well with narrative. They activate similar cognitive processes, but may appeal more to different learning styles or skill levels. We recommend choosing strategies that best meet the current needs of your students. Once they master a certain strategy, you may introduce a new one to broaden their strategy use.

To incorporate writing into the lesson, we recommend doing a summary after the Story Grammar and a Character Sketch after the Literary Report Card.

BACKGROUND KNOWLEDGE STRATEGY:
Semantic Map

A Semantic Map (Johnson & Pearson, 1984) is a visual representation of ideas underlying a concept or topic discussed in the text. It clarifies information about the topic and provides a way to show relationships among ideas in the text in a simple way.

The level of detail you go into will depend on the needs of your students. Figure 2A shows a semantic map a first-grade class created to explore the concept of naughtiness before reading *Babushka's Doll* (Polacco, 1990). In this example, students simply described instances of being naughty. A more elaborate map is shown in Figure 2B. Here, students generated ideas about wilderness, which they then placed

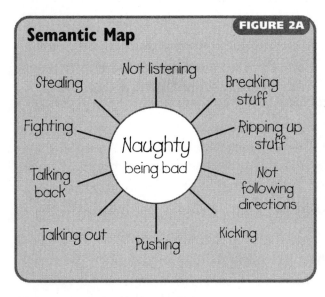

A Semantic Map created by first graders exploring the concept of naughtiness

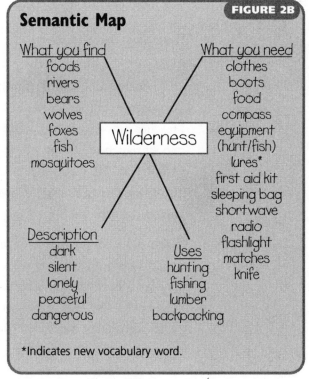

A Semantic Map in which sixth graders categorized their ideas about the wilderness

into four categories. In addition, the teacher introduced the word *lures* into the discussion of items that would be needed in the wilderness. The word was easy for students to understand once they had discussed its meaning and its association with other words that would be important for survival. You can include as many vocabulary words as are needed to understand the critical concepts in the text.

Before the Lesson

- Select a key concept from the story that you want your students to understand. In our first-grade example, the teacher chose to focus on naughtiness in preparation for reading *Babushka's Doll*. A sixth-grade teacher decided to work with the concept of wilderness before students read *Hatchet* (Paulsen, 1987).

- Determine if there are any unfamiliar words from the text that are critical to understanding the key concept. For example, in the Semantic Map for wilderness (shown in Figure 2B), the teacher knew he wanted to include one new word, *lures*. With other concepts, however, you may need to select up to 5 or 6 words so that students can understand the reading. By introducing vocabulary words through the Semantic Map, you're helping your students develop an initial understanding of the words and their relationship to the concept; you may reinforce these words during the vocabulary portion of the lesson. There are two Semantic Map templates on the CD in the back of the book.

Teaching the Strategy

- Tell your students the major concept they'll be learning about in preparation for their upcoming reading. Explain that a Semantic Map will help them discover and organize what they know about a concept. In the *Babushka's Doll* example, the teacher introduced the concept of naughtiness this way: "Today we're going to talk about naughtiness. Soon we'll be reading a story about a girl who behaved mischievously, and I'd like us to think about what it means to be naughty to get us ready to read. We'll use a strategy called a Semantic Map to help us gather our thoughts about naughtiness."

- Have students generate ideas about the target concept; record them on chart paper or the overhead. For young students, you may simply list them around the main concept, as shown in Figure 2A for the *Babushka's Doll* example. Older students can brainstorm ideas and then categorize them, as shown in Figure 2B. In this case, the teacher was sure to add the word *lures* to the map because he thought it would be unfamiliar to students and important for their comprehension of the story. Encourage students to discuss how the words are related to the main concept.

- Display the map so students can consult it while they're reading. You can orally review the information on the Semantic Map for younger students.

- After students read (or you read aloud to them), gather the group together to discuss and add information to the map—including new categories—as students refine their ideas.

- Use the map for study and review after reading.

A modification of the Semantic Map strategy is List Group Label (Taba, 1967). Similar to a Semantic Map, students generate a list of all the words associated with a key concept, just as they do in the brainstorming for a Semantic Map. List the words in random order, and add any vocabulary you want students to know. Then have students group the words into categories and label each one. They should be able to provide a rationale for their category labels. This strategy differs from the Semantic Map because there is no visual outline or map of the categorized information. Like a Semantic Map, this strategy helps students activate and build background knowledge. It also introduces them to important vocabulary words. It is easy for students to do the List Group Label strategy independently or with tutors or parents.

Assessment

To evaluate the effectiveness of a background knowledge strategy such as Semantic Map, you need to determine if the strategy achieved its purpose, which is to activate and build relevant background knowledge. Simply asking students questions about the concepts will suffice. The questions could be asked in writing or in an oral discussion. Either mode would tell you what you need to know before reading: do the students have the necessary background information to understand the text? If the answer to that question is *yes*, then you can proceed with the lesson; if the answer is *no*, then you will have to review the contents of the map with them or extend the categories of information on the map.

VOCABULARY STRATEGY:
Concept Circles

Activating and building background knowledge is the first step. Now you must consider any vocabulary in the text that might impair students' comprehension. We chose Concept Circles (Vacca & Vacca, 1999) for this lesson because it makes a nice follow-up to the Semantic Map presented above. With Concept Circles, you develop more fully students' understanding of key concepts you've chosen for the Semantic Map. You may use words you selected in preparation for the Semantic Map, or you may preview the text for other important concepts or words. Once you've identified target words, create one or more Concept Circles to help students explore the central ideas and vocabulary they'll encounter in the text. We've found that students really enjoy exploring words in this way.

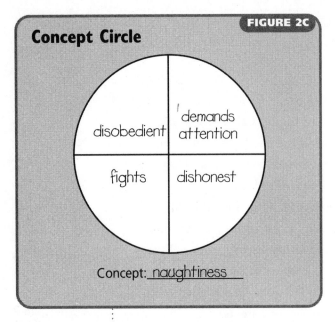

Concept Circle

disobedient | demands attention

fights | dishonest

Concept: _naughtiness_

A Concept Circle for first graders exploring the concept of naughtiness

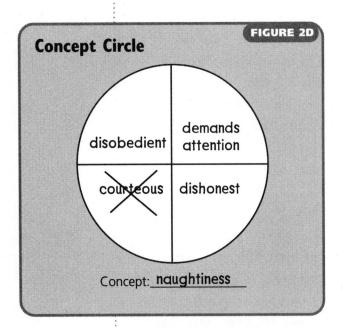

Concept Circle

disobedient | demands attention

~~courteous~~ | dishonest

Concept: _naughtiness_

A more challenging Concept Circle for the concept of naughtiness; here first graders had to cross out the antonym.

The Concept Circle invites students to study a group of words that are related to one another. To prepare a simple Concept Circle, divide a circle into four (or more) sections and fill the sections with related words or phrases. Students must name the concept represented by the words. Some of the words in the circle should be familiar to your students, while others may be unknown. When you include one or two unknown but related words, your students learn new vocabulary and place it in the context of the concept you are teaching. For example, in the Concept Circle for naughtiness (see Figure 2C), *dishonest* was a new vocabulary word. Students learned the meaning of *dishonest* through a group discussion about all the words in the Concept Circle. They determined that *dishonest, disobedient, fights,* and *demands attention* pertain to the concept of naughtiness.

Concept Circles can be used across grade levels at different levels of sophistication. In a more challenging variation, each Concept Circle contains three related words or phrases and one antonym or completely unrelated word. Students first cross out the unrelated word or antonym and then write in the word for the concept that's represented by the remaining three words (see Figure 2D).

Finally, you can make Concept Circles more difficult still by leaving one or two of the areas in a circle empty and directing students to fill in these sections with words or phrases that relate to the other terms in the circle. Make sure that students understand the given words. Then students can brainstorm words to put in the remaining space(s). A thesaurus is useful for this activity. Students will have to justify their choices by naming the concept that represents all of the

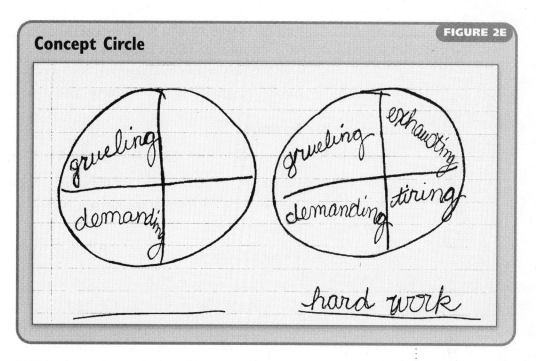

Concept Circle

FIGURE 2E

In this version of a Concept Circle, students were asked to complete the circle with words related to the original ones and then name the concept the four words together describe.

words or phrases in the circle. Figure 2E shows an example of this type of Concept Circle for the concept of hard work.

The Concept Circle strategy is best used when your students need to fully understand one or more concepts before they read a story. It is a strategy that requires a good deal of time on your part and on the part of your students, but it is time well spent because your students will learn new ideas and vocabulary. There are four Concept Circle templates on the CD.

Before the Lesson

- Examine the story your students are going to read and determine which concept or concepts they will need to understand in order to appreciate the story.

- Select words or phrases from the story that relate to the concept(s) you want to teach and that may be unfamiliar to students.

- For each concept, draw a large circle on chart paper with as many sections as are necessary to accommodate the words or phrases for teaching the concept. Typically there are four sections to allow students to learn one or two new related words. You can use one of the templates from the CD, if desired.

- Decide which level of difficulty you want to work at and prepare the circle(s) on chart paper accordingly. For example, if you simply want your students to name the concept depicted in the circle, put all of the words or phrases in the circle segments and leave the line for naming the concept blank. If, on the other hand, you want them to come up with other examples of a concept, leave two segments of the circle empty. This is an opportune time to extend students' vocabulary knowledge by introducing synonyms and antonyms related to the concept.

Teaching the Strategy

• Distribute to students papers with one or more blank Concept Circles.

• Give students a quick preview of the story. Tell them that you have selected some words or phrases from the story that you think might be difficult for them to understand.

• Explain how a Concept Circle will help them learn words related to an important idea in the text.

• Discuss the words or phrases on the Concept Circle(s) that you have prepared on chart paper. Ask students what the words in each Concept Circle have in common (e.g., What do they all describe or tell about?). Have students write down related words in the blank segments of the circle. Guide students to name the concept represented by all of the sections.

• Lead students in a discussion of the concept using the words or phrases in the circle. Talk about the attributes of the concept and give some non-examples of the concept as well as examples. At the end of the discussion, students should be able to talk about the concept using the words or phrases in the circle.

Concept Circles can be completed initially through whole-class discussion when you want students to fully understand one or more concepts before they read a story. Alternatively, students can complete teacher-prepared Concept Circles in small groups or independently. In this situation, students make the decisions of which words to include, eliminate, and substitute. They name the concept that includes all four of the words they have chosen. If students complete the Concept Circles themselves, in small groups or independently, you will have a way of checking their understanding of key vocabulary and ideas.

Writing Extension

A benefit of the Concept Circle strategy is that it encourages students to learn and retain vocabulary words. Students can incorporate the new words into their writing as they use the comprehension and application/extension strategies presented next in this chapter.

Assessment

The accuracy of students' completed Concept Circles can serve as a method of evaluating the effectiveness of this strategy.

COMPREHENSION STRATEGY:
Story Grammar

After you have provided the link from reader to text with prereading strategies such as Semantic Mapping and Concept Circles, your students are ready to read. However, they will still need support to understand the text while they are reading. Using a Story Grammar is one strategy that helps students understand the various components in a story and how they function.

The Story Grammar strategy (Mandler & Johnson, 1977) focuses on the structure of narrative text. You can vary the difficulty of this strategy by altering the elements included. For instance, early elementary students might work with

beginning, middle, and end (see Figure 2F), while older students can handle character, setting, plot elements (problem, events, solutions), and theme (see Figure 2G). The elements in a Story Grammar can vary according to genre as well. For example, many Native American stories are called How and Why stories because they use animal characters to explain natural phenomena. These stories have different elements in their Story Grammars. You'll find five Story Grammar templates at various levels on the CD.

Students should complete a Story Grammar in reading situations where the act of identifying and understanding the important elements of a story will greatly enhance comprehension. If students know that they have to identify the elements of a story, they will read with a purpose, attend to important concepts, and monitor their understanding as they read (Marshall, 1983). In addition, identifying story elements provides a solid basis for visualizing characters and their actions. At first, work together to help your students complete Story Grammars as a whole class. As students become more familiar with the strategy, they can complete Story Grammars in small groups or individually. Ultimately, students will use the information they glean from story elements to enhance their comprehension. In time, they will internalize the components of the Story Grammar and be able to focus on important story elements even without a graphic prompt.

Before the Lesson

- Determine what story elements you will include in the Story Grammar; prepare a blank template with those elements. (You may choose one of the five templates on the CD or create your own.)

FIGURE 2F

Simple Story Grammar

Name Sam (Samantha)

Title Whistle for Willie   Author _____

Characters P Peter, Willie _____

Setting outside _____

Beginning Peter Wisht he cud Wiso _____

Middle then he sall A littk Boy Wiso at his Dog _____

Ending then he Lvd hm to Wiso _____

A Simple Story Grammar for *Whistle for Willie*

Teaching the Strategy

- Explain to students that you are going to teach them a strategy that will help them identify the elements of a story, which in turn will increase their comprehension. Tell students that the identification of story elements also will help them visualize what is happening in the story.

- Show the template of the Story Grammar on chart paper or the overhead and discuss each element so students have a framework for identifying important story elements.

- Have the students read the text silently. You can read the story aloud to young students.

- Complete the Story Grammar together as a class. You can guide students in completing the Story Grammar by asking questions such as: Where does the story take place? What is the problem? Who are the important characters? How do they try to solve the problem? How is the problem solved? What is the theme of the story? Information in the Story Grammar can be listed as phrases or as sentences.

FIGURE 2G

Story Grammar

Characters: Quentin, Flan, Mom, Dad, President, U.S. Army Personnel

Setting: Present-day on a farm outside a small town

Problem: Quentin has all the money in the world and needs to find a way to get it all back to the original owners so cities, businesses, and people can survive.

Events:

Quentin is granted his wish of having all the money in the world by Flan, a leprechaun he rescued from a well.

After huge piles of money appeared on Quentin's father's farm, the U.S. Army came and loaded it into trucks, but the money kept magically reappearing on the farm.

People from all over began to panic because all their money had vanished and banks, businesses, and the government could no longer run.

Quentin realized the suffering going on and wanted to take back his wish, but the law of the leprechauns would not allow it.

Quentin and Flan were flown to the White House and urged by the president to somehow get the money back to the owners or the other countries would start a war with us.

The next day Flan got stuck in a broken step and was rescued again by Quentin.

Solution: Quentin was granted one more wish by Flan, and he wished for all the money to go back where it came from.

Ending: The president bought Quentin a bike that he had always wanted as a reward for doing the right thing.

Theme: Be careful what you wish for, or, Money doesn't always solve problems.

A detailed Story Grammar completed by a sixth grader for *All the Money in the World*

Story Chart

Title	The Talking Eggs	Ashpet
Country	Europe	United States
Author	Robert D. San Souci	Joanne Compton
Illustrator	Jerry Pinkey	Ken Compton
Setting	Woods Her house Old woman's house	House Church Granny's house
Characters (describe) (put a * by bad guys)	*Widow (mother) *Rose (sister) Blanche (nice) Old Woman (nice)	Ashpet (nice) *Widow Hooper (mean) *Ethal (ugly) *Myrtle (ugly) Granny (old)
Problem	Blanche lives with a poor and mean family and is treated badly.	Ashpet lives with Widow Hooper and her cranky daughters and she has to do too much work.
Events (plot)	• Goes to woman's house • Very nice to her and gets eggs (Blanche) • Goes to woman's house • Very mean and gets bad eggs (Rose) • Blanche lives in city	• Ashpet goes to Granny's house • Granny helps Ashpet clean and get dressed for the meeting • Ashpet meets doctor's son • Ashpet loses shoe • They get married
Solution	Blanche gets the eggs from the old woman and lives grandly in a city.	Old Granny helps Ashpet clean and Ashpet goes to the meeting and meets the doctor's son.
Theme	You reap what you sow.	If you're good, you get rewarded.
Special Effects/ Magic	Talking eggs Woman taking off head Two headed cow Colorful chickens	Granny New dress New shoes Clean house
Literary Devices • Simile	Horns like corkscrews Sharp as forty crickets	Ugly as they were lazy Mad as a wet hen
• Imagery	Goes to fancy balls wearing trail train dresses	Deep in the shadow of Eagle's nest
• Foreshadowing	You've got a spirit of do-good in your soul. God is gonna bless you. Ah, child, you're a wicked girl.	...muttered something... Tapped her walking stick three times
• Poetic Justice	Blanche went to the city to live like a grand lady.	Ashpet walked out and married a doctor's son.
Vocabulary	Plaited Contrary Silver Dawdled	Gussy Skedaddled Gaped Commotion

A fifth grader uses a Story Chart to compare two versions of the Cinderella story.

- Ask questions and encourage discussion about the story using information from the Story Grammar.

- Extend your students' learning by having them use the Story Grammar to compare the story they have just read with other pieces of literature.

- Provide students with many opportunities to practice completing Story Grammars, so they can complete them independently with stories of various lengths and levels of difficulty.

A Story Chart is similar to a Story Grammar but is more comprehensive. It includes elements that you want the reader to reflect on that extend beyond a Story Grammar, such as theme, point of view, expressive language, or literary devices; there are two Story Chart templates on the CD.

Figure 2H is a Story Chart completed by a fifth-grade student. In this example, the teacher has the student identify the author's use of special effects, reflect on literary devices, and note descriptive vocabulary. The student also has to compare two different versions of the Cinderella story, "The Talking Eggs" (San Souci, 1989) and "Ashpet" (Compton, 1994).

Writing Extension

Students can use their completed Story Grammar to write a summary or give a retelling (Heller, 1991). A retelling consists of a fairly detailed account of the story, while a summary is more concise and includes only the critical elements of the story. The Story Grammar provides an outline for students to follow. Their summary or retelling should be in chronological order and include the vocabulary words studied with Concept Circles. Encourage students to write summaries in their own words. Summaries can be written by students at all levels and writing them will get easier with practice. See the summaries written from the simple Story Grammar of *Whistle for Willie* (see Figure 2I) and the more sophisticated one written on the Story Grammar for *All the Money in the World* (see Figure 2J).

> **FIGURE 2I**
>
> ## Simple Summary
>
> Peter wisht he cod wiso. Then he saw a littl boy wiso at his dog. Then he lrd ho to wiso.

A first grader's summary of *Whistle for Willie*, based on a Story Chart

Assessment

You can evaluate the effectiveness of the Story Grammar strategy by examining students' summaries, for if students can successfully summarize all of the important elements of the story, the strategy has achieved its purpose. See Chapter 8 for an explanation of how to obtain both a comprehension and a writing grade for student summaries. You can also evaluate the strategy by having students give written or oral retellings of the story.

Summary

The book *All the Money in the World* which took place on a small farm outside of a small town, was about a boy named Quentin who rescued a leprechaun named Flan from a well. Quentin was granted his wish of having all the money in the world by Flan, and before long, huge piles of money appeared on Quentin's father's farm. When the U.S. Army heard about this they came and loaded the money into their trucks, but as they drove away, the money vanished from the trucks and reappeared on the farm. It was then that Quentin and his family realized that the money could not leave the farm and not even Quentin could spend it because then he wouldn't have all the money in the world.

As people found out their life savings had disappeared and banks, businesses, and even the government could no longer run, they began to panic. Quentin knew he had to do something about all the suffering taking place, but the Law of the Leprechauns would not allow him to take back his wish. Then the President of the United States invited Quentin and Flan to the White House and urged them to somehow reverse the wish and return the money because the other countries were threatening war. Quentin didn't know what he was going to do, but he knew he had to do something.

Luckily, the next day, Flan got stuck in a broken step and was again rescued by Quentin. This time when Quentin was granted a wish, he wished for all the money to go back where it came from. The President was so pleased with Quentin that he bought him the bike that Quentin had always wanted. Everyone was happy to have their money back in their pockets, and Quentin was glad to have his normal life back.

A sixth grader's summary of *All the Money in the World*, based on a Story Grammar

APPLICATION/EXTENSION STRATEGY:

Literary Report Card

Once students have read and understood the text, their learning continues when they apply what they have read to new situations or extend what they have learned in some way. Generally, application/extension strategies encourage students to do something with the material they have just read. By thinking—critically, logically, and creatively—about the information and ideas that emerge from their reading, students transform their thinking into actions and become producers of knowledge (Graves et al., 1998; Zull, 2002). Strategies to apply and extend learning flow from strategies used prior to reading and during reading. These strategies involve students, at all age levels, in aesthetic responses such as enjoying text and in cognitive responses such as analyzing, synthesizing, justifying, and evaluating information. If students respond to the text in one or more of these ways, they will better remember what they read, have a greater appreciation for the important concepts and ideas in the text, and express themselves in a variety of ways.

To have a complete lesson that encourages students to apply or extend their learning, select a strategy that has them use the cognitive processes of analysis, synthesis, evaluation/justification, and creation/invention. Since an understanding of character development is a very important objective of understanding narrative texts, we have chosen to showcase the Literary Report Card in this lesson.

The Literary Report Card (Johnson & Louis, 1987) is a versatile strategy that extends students' learning by inviting them to analyze text and evaluate characters' actions and traits. Based on the format of a school report card, the Literary Report Card asks students to select character traits, such as intelligence or courage; to grade the story character on those traits; and to support the grade with comments or evidence drawn from the story. The grades given by the students involve them in evaluation, and their supporting comments involve them in justifying the evaluation.

Using an overhead, list the subjects to be graded or the traits of the major character. Figure 2K is an example of a Literary Report Card completed by a first-grade class on Natasha from *Babushka's Doll*. After sufficient practice, the students themselves can come up with the subjects by reviewing characters' actions and formulating a list of qualities to be judged.

Before the Lesson

- Prepare a Literary Report Card template on chart paper or an overhead; also make copies for all students. (There are four Literary Report Card templates included on the CD.) We recommend focusing on one character when introducing the strategy and limiting the traits to two at first.

Teaching the Strategy

- After students have read the story, distribute the Literary Report Card templates and display a copy on the overhead or chart paper.

- Discuss with your students the characters' actions and traits that they observed from the story.

- Help students select a character from the story and write down the name of the character on the overhead. Students can choose the main character or another character that is interesting to them. You can guide students to select strong characters with a range of traits.

- Help students decide which of the character's traits will be evaluated and write the traits under the subject heading on the overhead. Be sure to use traits that are both positive and negative and will engender good discussion. For example, in Figure 2K, students selected *thoughtfulness* and *naughtiness* for Natasha. Many schools have "Character Counts" or similar citizenship programs. When possible, add one or more of the traits from your school's program to the Literary Report Card.

Literary Report Card

Character: Natasha

Subject	Grade	Comments
naughtiness	A	She wanted to do everything "now." When Babushka was busy she wanted to swing, eat lunch and have a ride.
thoughtfulness	D	She asked Babushka to rush and do everything for her when she was busy.
politeness	B	She asked permission to play with Babushka's doll.
responsibility	A	Natasha stayed alone and took care of the doll.

A first-grade class's evaluation of the character Natasha from *Babushka's Doll*

- Divide your students into small groups and assign them the task of discussing the character's actions and awarding grades on each subject; have them record a letter grade for each trait on the report card.

- Have students write comments to support each grade. If students are going to write about a trait, make sure they have three justifications for their grade.

You can use this strategy at all grade levels. In primary grades, students can evaluate the characters in a story based on their actions. In the upper grades, students can compare characters from different stories on a number of character traits; see the example in Figure 2L. The strategy also can be adapted so that students can evaluate characters from their reading in content areas such as history or social studies. After sufficient practice, the students will be able to apply the Literary Report Card strategy independently.

Writing Exercise: Character Sketch

The Literary Report Card lends itself very well to writing a Character Sketch, which consists of one or more paragraphs that describe personal characteristics of a character in the story. In a Character Sketch, the student presents his or her beliefs or opinions about a character by noting what kind of person the character is. Students can use the information generated in the Literary Report Card discussion. For example, when doing a Literary Report Card for *Babushka's Doll*, students can grade Natasha on specific traits and behavior toward her grandmother. All of that information can be used when they write a Character Sketch of the little girl.

Literary Report Card

Character: Natasha   Manyara

Subject	Grade	Comments	Grade	Comments
pride	D	She was humble about going to meet the prince.	A	Manyara boasted that the prince would choose her to be his wife.
gentleness	A	Natasha handled the snake carefully and was kind to the old lady in the woods.	F	She kicked the old woman and spoke unkindly to others.
honesty	A	Natasha was always truthful and open with others.	C	She was sneaky when she left for the city ahead of everyone but she did not lie about the trip.
generosity	A	Natasha always thought of others and even let her sister live in the castle after she was married.	F	She thought only of herself and did not care about her sister.

In this version of the Literary Report Card, students compare two characters on four traits.

To organize information for their Character Sketch, students can use the About Point Writing Response strategy, which provides a structure for all types of writing, including Character Sketches. This strategy is explained in detail on page 17. Give your students an About Point Writing Response Planning Guide (see template on facing page; it is also on the CD). To complete the outline for a Character Sketch of Natasha, they would do the following:

1. Write down who the Character Sketch is about (Natasha) and the main point (e.g., She was naughty because she wanted her grandmother to do everything for her when she was busy).

2. Write at least three sentences consisting of details that support the About Point. The details can come from the Literary Report Card.

3. Write a closing sentence that restates the About Point.

4. Write a Character Sketch (or summary) using information in the outline. First, use the About Point information to write a topic sentence. Then, if needed, flesh out ideas in the three supporting details. Finally, add a closing sentence from the outline.

Figure 2M is a Character Sketch of Natasha from *Babushka's Doll*. The About Point and closing were completed by the whole class, while the supporting details were completed by individual students.

Assessment

To evaluate the effectiveness of the Literary Report Card for promoting analysis and evaluation skills, engage students in an oral discussion about the character in the story, making observation notes on your students' responses. An alternative would be to use the Character Sketch as a means of evaluating the strategy. If your students write a Character Sketch, you can evaluate their writing ability by scoring it holistically with a writing rubric or by using a Character Sketch Checklist. Please see Chapter 8 for a description of both of these assessment measures.

ABOUT POINT WRITING RESPONSE PLANNING GUIDE

Outline	Summary
About:	
Point:	
1.	
2.	
3.	
Closing:	

FIGURE 2M

Character Sketch

About: Natasha

Point: was naughty because she wanted her grandmother to do everything for her when she was busy.

Supporting Details:

Babushka was washing the clothes but Natasha wanted to swing.

Babushka was feeding the goats. Natasha was hungry and wanted to eat lunch.

Babushka was hanging up clothes but Natasha wanted a ride.

Closing: Natasha was not thoughtful.

Natasha was naughty because she wanted her grandmother to do everything for her when she was busy. Babushka was washing the clothes but Natasha wanted to swing. Babushka was hanging up clothes but Natasha wanted a ride. Babushka was feeding the goats. Natasha was hungry and wanted to eat lunch. Natasha was not thoughtful.

This Character Sketch was completed by a first-grade class using the About Point Writing Response Guide (see page 17).

Alternative Comprehension and Application/Extension Strategies for Understanding Narrative Text Structure

The goal of this chapter is to present a coherent lesson plan for helping students understand a narrative text. Semantic Maps and Concept Circles are also effective with expository texts, but Story Grammar and Literary Report Cards focus on key aspects of narrative and enhance comprehension by helping students become skilled in recognizing and analyzing story elements.

In this section we present five additional strategies that facilitate comprehension of narrative text. Three alternative comprehension strategies are Circle Story, Story Pyramid, and Plot Relationships Chart. The two alternative application/extension strategies are Character Rating Scale and Emotions Chart. You may substitute these for the Story Grammar or Literary Report Card, depending on your students' needs and interests. Alternative strategies develop the same skills and cognitive processes as the strategies previously discussed in the lesson sequence, but they have different characteristics that help you differentiate instruction to meet the needs of all learners. For example, while some students complete a Story Grammar, other students who need a simplified version might complete a Plot Relationships Chart. Still others might do advanced work with a Story Pyramid. As students develop competency, they can be exposed to all of the strategies throughout the elementary grades.

COMPREHENSION STRATEGY:

Circle Story

Circle Stories (Jett-Simpson, 1981) involve students in the same cognitive processes as a Story Grammar, but instead of writing about story elements, students draw them. The drawing option encourages students to visualize what occurred in the story, which enhances comprehension. Drawing also supports students with limited English proficiency and provides a new modality for students who show strength in drawing. The strategy is often used to introduce young children to the elements of story structure and helps them learn to summarize or retell stories. Circle Stories can integrate reading, listening, viewing, speaking, and writing. A sample Circle Story for *Where the Wild Things Are* (Sendak, 1963) is shown in Figure 2N. In this instance, the first-grade student went on to write a summary on the computer, which he then added to his Circle Story.

Circle Story

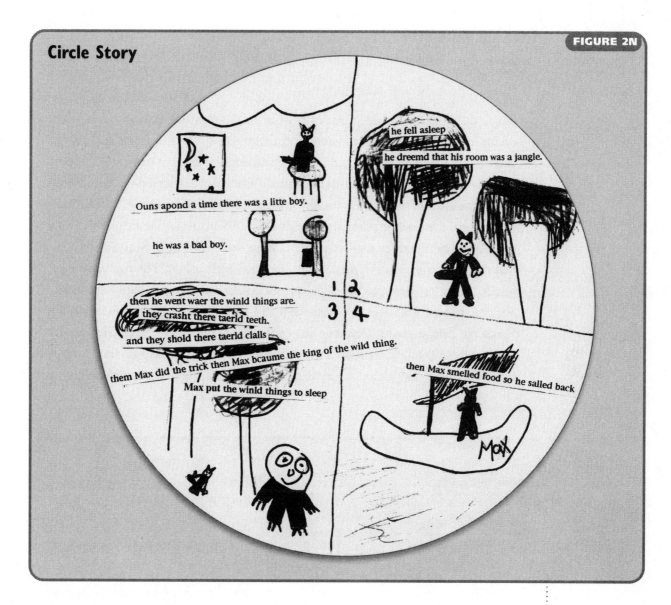

This is a Circle Story completed by a first-grade student for *Where the Wild Things Are* (Sendak, 1963). The story is about an adventure a boy imagines when he is punished and sent to his room. The student completed a summary on the computer and added it to the Circle Story.

Before the Lesson

- Draw a large circle on chart paper and divide it into as many parts as are necessary to depict the significant events in the story. You can begin with three sections for beginning, middle, and end. As students develop competency, you can add more sections to represent the number of significant events in the story. Make copies of the Circle Story template with the same format for students. (You will find several Concept Circle templates on the CD.) You may adapt this for younger students by having them focus on only one event, as shown in Figure 2O. Then you can sequence the individual circles as a whole-class activity.

Teaching the Strategy

- Have your students read the story for enjoyment.

- Discuss the story with your students.

- Guide the students, either individually or in small groups, to select and sequence events in the story. Write the events in the segments of your large circle. In time you can list the main events and have the students place them in the appropriate sections in the circle. Use questions to guide students to describe the beginning (goal), the middle (problem), and the ending (resolution) events. For "The Three Little Pigs," the teacher asked these questions: "Think about the beginning of the story. What did the three pigs want to do? What was their goal?" Students responded that the pigs wanted to go live on their own (see Figure 20). The teacher then asked, "What problem did the pigs have after they built their house?" Students decided that the wolf wanted to eat them and blew two of their houses down. Finally, to help students decide on the resolution of the story, the teacher asked, "How did the third pig trick the wolf and protect himself?" These guiding questions helped students skip various story details and identify the major events in the story.

FIGURE 20

Circle Story

This is a kindergartner's artwork and writing describing the first event in *The Three Little Pigs*. In this modification of a circle story, eight students in a kindergarten class created a circle for one of the eight events in *The Three Little Pigs*. Then they wrote about their drawing on another circle. The teacher then sequenced the circles on a large sheet of paper.

- Distribute the Circle Story templates. Ask individual students or students in groups to draw a picture representing designated events in the appropriate section of the circle. NOTE: Mark the initiating event to indicate where the story begins.

- Using a completed Circle Story as a prompt, have the students retell the story, either individually or cooperatively in a round-robin format. Working in groups, the students can write a summary of the story, which could also serve as the writing and assessment components.

COMPREHENSION STRATEGY:
Story Pyramid

The Story Pyramid (Macon, Bewell, & Vogt, 1991) is a strategy that helps students identify important elements of a story and describe them using a limited number of words. Requiring concise descriptions stretches students' thinking and is a fun alternative to a traditional Story Grammar. A completed Story Pyramid will have the following information:

LINE 1. First name of the main character

LINE 2. Two words describing the main character

LINE 3. Three words describing the setting

LINE 4. Four words stating the problem

LINE 5. Five words describing one main event

LINE 6. Six words describing a second main event

LINE 7. Seven words describing a third main event

LINE 8. Eight words stating the solution to the problem

STORY PYRAMID TEMPLATE

1. ___
2. ___ ___
3. ___ ___ ___
4. ___ ___ ___ ___
5. ___ ___ ___ ___ ___
6. ___ ___ ___ ___ ___ ___
7. ___ ___ ___ ___ ___ ___ ___
8. ___ ___ ___ ___ ___ ___ ___ ___

Students enjoy the challenge of completing a Story Pyramid, but they need a great deal of guidance in getting started with this strategy. Once they understand the elements they are to describe, they will need to practice compressing into very brief phrases ideas that have been expressed in complete sentences during discussion. Thinking aloud as you complete a Story Pyramid for a book you've read as a class is a great way to model the process before asking students to do it independently.

Story Pyramid and Summary

FIGURE 2P

Story Pyramid

1. Daughter
2. sad, lonely
3. On grandparents farm
4. She misses her dad
5. Her dad is always leaving
6. Her dad comes to visit them
7. He leaves again for a new job
8. Dreaming about her dad makes her remember him

Summary

This is about a girl who has a problem with her Dad because he's always leaving and leaves again for a new job. And she really misses him. The only thing she can remember him by is if she dreams about him. This girl lives with her grandparents on a farm. And she's really lonely and sad too, but her dad comes to visit sometimes and that makes her very very happy because she doesn't see him that much because he's busy with this job. At the end of the story, her dad comes to see her at the farm and she runs to him with happiness and is glad to see her father again.

A Story Pyramid and summary completed by a fifth-grade student for *Always My Dad*, a story about a girl who misses her father, who must travel frequently

Teaching the Strategy

- Show students a Story Pyramid and discuss the elements with them; there is a template on the CD. Discuss some specific examples of setting descriptions, problem statements, and event summaries from stories familiar to the class.

- Ask students to read the story, focusing on the important story elements called for by the Story Pyramid. You can read the story aloud to younger students.

- Guide students in their reading by having them stop to predict story events or to describe key elements. For example, prompt students to predict what the problem is and how they think the main character will solve it.

- Discuss the story after reading. Encourage students to form images in their minds of what occurred in the story.

- Complete the Story Pyramid, first as a whole-group activity. When students become familiar with the strategy, have them complete it in small groups and then individually.

Students may need help in deciding which events to select for lines 5 through 7 of the pyramid. Suggest that they use an event from the beginning, middle, and end of the story to complete the lines. They might also choose the three most significant events, making sure that the events are written in the correct sequence. If students have difficulty selecting a specific number of words to complete a line of the Pyramid (e.g., four words to describe the problem), have them state their ideas in sentence format and then select kernels of information from their sentences to find words for completing the lines. After a Story Pyramid is completed, students can write a summary of the story, which can also serve as an assessment/evaluation of the strategy. A summary should be easy to write, because students have already selected and organized a limited number of key elements of the story. Figure 2P shows a Story Pyramid and summary completed by a fifth-grade student for *Always My Dad* (Wyeth, 1995).

Plot Relationships Chart

The Plot Relationships Chart (Schmidt & Buckley, 1991) helps students identify the major parts of a story. This strategy provides students with a structure to help them understand the relationships among characters, goals, problems, and solutions. Figure 2Q shows an example of a completed Plot Relationships Chart for *Stone Fox* (Gardiner, 1980). You will find a template for the chart on the CD.

Before the Lesson

- Prepare a chart with four columns. Label the columns with the four guide words: *Somebody*, *Wanted*, *But*, and *So* (see the example in Figure 2Q and the template on the CD).

FIGURE 2Q

Plot Relationships Chart

Somebody	Wanted	But	So
Little Willy	to win the dogsled race and earn first prize of $500 so he could pay the back taxes on Grandpa's farm.	Stone Fox, a Shoshone Indian, enters the race with his dog team of Samoyeds so he can win the $500 prize and buy back the lands his tribe has lost.	Little Willy and Stone Fox race, and close to the finish line when they are neck-and-neck, Willy's dog, Searchlight, drops dead from exhaustion. Stone Fox lets Willy carry Searchlight across the finish line and win the $500 prize.

Summary:
Little Willy wanted to win the dogsled race and earn the first prize of $500 so he could pay the back taxes pm Grandpa's farm. But Stone Fox, a Shoshone Indian, enters the race with his dog team of Samoyeds so he can win the $500 prize and buy back the lands his tribe has lost. So Little Willy and Stone Fox race, and close to the finish line when they are neck-and-neck, Willy's dog, Searchlight, drops dead from exhaustion. Stone Fox lets Willy carry Searchlight across the finish line and win the $500 prize.

A completed Plot Relationships Chart for the story, *Stone Fox*, along with a summary based on the chart.

Teaching the Strategy

- Ask a question for each guide word and write the students' response in the appropriate column. For example, Who is the main character in the story? (Somebody) What was his or her goal? (Wanted) What was the problem? (But) What happened? (So)

- Read the responses on the chart so students can see the relationship of the elements (character, goal, problem, solution). Ask students to visualize what happened in the story as you read. When discussing *Stone Fox*, the teacher asked students to create an image in their mind of Willy and Stone Fox in a close race, each eager to win.

- If appropriate, have the students select another character in the story and repeat the four questions, answering them from the new character's perspective. Once again, model the use of the chart.

- Discuss alternative solutions to the problem as a class. Ask students how else the author could have solved the problem the story presents.

- After you have modeled this strategy several times, have the students apply the strategy in pairs or in small groups.

As is the case with the Story Pyramid, students are going to need guidance and practice with the Plot Relationships Chart. Once they understand the structure, they can use it to share personal reading, create story ideas, and write summaries of stories.

APPLICATION/EXTENSION STRATEGY:
Character Rating Scale

The Character Rating Scale (Johnson & Louis, 1987) is a strategy that, like the Literary Report Card, encourages readers to make judgments about characters in a story and then justify their opinions. With this postreading strategy, students evaluate characters by rating them on several key qualities or traits using a three-, five-, or seven-point scale. You can use a three-point scale with young students and increase the number of levels for older students who can discern degrees of differences more easily. After you have read the story with your students, help them complete the Character Rating Scale using character qualities and their opposites (see a sample Character Rating Scale for *The True Story of the 3 Little Pigs* [Scieszka, 1996] in Figure 2R).

Character Rating Scale

Directions: Complete the Character Rating Scale. Then choose one trait and write a Character Sketch of the Wolf. Be sure to have three reasons to justify your rating for the trait about which you will be writing.

CHARACTER RATING SCALE: Wolf

CHARACTERISTIC						OPPOSITE TRAIT

Devious ✔ _____ _____ _____ _____ Straightforward
Justification: 1. He pretended to need sugar so he could get into the houses of the three pigs. 2. He claimed the third pig insulted his Granny so he tried to break in. 3. He blamed the news reporters for making him look guilty.

Clever _____ ✔ _____ _____ _____ Dull
Justification: He tried to present a different slant to the story but he was not clever enough to have people believe him.

Creative _____ ✔ _____ _____ _____ Unimaginative
Justification: He tried to think of a good explanation for breaking into the pigs' houses.

Honest _____ _____ _____ ✔ _____ Dishonest
Justification: Though he was honest about eating the pigs, the rest of the story is a lie.

Character Sketch: The Wolf is a devious character. He pretended to need sugar to bake his Granny's cake so he could get into the homes of the two pigs so he could eat them. He also claimed that the third pig insulted his sweet Granny and that is why the police caught him banging on this door. The Wolf lays the blame for this poor image on news reporters who make him look guilty. The Wolf slants the truth.

A completed Character Rating Scale and Character Sketch for *The True Story of the 3 Little Pigs*. The student chose the characteristic "devious" to use for the basis of his sketch. The Character Sketch uses the About Point Writing Response format (see page 53) with a topic sentence consisting of an About (the Wolf) and a Point (is a devious character), three sentences of justification, and a closing statement, "The Wolf slants the truth."

Before the Lesson

• Choose the main character or another strong character from the story and list one or several of his or her characteristics on the left-hand side of the rating scale; you'll find a template on the CD.

• Leave space on the right-hand side of the scale to list the opposite of each characteristic; the class will generate the opposite traits during the lesson. For instance, if you choose *devious* as one trait, you might use *straightforward* as the opposite.

Character Rating Scale and Character Sketch

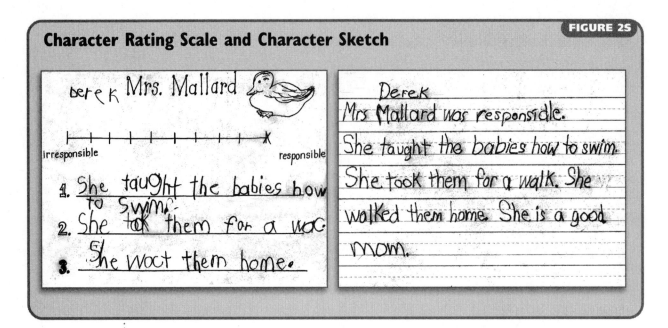

A completed first grader's Character Rating Scale and a Character Sketch for *Make Way for Ducklings* (McCloskey, 1941), a story about the search for a home for a family of ducklings in Boston. The Character Sketch follows the About Point Writing Response format (see page 17). The topic sentence is constructed from the About (Mrs. Mallard) and the Point (was responsible). There are three sentences with supporting details and a closing statement, "She is a good mom."

Teaching the Strategy

- Discuss the story, guiding students to talk about the qualities or traits of the characters.

- Focusing on the characteristics you've listed on the Character Rating Scale, ask students what the opposite quality of each characteristic would be; write the opposite characteristics on the right-hand side of the rating scale.

- Ask students to rate the character on each characteristic by putting a check mark on one of the blank spaces between the opposite qualities. A check mark on the space right next to the quality indicates that the character has that quality, while a check in the middle of the scale indicates that the character is not strong on either quality.

- Have students justify each rating by writing down (or asking you to write down) one to three of the character's actions in the story that support the rating.

Students can use the information from the Character Rating Scale to write a Character Sketch, which was discussed earlier as a possible writing activity for the Literary Report Card (see page 49). The Character Sketch, along with oral discussion, can be used for evaluating the effectiveness of the Character Rating Scale strategy. Figure 2S shows a Character Sketch written by a first grader for Mrs. Mallard from *Make Way for Ducklings*; the student's Character Rating Scale is also shown.

Emotions Chart

Another strategy that requires students to apply or extend what they have read is an Emotions Chart, which presents a visual display of events in a story. As students complete an Emotions Chart, they are analyzing the story while looking for the impact of events on characters' feelings and emotions. Students are also making judgments about how an event has affected a character.

Before the Lesson

- Prepare an Emotions Chart (see the sample below and the template on the CD).

- Number and list the events in the story below the chart using the information collected on the Story Grammar, Circle Story, or the Story Pyramid (whichever comprehension strategy you used) as a guide.

- Along the horizontal axis of the chart, place the numbers corresponding to the events; see the examples in Figures 2T and 2U.

- Select a character from the story that you think exhibits the full range of a particular emotion (e.g., happy, sad, angry, etc.) throughout the events of the story.

- Along the vertical axis, write the word *Emotions* at the top, followed by three short blank lines (which show three levels of intensity for the emotion). By connecting each of the events on the horizontal scale with one of the emotions on the vertical scale, students create a graph of the emotions experienced by one or more of the story characters at each point in the story.

> **EMOTIONS CHART TEMPLATE**
>
> Emotions:
>
> _____
>
> _____
>
> _____
>
> Events:
>
> 1. _____
> 2. _____
> 3. _____
> 4. _____
> 5. _____
>
> 1   2   3   4   5

Teaching the Strategy

- Discuss the story with the students, focusing on how the chosen character must have felt at certain points in the story (consult the graphic organizer used with the comprehension strategy as necessary).

- Write a range of related emotions on the board. The emotions can be either one emotion with degrees of intensity (e.g., annoyed, angry, furious) or three different emotions, the first and last being polar opposites and the middle representing a moderate stance (e.g., shy, sociable, gregarious).

- Help students relate to the range of emotions by asking them to respond to three brief scenarios. For example, if the emotion is happiness, you might have students imagine scenarios that would elicit three degrees of happiness, ranging from mild to strong. For instance, you might ask, "How do you feel about having dinner with your family?" (Okay or Good) "How do you feel when your mother says you can have ice cream on a hot day?" (Happy) "How do you feel when your parents take you to an amusement park?" (Excited).

- Ask the students how the character in the story felt at the time each of the numbered events took place. Mark their responses on the chart with dots.

- Have the students take turns drawing lines between each point—connecting the dots—so they can understand how the events that took place in the story affected a character.

- If you want your students to understand the impact of events on different characters in the story, follow the same procedure with another character, using a little square instead of a dot. Have the students draw the lines with different colored markers, so they won't confuse the characters; see Figure 2T for an example of a Emotions Chart depicting the emotions of three characters at once.

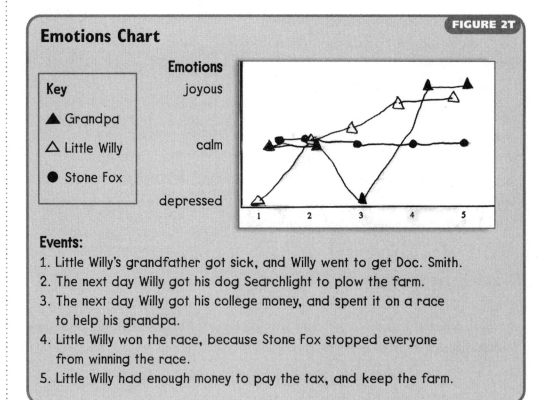

FIGURE 2T

Emotions Chart

Key

▲ Grandpa

△ Little Willy

● Stone Fox

Emotions

joyous

calm

depressed

Events:
1. Little Willy's grandfather got sick, and Willy went to get Doc. Smith.
2. The next day Willy got his dog Searchlight to plow the farm.
3. The next day Willy got his college money, and spent it on a race to help his grandpa.
4. Little Willy won the race, because Stone Fox stopped everyone from winning the race.
5. Little Willy had enough money to pay the tax, and keep the farm.

An Emotions Chart for *Stone Fox* that was completed independently by a low ability sixth-grade student and depicts three different emotions for three characters in the story.

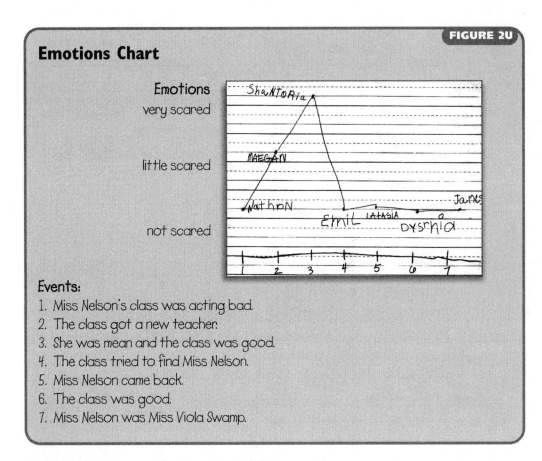

Emotions Chart

FIGURE 2U

Emotions

very scared

little scared

not scared

ShaNTORia

MAEGAN

NathoN

EmiL   LATASIA   James

DYShia

1   2   3   4   5   6   7

Events:
1. Miss Nelson's class was acting bad.
2. The class got a new teacher.
3. She was mean and the class was good.
4. The class tried to find Miss Nelson.
5. Miss Nelson came back.
6. The class was good.
7. Miss Nelson was Miss Viola Swamp.

This Emotions Chart was completed by a group of kindergarten students.
The chart depicts the level of fear the fictional class was feeling throughout
Miss Nelson is Missing (Allard & Marshall, 1977), from not scared to
very scared. Students wrote their names alongside their responses.

After completing an Emotions Chart, students can write a paragraph explaining why a character feels a particular emotion related to one of the events in the story. Students can use the About Point Writing Response strategy (see page 17). You can use students' paragraphs and oral discussion to evaluate the effectiveness of the Emotions Chart strategy.

ThinkingWorks Lesson Planning Guide

A number of strategies have been introduced in this chapter that will enable you to teach a complete lesson for narrative text. The ThinkingWorks Lesson Planning Guide provides you with a way of organizing the strategies and making a record of which cognitive and language processes you have addressed in your lesson. Simply write the name of the strategy under each component of the lesson plan (e.g., background knowledge, vocabulary, comprehension, and application/extension). Then check off the processes that each of the strategies encourages students to use. Figure 2V shows two completed planning guides using strategies introduced in this chapter.

ThinkingWorks Lesson Planning Guides

	STRATEGIES			
	Background Knowledge	Vocabulary	Comprehension	Application/ Extension
COGNITIVE PROCESSES	Semantic Map	Concept Circles	Story Grammar/ Summary	Literary Report Card/Char. Sketch
Develop Background Knowledge	✔	✔		
Expand Vocabulary Knowledge	✔	✔		
Use Text Structure			✔	
Set a Purpose for Learning	✔		✔	
Infer/Select Information			✔	
Create Images			✔	
Relate/Connect Ideas			✔	
Clarify/Monitor Understanding			✔	
Analyze				✔
Synthesize				✔
Evaluate/Justify				✔
Create/Invent				✔
LANGUAGE PROCESSES				
Read			✔	
Write			/✔	/✔
Listen/View	✔	✔		✔
Communicate Orally	✔	✔		✔
COGNITIVE PROCESSES	Semantic Map	Concept Circles	Circle Story/ Summary	Character Rating Scale/Char. Sketch
Develop Background Knowledge	✔	✔		
Expand Vocabulary Knowledge	✔	✔		
Use Text Structure			✔	
Set a Purpose for Learning	✔		✔	
Infer/Select Information			✔	
Create Images			✔	
Relate/Connect Ideas			✔	
Clarify/Monitor Understanding			✔	
Analyze				✔
Synthesize				✔
Evaluate/Justify				✔
Create/Invent				✔
LANGUAGE PROCESSES				
Read			✔	
Write			/✔	/✔
Listen/View	✔	✔	✔	
Communicate Orally	✔	✔	✔	

Analyzing Narrative Text

In This Chapter:

As noted in Chapter 1, the purpose of the ThinkingWorks Model is to help teachers systematically implement strategies instruction in their classrooms. The previous chapter outlined a lesson sequence aimed at helping students learn about story structure to enhance their comprehension of narrative texts. This chapter builds on the fundamental understandings developed by the comprehension and application/extension activities presented in Chapter 2. The strategies in this chapter challenge students to analyze narrative text by relating story problems to their own lives, examining story events from different perspectives, comparing and contrasting story elements, and inferring information about characters. Students will also write original stories based on key vocabulary and concepts from a text.

ThinkingWorks Lesson Plan Sequence for Analyzing Narrative Text

To help students extend their understanding of narrative text and deepen their comprehension, we have designed the following lesson sequence:

BACKGROUND KNOWLEDGE: . . . . .Problem/Solution Guide

VOCABULARY: . . . . .Concept of a Definition

COMPREHENSION: . . . . .Story Map from Characters' Perspectives

APPLICATION/EXTENSION: . . . . .Compare/Contrast Venn Diagram

In addition, we present three alternative strategies for comprehension and application/extension that you may choose for variety or to meet your particular students' needs: Probable Passage, Action Belief Chart, and SCAMPER. You can be flexible in terms of how you implement these strategies. However, each lesson should provide at least one assessment and one writing opportunity for students. In this sequence, we recommend that students write an editorial after the comprehension activity.

BACKGROUND KNOWLEDGE STRATEGY:

Problem/Solution Guide

A Problem/Solution Guide (Johnson & Louis, 1987) is a highly motivating activity because it piques students' interest in a topic by asking them to look at a novel situation and resolve a problem. As a prereading strategy, it activates students' background knowledge about an important concept or idea in a story. Figure 3A shows the problem we posed to third graders to get them ready to read *Stone Fox* (Gardiner, 1980). Beneath the problem are the varied solutions students generated. As students thought through the hypothetical problem, they drew on their background knowledge and shared how they might approach the problem of getting money to help with family finances. This experience prepared them to read and understand the story about a boy facing a similar situation.

Before the Lesson

- Identify a problematic situation in the story that students need to understand in order to comprehend and appreciate the events of the story. In our example using *Stone Fox*, Little Willy and his sick grandfather are in danger of losing their home.

- Create a hypothetical situation similar to the one in the story you're about to read that will stimulate students' interest in the story and help them to understand the problem. Develop a question that will spark discussion about the problem. We asked students to think about what they could do to earn money if their family needed it. You can write the question on the board or prepare copies of a Problem/Solution Guide (see the template on the CD) with the question at the top; students write their solutions beneath the problem (see the example in Figure 3A).

Teaching the Strategy

- Tell students that they will be working on a Problem/Solution Guide to build their background knowledge before reading a story.

- Pose the question you created that invites students both to think about the problem and devise possible solutions. We asked, "What would you do if your family needed money to pay the rent and your mom, dad, or grandparents were sick and couldn't pay it?"

- Divide the students into groups, so they can discuss the problem and develop possible solutions. Have them record their solutions on the Problem/Solution Guide.

- Bring the students together and have each group present its solutions to the hypothetical problem. Write the solutions on the board.

- Summarize the discussion and link it to the story. The teacher in our example tied the discussion up this way: "These are all good solutions to the problem. They tell me that you know a lot about the situation you discussed, and you used this knowledge to come up with possible solutions to the problem. The story you are

Problem/Solution Guide

Problem

What would you do if your family needed money to pay the rent and your mom, dad, or grandparents were sick and couldn't pay it?

Solutions

Student A: Borrow money from my uncle.

Student B: Deliver papers.

Student C: Baby sit for my neighbor.

Student D: Buy a lottery ticket.

Student E: Hold a fund-raiser.

A Problem/Solution Guide third graders completed in preparation for reading *Stone Fox*.

going to read is about a boy who has to confront a problem similar to the one you've discussed in your groups. However, while your solutions are good for those who live in the city, the boy in the story, *Stone Fox*, lives with his grandpa in Wyoming. They are in danger of losing their farm, and he doesn't have a lot of people around who will buy his papers or candy or hire him to babysit. As you read, you will see what he does to try and earn money to save his farm."

- Have students read the text for the purpose of identifying the problem in the story and determining how the character in the story solved the problem.

Writing Extension

You can add a writing component to this strategy by having students write a one-paragraph summary developing their suggestion for how they would solve the problem stated in the Problem/Solution Guide. Students can use the About Point Writing Response strategy to plan and write their paragraph (see page 17).

Assessment

You can analyze your students' summaries to determine if the Problem/Solution Guide helped them use their background knowledge and information to understand the problem situation in the story. If students are unable to identify the problem and develop solutions, the strategy was ineffective.

VOCABULARY STRATEGY:
Concept of a Definition

Concept of a Definition (Schwartz & Raphael, 1985) is a strategy for learning vocabulary words in depth. There are times in their reading when students need to thoroughly understand the vocabulary in order to comprehend the story; a simple definition is not enough. At these times, you can use the Concept of a Definition strategy, which provides students with guidelines for understanding the components of a complete and thorough definition. You help your students achieve this understanding by having them ask themselves three questions about a word:

- What is it? (categorization)

- What is it like? (characteristics of the word)

- What are some examples? (illustrations)

Students should be able to answer all three questions if they have a solid grasp of the word.

Figure 3B features Concept of Definition diagrams for three words chosen for *Stone Fox*. When using this strategy, select words that are critical to understanding the central ideas in the text (usually five or six words per chapter of a book). You can also select one or two words that are interesting and that students will use again. In our example from *Stone Fox*, the words *strongbox* and *forged* are critical to understanding two important points in the text. Will realized the enormity of his problem when he finds there is no money in the strongbox to pay the taxes. The speed and determination of the dog Searchlight are also important; Searchlight is described as having "forged ahead."

Note that the category can be concrete—for example, *astronaut* is a *person*, who has characteristics such as *understands science* and *is courageous and healthy*. Examples would include people such as *John Glenn* and *Neil Armstrong*. Or the category can be abstract—for example, *irrigation* is a *process*, which has characteristics such as *helps crops grow* and *uses pipes*. Examples might include *farms out west* and the *Nile River*.

Before the Lesson

- Select a few words from the text students are going to be reading that are important for an understanding of the story.

- Prepare copies of Concept of a Definition graphic organizers for the class; you'll find a template on the CD.

Teaching the Strategy

- Write the words on the board and define them in student-friendly language, giving examples to clarify meaning.

- Distribute the Concept of a Definition graphic organizers.

- Discuss the three components of the diagram, emphasizing how this strategy will help them learn words they need to know to understand the text.

- Brainstorm responses to the questions with the class.

- Have students complete the diagram as a class. Students can also work in small groups and then share results with the class. You can support groups by reviewing definitions and examples of the words when necessary.

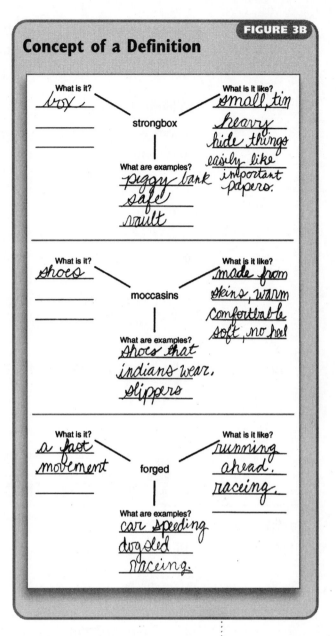

FIGURE 3B

Concept of a Definition

Third graders used Concept of a Definition to learn about these three words from *Stone Fox*.

- Remind students that they are better prepared to read the text now that they fully understand the vocabulary for the important concepts. They can refer to their graphic organizers as they read if they need extra support.

Writing Extension

You can ask students to write a one-paragraph summary for each of the words they defined with the Concept of a Definition diagram, using the About Point Writing Response strategy if desired (see page 17).

Assessment

If you choose to have students write at this point in the lesson, you can use their paragraphs to assess the effectiveness of the Concept of a Definition strategy for learning vocabulary. If you are not going to assign a writing component, you can have students write a definition for each of the words that includes telling what the word is, what it's like, and what some examples are.

COMPREHENSION STRATEGY:

Story Map from Characters' Perspectives

Story Map from Characters' Perspectives (Shanahan & Shanahan, 1997) is a strategy that helps students think critically about story elements. Students examine the problem and events of a story from the perspectives of two different characters. Figure 3C shows how students interpreted events in *Stone Fox* from the points of view of Willy and Stone Fox. Considering different points of view deepens students' thinking about a text. In this case, the strategy helped students discover the different motivations Willy and Stone Fox had to achieve the same goal of winning money. This is a sophisticated strategy, and students need guidance—which you can provide through questioning and discussion—to use it effectively.

Before the Lesson

- Prepare handouts of the Story Map from Characters' Perspectives for students; see the template at left, which is also on the CD.

STORY MAP FROM
CHARACTERS' PERSPECTIVES

Setting: Setting:

Character: Character:

Characters' Perspective of: Characters' Perspective of:

    Problem: Problem:

    Events: Events:

    1.   1.

    2.   2.

    3.   3.

    Ending: Ending:

Story Map from Characters' Perspectives

Setting: Wyoming
Character: Willy

Character's Perspective of:

Problem: Willy and his sick Grandpa will lose their farm without money to pay the taxes.

Events:
1. Willy believes he can win the race because he has a fast dog and they know the course.
2. Willy tried to talk to Stone Fox.
3. Willy petted the Samoyeds.
4. Willy raced his dog hard and led the race. He was determined to win.
5. Willy's dog died before reaching the finish line.

Ending: Willy carried his dog across the finish line and won money to save the farm.

Setting: Wyoming
Character: Stone Fox

Character's Perspective of:

Problem: Stone Fox is determined to buy land so his tribe can leave the reservation.

Events:
1. Stone Fox believes he will win because he has five strong dogs and never has lost a race.
2. Stone Fox never talked to white people because of the way they treated his people.
3. Stone Fox hit him for touching his dogs.
4. Stone Fox let his dogs take a gradual lead and caught up to Willy. He was determined to win.
5. Stone Fox stopped his sled and saw that Willy's dog Searchlight was dead.

Ending: Stone Fox stopped the other racers and let Willy carry his dog across the finish line.

Students used this version of a Story Map to see events in *Stone Fox* from different perspectives.

Teaching the Strategy

• Distribute the Story Map from Characters' Perspectives handouts.

• Review the elements of Story Grammar so students can attend to the important story elements while reading (setting, character, problem, events, ending).

• Have students read the text or read it aloud.

• Ask students questions that will help them understand main elements of the story (e.g., characters, setting, problem, resolution). Then ask questions that will help them interpret the story elements from the different points of view of two characters in the story. The teacher in our *Stone Fox* example asked students why Willy and Stone Fox wanted to win the race and why Stone Fox stopped before the finish line. These questions helped students see events from different perspectives.

• Explain how seeing events from different perspectives can enhance our understanding of a situation or story.

- Have students complete this version of a Story Map (Grammar), first from one main character's perspective and then from the perspective of another main character with a different view. Initially, the strategy should be completed as a class; as the students become familiar with the strategy, they can complete the Story Map in small groups or individually.

- Engage your students in comparing the characters' interpretations of the problem, the events in the story, and the resolution of the problem.

Figure 3D shows an adaptation of the strategy in which students compare characters from different versions of a story.

Writing Exercise: Editorial

This is an excellent place to include a writing component. The Story Map from Characters' Perspectives lends itself very nicely to the writing of an editorial—a short, persuasive essay presenting the writer's opinion of an event. Students can

---

FIGURE 3D

Adaptation of a Story Map from Characters' Perspectives

Name: Dawn

Three Little Pigs Comparing the Wolf Version and the Pig Version

	Wolf's Version (*The True Story of the Three Little Pigs*)	Pig's Version (*The Three Little Pigs*)
Why did the wolf go to the pigs' houses?	He needed a cup of sugar to make a cake for his granny.	He wanted to eat the pigs.
Why did the wolf huff and puff?	He had a terrible cold and kept sneezing.	He did it to blow the pigs' houses down.
How did the first and second pig die?	They were killed when their poorly built houses caved in on them.	The wolf ate the pigs.
What happened after the wolf went to the third pig's house?	The pig insulted the wolf's granny so the wolf became angry and pounded on the door. At the same time he was huffing, puffing and sneezing from his cold. The police arrested him and put him in jail.	The wolf tried to break in but the house was too sturdy. The wolf tried to get the pig to meet him in an open area 3 times but the pig outsmarted him. Finally the wolf tried to get in the house through the chimney. The pig caught him in a pot, cooked him and ate him.

This is an adaptation of a Story Map from Characters' Perspectives completed by a fourth-grade student. It shows the different perspectives of the wolf in *The True Story of the Three Little Pigs* (Scieszka, 1996) and the third pig in *The Three Little Pigs*. The questions on the Story Map focus attention on the important points of controversy.

write the editorial from their own perspective or from the perspective of one of the characters in the story they have just analyzed using the Story Map.

An Editorial Planning Guide (see the sample below and template on CD) can prepare students for this writing task. On the planning guide, they write down the name of the author of the editorial, which can be either themselves or a character in the story. They then write a statement expressing their opinion in support of an action they feel should be taken. They list reasons justifying their opinion and include a closing statement. From this planning guide, students can write their editorial. Figure 3E shows an Editorial Planning Guide and an editorial written from the perspective of Doc Smith using information from the Story Map for *Stone Fox* shown in Figure 3C. Note that the About Point Writing Response strategy (see page 17) can be adapted and used to plan and write an editorial. Figure 3F shows another writing extension based on the Story Map from Characters' Perspectives.

Assessment

You can assess comprehension by examining students' editorials to see if they took a stance and supported it with evidence from the story. You can also assess the editorials to obtain a measure of students' writing ability. To do this, use a rubric to score their editorials holistically as explained in Chapter 8.

Editorial Planning Guide and Editorial

Editorial Planning Guide

Author: Doc Smith

Audience: Residents of Jackson, Wyoming

Opinion
- About: The sponsors of the dogsled race
- Point: should award two prizes to both Willy and Stone Fox this year

Reasons
- Willy raced well and led the racers.
- Stone Fox let him carry Searchlight across the line.
- Stone Fox is a champion racer and never lost a race.
- He could have won but stopped for Willy.
- Willy and Stone Fox acted like winners and showed good sportsmanship.

Closing: Both deserved to win.

Editorial

The sponsors of the dogsled race should award two prizes this year to Willy and Stone Fox. Willy deserves the prize. He raced well and was ahead of the racers until the finish line. When his dog, Searchlight, died from exhaustion, his opponent, Stone Fox, let him carry his dog and cross the finish line first.

Stone Fox should win the race as well. He is the champion dogsled racer and has never lost a race. Stone Fox could have crossed the finish line first but he stopped out of respect for Willy. Stone Fox and Willy acted like winners and showed good sportsmanship throughout the race. Both deserved to win.

A fourth grader's editorial persuading readers that both Willy and Stone Fox be awarded prizes; it is written from the perspective of a third character in the story.

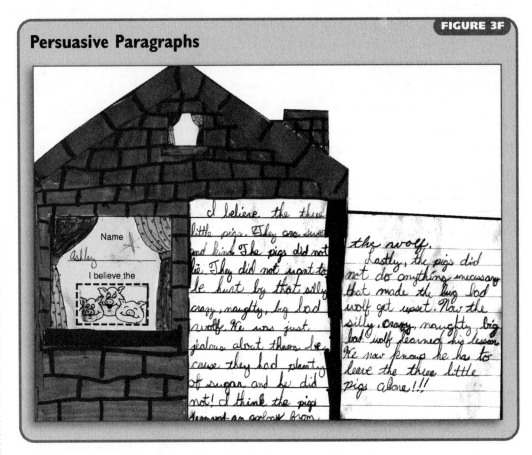

Persuasive Paragraphs

FIGURE 3F

Here is another writing option based on the Story Map from Characters' Perspectives. Fourth graders wrote persuasive paragraphs in support of a character from *The Three Little Pigs*. These paragraphs are similar to an editorial because the student takes a stand and supports it. However, they are different from an editorial because they are not addressed to a specific audience.

APPLICATION/EXTENSION STRATEGY:
Compare/Contrast Venn Diagram

The Venn Diagram (Macon, Bewell, & Vogt, 1991) is a visual aid that allows students to see how two or more people, places, events, or ideas are alike and different. Students can easily extend their learning by comparing and contrasting characters from different stories or story elements from two different versions of a text. See Figure 3G for a comparison of Willy and Matuk, characters from two different books, in a Venn Diagram. Figure 3H shows how students used a Venn Diagram to compare how a character was presented in two versions of a story.

Students can complete the Venn Diagram in groups or on their own and then use the diagram to discuss the similarities and differences between the items being compared and contrasted. The completed diagram can also be used as a basis for writing, as shown in Figure 3I. The strategy can also be adapted for younger students, as shown in Figure 3J, where it was used to help students comprehend a story.

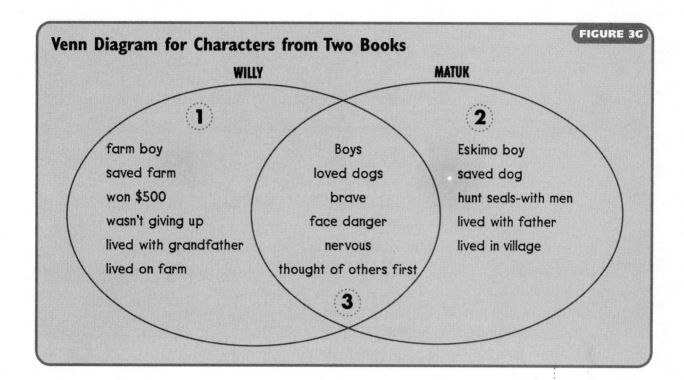

Venn Diagram for Characters from Two Books

WILLY

MATUK

1

farm boy
saved farm
won $500
wasn't giving up
lived with grandfather
lived on farm

Boys
loved dogs
brave
face danger
nervous
thought of others first

2

Eskimo boy
saved dog
hunt seals-with men
lived with father
lived in village

3

Before the Lesson

• Prepare a Venn Diagram handout by drawing two interlocking circles and numbering each portion of the circles; see template on the CD. Also draw an enlarged version on chart paper, the overhead, or the board.

Teaching the Lesson

• Tell students that a Venn Diagram can help them compare and contrast two characters, plots, settings, or other literary elements and is very useful in analyzing texts.

• Distribute the Venn Diagram handout after the students have read the story and completed the Story Map from Characters' Perspectives. Review characters and elements from a story that students have read previously. Explain that they will be comparing and contrasting main characters from two books. In our example, students worked with Willy and Matuk.

• Ask the class to brainstorm qualities and characteristics of each element being compared. You can guide students in their brainstorming by asking questions to help them organize the points they want to compare, e.g., character traits. Write the properties unique to each inside its circle. Write the properties that are common to both in the place where the circles intersect. Students can number the properties in each section to indicate their order of importance.

• Ask students questions that encourage them to process and synthesize the information from all three parts of the circle. To compare Willy and Matuk

(Figure 3G), for example, the teacher directed students to look at what they wrote in the intersection of the circle and asked, "In what ways are the boys similar?"

- Remind students that, when analyzing stories, they often find that certain characters or other elements in stories are similar in some respects and different in others.

Writing Extension

Like the Story Map from Characters' Perspectives, the Venn Diagram lends itself naturally to a writing activity, in this case, writing paragraphs about the similarities and differences the students discovered while completing the Venn Diagram. Students can write a paragraph for each of the three sections on the Venn Diagram using the About Point Writing Response format (see page 17):

- Topic sentence that introduces the subject (About) and states the main point (Point).

- Reasons/details to support the topic sentence.

- Closing statement which reinforces the message stated in the topic sentence.

You can find a more thorough explanation of the structure of paragraphs and the proper form for writing them in Chapter 6. Figure 3I is an example of compare/contrast paragraphs about two characters from two different books.

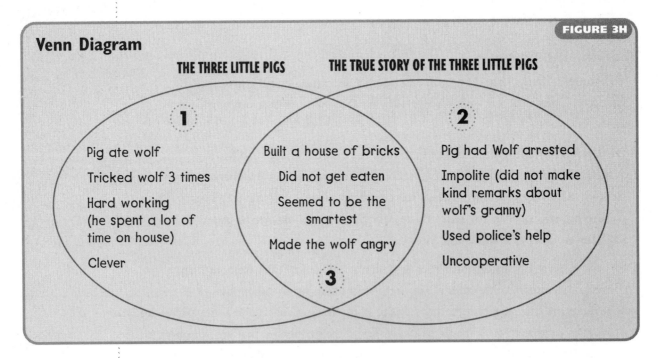

FIGURE 3H

Venn Diagram

THE THREE LITTLE PIGS   THE TRUE STORY OF THE THREE LITTLE PIGS

1
Pig ate wolf
Tricked wolf 3 times
Hard working
(he spent a lot of
time on house)
Clever

Built a house of bricks
Did not get eaten
Seemed to be the
smartest
Made the wolf angry

2
Pig had Wolf arrested
Impolite (did not make
kind remarks about
wolf's granny)
Used police's help
Uncooperative

3

This Venn Diagram was completed to analyze the third pig
as portrayed in two versions of "The Three Little Pigs."

Assessment

The evaluation of the Compare/Contrast Venn Diagram is built into the strategy itself. If students can successfully write the paragraphs, the strategy has accomplished its purpose, which is to help students compare and contrast characters and other story elements. The paragraphs can be scored holistically with a writing rubric or you can use a comprehension checklist. See Chapter 8 for an explanation of both of these assessment measures.

FIGURE 31

Compare/Contrast Summary for Two Characters

About Willy and Matuk

Willy is a farm boy who lives with his grandfather on a farm in Wyoming. Willy had seen a poster about a dogsled race. Then he decided to go on the race. But he didn't have any money for the race. So he went in the bank. He tried to get his money his mom saved in the bank. Then when Willy came out from the bank, he had $10 for the dogsled race. Then the race had come. Willy saw another racer Stone Fox but Willy still thought he was going to win. The race begins and at the end Willy still thought he was going to win. But when he almost got to the end his dog Searchlight died. Stone Fox let Willy carry Searchlight to the finish line. Willy won the race and got $500. He used the money to save his grandfather's farm.

Matuk is an Eskimo boy who lives with his father in a village. One day Matuk saw two seals walking on the ice. Then he went home and came back. The next day he saw the two seals again. Then Tupak was playing around and fell in the ice hole. Matuk tride to help Tupak. But he was too weak so he called for help. But nobody came. Then when Matuk helped Tupak from falling down the ice hole, Matuk's father came. Matuk's father had heard about Matuk saving Tupak from falling. He decided to help Matuk hunt for the seals and have a feast at the village. Matuk was then allowed to hunt seals with his father and the men in the village.

Willy and Matuk are alike because they are both boys. Willy and Matuk both love dogs. Will loves his dog Searchlight because Searchlight is Willy's only dog. Matuk loves his dogs Tupak and Kunik because Tupak and Kunik are Matuk's only dogs. Willy and Matuk are brave and face danger, and they thought of others first. Even though they have very different lives, Willy and Matuk are a lot alike.

Students extend their learning by using the Venn Diagram as the basis for a compare/contrast summary, as shown in this figure.

Venn Diagram

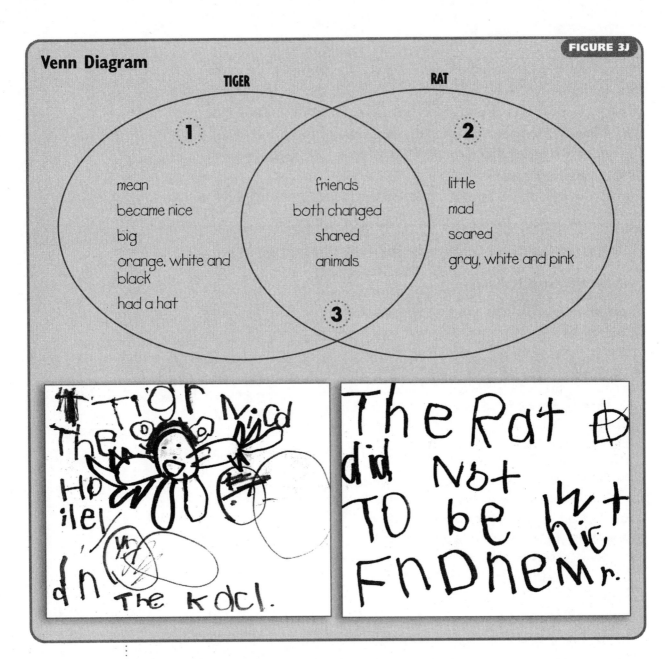

A Venn Diagram completed by a kindergarten class to help
students comprehend the story *The Rat and the Tiger* (Kasza, 1993).
The response was written independently by one student.

Alternative Comprehension and Application/Extension Strategies for Analyzing Narrative Text Structure

The goal of this chapter is to present a coherent lesson plan for helping students analyze narrative texts. In addition to the strategies presented in the previous section, we offer three others to choose from, based on your students' needs and lesson objectives. They are Probable Passage, Action Belief Chart, and SCAMPER.

COMPREHENSION STRATEGY:
Probable Passage

Probable Passage (Wood, 1984) is a motivational reading strategy that invites students to use their creativity to write an original story using vocabulary from a story they are about to read. The activity helps students activate background knowledge, improve vocabulary retention, set a purpose for reading, create images, and practice writing. Students use their knowledge of story structure and the words studied with the Concept of a Definition strategy to create their own story. Your students will enjoy creating the stories, and the idea of comparing their story with the actual story motivates them to read the text. Probable Passages can be done in writing or developed in oral discussions. Students can collaborate as a class or in small groups, or they can work individually to construct the story. Figure 3K shows a Probable Passage Outline and Summary created by second graders before reading *Strega Nona* (dePaola, 1975), about a witch with a magic pasta pot.

Before the Lesson

• Select vocabulary words from the story you want your students to read; be sure to include words from the Concept of a Definition activity.

• Prepare copies of the Probable Passage Outline sheet (see template on CD).

Teaching the Strategy

• Distribute copies of the Probable Passage Outline sheet and review story elements (setting, character, events). Tell students the purpose for writing a probable passage, saying something like, "This is a fun activity in which you get to choose how a story might develop. The meaning of the vocabulary words we discussed earlier will help you think of characters, a setting, and a plot. Then you get to create your own story! After, we'll read the story the author wrote and compare the two. This activity helps us set a purpose for reading."

Probable Passage Outline and Summary

Vocabulary: peeking potions magic pasta

Setting: In a town a long time ago

Characters: witch, cat

Events:
1. Once upon a time a lady was making pasta.
2. She saw a cat peeking from behind her stove into the pot.
3. The woman yelled at he cat to get away.
4. The cat ran off but his tail hit a jar.
5. The jar held magic potions that spilled on the pot.
6. Every time she cooks the lady makes magic food.
7. Everyone thinks the lady is a witch.

Once upon a time a lady was making pasta. She saw a cat peeking from behind her stove into the pot. The woman yelled at the cat to get away. The cat ran off but his tail hit a jar. The jar held magic potions that spilled on the pot. Every time she cooks the lady makes magic food. Everyone thinks the lady is a witch.

A Probable Passage in both outline and summary forms written by second graders for the story *Strega Nona* (dePaola, 1975). The Story Grammar format and selected vocabulary words (*magic, potions, peeking, pasta*) prompted students to think of ideas that could serve as the basis of their own stories.

- Have students write the vocabulary words you have selected in the box on the top of the page.

- Using the Story Grammar as a guide and vocabulary words as a prompt, help students develop a story line that incorporates the vocabulary words.

- Have students write a story based on their storylines, incorporating the vocabulary words and their ideas, working either individually or in small groups.

- Have your students read the assigned story.

- Invite small groups of students to compare their original stories with the assigned story.

COMPREHENSION STRATEGY:
Action Belief Chart

In order to understand characterization, students must be able to infer characters' beliefs and attitudes from their actions. The Action Belief Chart (Beach & Marshall, 1991) helps students make these inferences. Figure 3L presents an example of an Action Belief Chart completed by a sixth-grade student for the story, *The Amistad Slave Revolt* (Zeinert, 1997), in which the student infers that Cinque believes in equality for everyone based on his fight for the freedom of the slaves. Figure 3M shows how the strategy can be modified for younger students.

Action Belief Chart

Title: The Amistad Slave Revolt   Author: Zeinert   Name: Michael

Character	Action	Belief
Cinque	Cinque fought for freedom.	Cinque believed that all people should be treated equal.
Ruiz	Ruiz captured the slaves and beat them.	Ruiz believed that the Africans were nothing but slaves.
Yamba	Yamba argued and fought with Cinque.	Yamba believed that he should have been the leader.
Mother & Baby	The woman jumped into the ocean with her baby.	She believed that she shouldn't be treated this way.

A sixth grader's Action Belief Chart for *The Amistad Slave Revolt*

Before the Lesson

- Prepare the Action Belief Chart for students (see the sample in Figure 3L and the template on the CD).

Teaching the Strategy

- Before reading, discuss how a person's beliefs and attitudes can affect his or her actions. Give examples from everyday life, such as "We do not tolerate bullying in this school. We believe it is always wrong for one person to hurt or demean another. So if I see a student bullying one of you outside, I will go over and stop it. My strong belief about bullying will affect the action I take." Encourage students to share their own examples.

- Tell students that we can infer information about a character from his or her actions, just as we do for real people. Discuss some examples of characters that are familiar to students.

- Tell students that after they read the story, they will complete an Action Belief Chart to help them infer characters' beliefs.

- Have the students read the assigned story, thinking about what the characters' actions reveal about their beliefs. For example, say to the students, "While you are reading, pay attention when the author says or implies something about what a character believes. Then take note of the action that follows and see if there is a connection between what the character believes and what he does. Either way, see if you can explain the relationship between what the character does and what he

Action Belief Chart

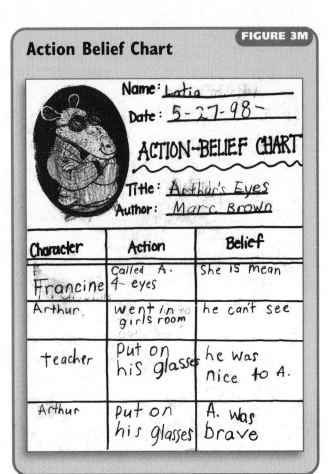

Name: Latia
Date: 5-27-98

ACTION-BELIEF CHART

Title: Arthur's Eyes
Author: Marc Brown

Character	Action	Belief
Francine	Called A. 4-eyes	She is mean
Arthur	went into girls room	he can't see
teacher	Put on his glasses	he was nice to A.
Arthur	put on his glasses	A. was brave

This Action Belief Chart for *Arthur's Eyes* (Brown, 1986) was modified for first-grade students. In the belief column, students wrote about what they thought the action meant instead of what it revealed about a character's beliefs.

believes. Because writers may not always state a character's beliefs, it's up to us, the readers, to determine what their beliefs are based on their actions in the story."

- Distribute the Action Belief Chart handout after students read the story. Have students list the character(s) in the story they would like to analyze.

- Have students complete the chart by writing down an action for the character(s) and the belief implied by that action; students may work independently or in small groups. Students may choose one action for each main character, or they may select several actions from one character. Encourage students to choose actions they feel reveal something important about a character's beliefs.

- Discuss with the whole class how a character's beliefs and story events are interrelated—namely, that beliefs influence actions. Ask questions that encourage inferential thinking such as, "Why did Ruiz capture the slaves and beat them?"

Writing Extension

If you would like your students to do some writing in conjunction with the Action Belief Chart strategy, you can have them write descriptive essays about a specific character or a compare/contrast essay describing the similarities and differences among characters.

SCAMPER

SCAMPER (Manzo & Manzo, 1990) is an acronym for: **S**ubstitute, **C**ombine, **A**dapt, **M**odify or **M**agnify, **P**ut to use, **E**liminate, and **R**earrange or **R**everse. The strategy encourages creative thinking and can easily be adapted for students of all abilities because it allows for a variety of activities. Below is a SCAMPER activity developed by a first-grade teacher for *King Bidgood's in the Bathtub* (Wood, 1985). In the story, King Bidgood refuses to get out of the bathtub in spite of the efforts of his subjects. Finally, his page finds a way to get him out of the tub. Figures 3N–3P show examples of SCAMPER challenges completed by students.

Students are free to work independently or in groups to complete one or more of the challenges.

SAMPLE SCAMPER CHALLENGES

SUBSTITUTE: What do you think would have happened if the king fished for shark instead of trout?

COMBINE: What might have happened if the entire court wouldn't leave their bathtubs?

ADAPT: How do you think the page would adapt his plan if the drain were clogged?

MODIFY: How could the story change if members from another kingdom arrived?

PUT TO USE: How could one of the items or people in the tub be used to solve the problem?

ELIMINATE: Rewrite the story without the page to solve the problem.

REVERSE: Rewrite the story with a king who refused to get into the bathtub.

FIGURE 3N

Concept of a Definition

> Josh) The footworm and the elephant one day the footworm was cralen through the jungle. the footworm met a elephant the elephant said I will sep on you if you dot measure my trunk. so the footworm measure the elephant trunk and that was how the footworm sov his problem

This SCAMPER "challenge" was completed by a first-grade student for the story *The Inchworm*. In response to the SCAMPER challenge to substitute something in the story, the student substituted a footworm for an inchworm and rewrote the story using the simple Story Grammar format of beginning, middle, and end.

Before the Lesson

- Prepare one or more of the SCAMPER challenges and any materials students require. (After students become familiar with SCAMPER, they too can develop one or more challenges for a story. However, they would develop them after completing the comprehension portion of the lesson.)

Teaching the Strategy

- Give your students a preview of the story they are going to read and instruct them to read the story for understanding.

- Explain the SCAMPER strategy to your students through questions that will help them to understand what each of the challenges requires them to do. For example, after students have read the story *The Amazing Bone* (Steig, 1983), you can ask them, "What do you think would have happened if a donkey had found the bone instead of a fox?" To answer, they would have to substitute (S) one character for another. Asking students "How can you rewrite the story and save Pearl without changing the size of the fox?" requires them to adapt (A) the story.

- When the students understand what actions each of the terms in the acronym requires them to perform, break them into small groups and tell them their group assignment is to respond to one or more of the challenges (substitute, combine, adapt, magnify or modify, put to use, eliminate, rearrange, or reverse parts of the story or the end of the story).

FIGURE 30

SCAMPER

If Cinque and Ruiz traded places in the story the story would be really different. Cinque would not have been involved with the killing of the slaves. He would never have attacked them and captured them. I think Cinque would have turned the ship around if he was seeing all the bad things his friends were doing. Cinque would've also told his friend this was wrong and we need to let them free.

If Ruiz was a slave he would've tried to kill the men who captured him. Or Ruiz would've tried to escape. I think Ruiz would've made a plan to take over the ship. Ruiz would also save and protect his people. Ruiz would find a way to get his people free.

This figure shows how a sixth grader responded to the "adapt" challenge when asked to answer the question of what would happen if the characters Cinque and Ruiz traded places in the story *The Amistad Slave Revolt*. In this case, it was not necessary for the student to rewrite the whole story.

SCAMPER

Strega's Magic

A long time ago there was a Strega. She knew a lot of magic. She could cure people. She also had love potions so the boys would like the girls. She took young girls to her house to teach them magic. She hired BJ to help her around the house. He wanted to learn the magic but Strega would not teach it to him because he was a boy. He tried to learn the magic anyway. When Strega wasn't around BJ would try the magic. One day Strega went away and told BJ not to mess with her magic cappuccino machine. While she was gone BJ tried to make cappuccino. He got it to make cappuccino. It tasted really really good. He asked his friends over. When it got dark his friends had to go home. BJ could not get the cappuccino machine to stop making cappuccino. It overflowed. It kept flowing right out the door. It flowed so long it made a river. That river is still there.

This sample shows how a new story was constructed as a group by sixth-grade students with severe behavior disorders and/or developmental disabilities. The students chose to use the "substitute" challenge with the story, *Strega Nona*.

- As students rewrite the story incorporating SCAMPER changes, tell them to use the original Story Map (Grammar) as a guide and change the affected events on the Story Map to agree with their group changes.

- Have the groups share their work by reading their changes to the class.

   To continue the writing aspect of the SCAMPER strategy, suggest to your students that they use their responses as the basis for creative writing. They can use the reconstructed Story Map as an outline for writing a revised story.

ThinkingWorks Lesson Planning Guide

A number of strategies have been introduced in this chapter that will enable you to teach a complete lesson for narrative text. Remember to use the ThinkingWorks Lesson Planning Guide to help you organize your strategies and keep a record of the ThinkingWorks cognitive and language processes that you have addressed in your lesson. Figure 3Q shows two completed planning guides using strategies introduced in this chapter.

ThinkingWorks Lesson Planning Guides

	STRATEGIES			
	Background Knowledge	Vocabulary	Comprehension	Application/ Extension
COGNITIVE PROCESSES	Problem/ Solution Guide	Concept of a Definition	Story Map for C.P./ Editorial	Compare/Contrast C/C Paragraphs
Develop Background Knowledge	✔			
Expand Vocabulary Knowledge	✔	✔		
Use Text Structure			✔	
Set a Purpose for Learning	✔		✔	
Infer/Select Information			✔	
Create Images			✔	
Relate/Connect Ideas			✔	
Clarify/Monitor Understanding			✔	
Analyze			✔/✔	✔
Synthesize			/✔	
Evaluate/Justify			/✔	
Create/Invent			/✔	
LANGUAGE PROCESSES				
Read			✔	
Write			✔/✔	/✔
Listen/View	✔	✔	✔	✔
Communicate Orally	✔	✔	✔	✔
COGNITIVE PROCESSES	Problem/ Solution Guide	Concept of a Definition	Action Belief Chart	SCAMPER
Develop Background Knowledge	✔			
Expand Vocabulary Knowledge	✔	✔		
Use Text Structure				
Set a Purpose for Learning	✔		✔	
Infer/Select Information			✔	
Create Images			✔	
Relate/Connect Ideas			✔	
Clarify/Monitor Understanding			✔	
Analyze			✔	✔
Synthesize				✔
Evaluate/Justify				
Create/Invent				✔
LANGUAGE PROCESSES				
Read			✔	
Write				/✔
Listen/View	✔	✔	✔	/✔
Communicate Orally	✔	✔	✔	/✔

CHAPTER 4

Responding to
Narrative Text

In This Chapter:

BACKGROUND KNOWLEDGE:	Experience Text Relationship (ETR)
VOCABULARY:	Possible Sentences
COMPREHENSION:	Personal Response/ Literary Analysis
APPLICATION/EXTENSION:	Journal Response
ALTERNATIVE COMPREHENSION STRATEGIES:	Prediction, Prediction Chart
ALTERNATIVE APPLICATION/EXTENSION STRATEGIES:	Literary Poster, Pictoral Outline

The previous two chapters introduced strategies to help readers understand story structure and analyze story elements to deepen their comprehension of narrative texts. In this chapter, we turn to strategies that encourage students to read stories and respond to them on a personal and/or analytical level. Reader-response theory (Rosenblatt, 1989) centers on the belief that both the reader and the writer are crucial to the construction of meaning from a text. Any specific reading of a literary text will produce an interpretation that reflects both the meaning intended by the writer and the meaning constructed by the reader (Graves et al.,1998). The lesson sequence featured in this chapter includes strategies that promote thoughtful reader response to narrative text.

Personal response and literary analysis are often done in small-group settings, such as literature circles, in which students interact with and learn from one another. ThinkingWorks strategies can be integrated easily into this format. This chapter demonstrates how a set of strategies can be adapted to a unit in which students are reading and responding to different sets of books in small groups. A typical class might have four reading groups of four to six students who select the same book (sometimes with teacher guidance). Once groups are formed, your role is to facilitate the interactions of students in their groups as they complete strategies in the lesson sequence.

ThinkingWorks Lesson Plan Sequence for Responding to Narrative Text

To help students respond thoughtfully to narrative texts, we have designed the following lesson sequence:

BACKGROUND KNOWLEDGE: . . . . .Experience Text Relationship (ETR)

VOCABULARY: . . . . .Possible Sentences

COMPREHENSION: . . . . .Personal Response/Literary Analysis

APPLICATION/EXTENSION: . . . . .Journal Response

The Journal Response also fulfills the writing component of the lesson. In addition, we present four alternative comprehension and application/extension strategies that work particularly well to help students respond to narrative texts. The application/extension strategies, Literary Poster and Pictorial Outline, encourage students to use a visual mode of expression in their response to text. Choose the strategies that best meet your lesson objectives and students' needs.

Experience Text Relationship (ETR)

Experience Text Relationship (ETR) is a strategy that helps students make connections between their experiences and those presented in a given text. Originally developed by Au (1979) to benefit students with culturally different backgrounds, the strategy is especially effective in building motivation and giving students a purpose for reading because it helps them see how a text relates to their own experiences. Using this strategy before students read activates their background knowledge and helps them make predictions that will be confirmed or refined as they read. As you ask students questions designed to probe their relevant experiences, you can connect these experiences to those they'll encounter in the text. In doing this, you are motivating and preparing your students to read the story. See the examples in Figures 4A and 4B for how this can be done with fifth graders and first graders.

Since students are working in reading groups, you will be preparing a different set of ETR questions or statements for each book they are reading and then helping students activate and build their background knowledge through a small-group discussion of the questions. A practical way to do this is to introduce books to groups at different times during your language arts instructional block or on different days. While you are working with one group, students in the rest of the class can be involved in other activities such as learning centers or independent work.

FIGURE 4A

Experience Text Relationship

Teacher: Were you ever forced to do something that you didn't think was fair? What was it?

Student 1: I had to change schools because we moved. I didn't want to leave my friends.

Student 2: Yes, we had to stay in our room last year and miss a movie because our class was not behaving and doing work.

Student 3: I've had to stay in and take care of my brother when my mom had to work and no one was around to watch him.

Teacher: How we react to a situation can make it easier or harder to handle. For example, if we think to ourselves, I'll make the best of the situation until I can change it, instead of becoming angry about it, we often are better able to handle it and think of alternative plans for the future. We're going to begin reading a book called *Sing Down the Moon* in which a Navajo girl, Bright Morning, finds herself in some terrible situations that she has no control over. How she reacts makes all the difference in the outcomes.

An example of the ETR strategy used in a fifth grade with the story *Sing Down the Moon* (O'Dell, 1970)

Experience Text Relationship

Teacher: How many of you have been really busy doing something?

Student 1: Sometimes when I have a lot of homework and I have basketball practice the same night.

Student 2: I get really busy when my mom tells me to clean my room after I haven't cleaned it for a week!

Teacher: You sound like busy people! Have any of you ever been too busy to answer someone when they were talking to you? Or, have you spoken to someone like your moms or dads when they were busy and they didn't seem to hear you?

Student 3: One time when my mom was doing the bills I asked her if I could go to my friend's house and she didn't even answer me until the third time I said her name.

Student 4: One time I was playing Nintendo and my dad called me to go to dinner and I didn't hear him until he was right next to me. He was kind of angry.

Student 5: When I play basketball I don't usually hear people cheering for me or calling my name. They always say later, "Did you hear me?"

Teacher: Pretty crazy how it happens, isn't it? Well today we're going to read a story about a spider who was so busy she didn't hear the things people said to her, and we'll find out what she was doing that she was so busy!

An ETR lesson used in a first grade with the story *The Very Busy Spider* (Carle, 1985)

Before the Lesson

• Prepare several questions for each group that will help students connect their own experiences to those they will encounter in the text. For example, before reading *The True Story of the Three Little Pigs* (Scieszka, 1996), you might ask students if their actions were ever misinterpreted because people didn't understand the reasons for them. One teacher asked her first graders, "How would your mom react if you took a favorite toy away from an annoying younger brother and made him cry? Would she believe you if you said you did it because you wanted to save it for him when he became bored?"

Teaching the Strategy

• When you meet with each group, tell students that they'll soon be reading an interesting story and that to get ready for it, you're going to ask them about experiences they've had that might be similar to those in the text. Remind them that making personal connections helps them activate background knowledge, and set a purpose for reading.

- Ask students a question from your list.

- Encourage students to share their experiences related to the question.

- Now you may pose a more specific question that is directly related to the experience of a character or characters in the story. The first-grade teacher followed up her discussion of taking away toys from siblings with this: "You all know the story of 'The Three Little Pigs.' Would you believe that the wolf didn't really huff and puff on the pigs' houses, that they fell down accidentally after the wolf sneezed on them? Would you believe that a wolf would only eat the pigs because he didn't want to waste food? That's what the wolf claims in the story we're going to read!"

- Alternatively, you may make a statement that will help the students understand the similarities between their experiences and those in the story. In the discussion described above, the teacher could have made a statement such as "You all know the story of 'The Three Little Pigs.' Perhaps the wolf would like a chance to explain the events in that story from his point of view, just as you all said you'd want a chance to explain why you took the toy away from a younger brother or sister. Well, we're going to read a book in which the wolf does get to tell his side of the story."

- Conclude the discussion by stating that the book the group will be reading will have characters or events similar to the experiences they have discussed.

If the books that the groups are reading have a common theme, such as courage or heroes of the past, you can prepare one set of ETR questions and lead a whole class discussion. For the theme of courage, you might ask students: "How many of you know someone who has acted courageously? Describe what she or he did." After class discussion, you can connect students' experiences to the texts they will be reading by indicating that all the people they mentioned performed a courageous act, even if they were afraid or had a difficult time doing so. You can conclude the discussion by stating that the texts that the groups will be reading contain examples of courageous actions.

Writing Extension

A natural extension of ETR would be to have students write an essay in which they compare some aspect of the experience they encountered in the story to their own experience. Encourage students to illustrate the experiences they write about and share their stories and illustrations. If students have read other stories that contain similar experiences, they could write an essay comparing those two sets of experiences.

Assessment

One of the best ways to determine the effectiveness of ETR is through a postreading discussion that focuses students' attention on comparing a character or an event in the story with the experiences they had discussed before reading. If the students are able to answer questions about the text experience and, even better, respond to each other's answers, you can conclude that the strategy helped them use their background knowledge to understand the story.

VOCABULARY STRATEGY:
Possible Sentences

Possible Sentences (Moore & Moore, 1992) is an effective strategy for getting students involved in discussing, writing, and reading key vocabulary words from an assignment. To begin, select vocabulary words critical to understanding the text that each group is reading. Introduce the words to the group and discuss their meaning in student-friendly language, giving examples. Ask students to demonstrate their understanding of each word by using it in a sentence. When students read the text, remind them to note how the words are used in the context of the story. As a final step, after students read, have them write new sentences using the words. If you implement this strategy along with ETR, your students will be well prepared to read, understand, and respond to the story. Figure 4C is an example of the Possible Sentences strategy completed by a fifth-grade class for the story *Sing Down the Moon*.

FIGURE 4C

Possible Sentences

Vocabulary Words: plunder, mesa, haughty

Prereading Sentences:
1. The burglars plundered the house despite the piercing sound of the sirens.
2. The mesa lay between the ramparts.
3. The haughty man looked scornfully at others.

Postreading Sentences:
1. The Indian chief said he would fight enemies who tried to plunder his tribe.
2. The sheep would graze on the mesa above the canyon.
3. The young warrior was haughty after he killed a bear.

A fifth grader's Possible Sentences written about vocabulary words from *Sing Down the Moon.*

Before the Lesson

- Identify key vocabulary words from each of the books that groups are going to read. Choose four to six words that are critical to understanding the text and prepare sheets of paper for each group, with a list of those words across the top; there is a template on the CD.

Teaching Procedure

- Discuss each word on the list with members of the group, giving a definition in student-friendly language, with examples to clarify meaning. A fifth-grade teacher defined *plunder*, selected as a vocabulary word for *Sing Down the Moon*, this way: "To plunder is to rob, to take away what is valuable in a place. Victorious soldiers have been known to plunder villages and cities they've conquered, taking away money, gold, silver, jewelry, art and other valuable objects."

- Have students write a sentence for each word on the list, before they read the text. Students can work individually or in their small groups and may consult a dictionary. Check their work and clarify any misunderstandings.

- Have students read the text and look for how the author used the words in the context of the story.

- After reading, ask the students to create new sentences that reflect information they have gleaned from the text. They can do this individually or in their groups.

Writing Extension

The Possible Sentences strategy lends itself very nicely to a writing assignment that follows the About Point Writing Response format (see page 17). You can instruct students to write a paragraph using one of their sentences as the topic sentence followed by three or four sentences containing supporting details and examples from the story and their own experience. The closing statement could either be a restatement of the topic sentence or an opinion of the idea represented by the vocabulary word.

Assessment

The most logical method of assessing the value of the Possible Sentences strategy is to test students on the meanings of the key vocabulary words you identified at the beginning of the lesson. Students should do well on this kind of a test because they have worked with the words through reading, writing, and discussion.

COMPREHENSION STRATEGY:

Personal Response and Literary Analysis Through Discussion

Responding to text is not a passive activity. Rather, students must actively participate in such a way that their attention is shifted from simply reading the words on the page to purposefully interacting with ideas in the text through discussion with others (Beach & Marshall, 1991). Student-led discussions (which can take the form of literature circles or book clubs) provide forums for students to express their personal feelings, exchange ideas, enhance and refine ideas through text analysis, and think creatively and critically (Graves et al., 1998). When reading or discussion groups are part of your language arts instructional block, students learn to work together and value others' opinions by sharing their reactions and connections to a text.

Discussions centering on student response to text can vary in emphasis, and may range from students' personal feelings about the text to more formal literary analysis, with many discussions leaving room for both types of response. Personal response discussions motivate readers because they understand that a variety of responses is

Personal Response	Literary Analysis
Open-ended prompts	• Teacher-created prompts • Structured prompts
Student selection of text	• Teacher or student selection of text • Teacher or student led
• Variety of responses —no right or wrong • Reactions to the text in terms of feelings and opinions	• Use of a variety of cognitive processes (inferring, imaging, selecting information, clarifying and monitoring understanding) • Use of application/ extension skills of analysis, synthesis, and evaluation

Note: For personal response discussions, the teacher can initially construct the prompts and lead the discussion. As students gain experience, they should take turns leading discussions.

accepted; they feel comfortable knowing that they can respond to the text according to their beliefs and feelings. Literary analysis requires students to develop or refine their critical thinking skills. Both kinds of discussion require much modeling and discussion to establish an atmosphere in which students feel comfortable sharing their thoughts and discussing text in a meaningful way. The chart on the left shows the characteristics often associated with personal response and literary analysis.

The way you organize discussions will depend on whether you wish to emphasize personal response or literary analysis. Following are teaching procedures for each of these two types of discussion. Keep in mind that literature discussions can involve both personal response and analysis, and therefore your discussion may combine elements from each of the following procedures. You will find a list of resources that describe the use of literature discussion groups in more detail in the reference section at the end of the book.

Teaching Procedure for Personal Response to Text

- Set up a display of several books, either by the same author or by different authors. Allow students to select the book they would like to read. Be sure to have multiple copies of books or stories available. Students are then more likely to get their first or second choice.

- Form groups, each with four to six students who have selected the same book. It is important to change the groups with each new text selection to insure interactions among a wide range of students. Also, you will want to make sure that, at various times, students have assumed a variety of roles (i.e., leader, recorder, arbiter, listener, or devil's advocate) in their groups (Lynch-Brown & Tomlinson, 1993).

- Meet with the members of each group to help them formulate reading goals (i.e., the number of pages or sections to read) and make decisions regarding how long they need to read each day to meet their goals and when the group will meet again. Discussion times are based on the type and length of the chosen text. With short stories, students may read the whole text before convening for a 20–30 minute discussion. With longer texts, students may decide to read one or several chapters before group discussions. Beginning readers can listen to all or part of a story and discuss it.

- Meet with the groups periodically—as a participant, not as a leader—to observe student interactions and provide direction and instruction as needed.

- To encourage open-ended questions and free discussion, post a pocket chart with prompts in the classroom. Examples of prompts are: Talk about your favorite part. Relate the story to your life. Would you recommend the story? To whom? Why? Also see the sample prompts in Figure 4D.

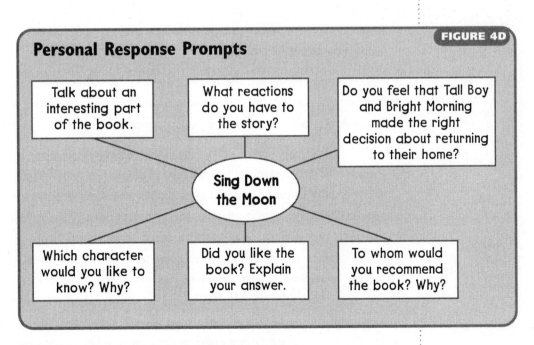

FIGURE 4D

Personal Response Prompts

Talk about an interesting part of the book.

What reactions do you have to the story?

Do you feel that Tall Boy and Bright Morning made the right decision about returning to their home?

Sing Down the Moon

Which character would you like to know? Why?

Did you like the book? Explain your answer.

To whom would you recommend the book? Why?

Questions to prompt personal response to *Sing Down the Moon*

- Encourage students to take turns leading the group in discussions that revolve around individual responses to the story they have read. One way to keep track of these responses is to have students record them in their response journals (described in the next part of this lesson).

Before a Lesson Focusing on Literary Analysis of Text

- Create a Literary Analysis Guide (Beach & Marshall, 1991) consisting of questions or prompts that will direct students to think more deeply about a story or book they read in their small groups. Like a Story Grammar, a Literary Analysis Guide helps readers form visual images and identify setting, characters, and plot; in addition, the guide helps readers bring out the central ideas in a literary work and assess the quality of the writing. The questions in the guide should help focus students' attention on the author's point of view and technique, story structure, and character development. The questions should also encourage students to both judge the quality of the work and respond to the story at a personal level; see the list of sample questions in Figure 4E. You'll find a template on the CD.

- Make copies of the Literary Analysis Guide for each member of the group.

Teaching Procedure for Literary Analysis of Text

- Distribute copies of the Literary Analysis Guide to each group member.

- Before students read, meet with each group and discuss with them the information in the guide for their book. Let them look over the questions so that they can set a purpose for reading.

- After students have read the story or sections of it, have them answer the questions that pertain to what they have read and discuss their responses in their groups. You may also have students write their responses to questions as part of a homework assignment that is later discussed in their group.

Figure 4E lists a number of question prompts that you can use to develop a Literary Analysis Guide. You will want to ask questions that are appropriate for a particular literary selection and the age of your students. Keep in mind that as many of the questions as possible need to be asked at various times in order to help your students think critically about stories and poems. Students should be familiar with the literary terms in a question before you ask it. Words used in the Literary Analysis Guide question (e.g., setting, plot) would be discussed when you go over the information in the guide before students read the story. You will need to help students with figurative language if it is used in the questions or in the story.

Figure 4F is an example of a Literary Analysis Guide created for *Tuck Everlasting* (Babbitt, 1975) and completed by a sixth-grade student. Figure 4G shows how the Literary Analysis Guide strategy can be applied to Wordsworth's poem, "I Wandered Lonely as a Cloud."

Literary Analysis Guide

- Where and when does the story take place? How do you know? If the setting were changed, how would that affect the story?

- How does the author begin the story?

- Does the story end the way you expected it to end? What clues does the author offer to prepare you for this ending?

- What kind of person is the main character? How do you know?

- Do any of the characters change during the story? How are they different? What caused them to change?

- What are the main ideas and theme(s) in the story? What techniques does the author use to make you think of the ideas and theme(s) as you read the story?

- Does the story create a mood or feeling? What is the mood? How is it created?

- What clues does the author use to alert you to future events in the story?

- How does the author use events that happened in the past to help you understand the present?

- Does the author use any figurative language to help you understand the characters and the action in the story? What are some examples?

- Why does the author use the analogy of _____ to explain_____?

- Is the story like any other you have read? Are characters in the story the same types of characters you have met in other stories?

- Did you have strong feelings as you read the story? What literary device (e.g., metaphor, simile, foreshadowing, mood, tone) does the author use to make you feel that way?

- What is the author's purpose in writing the story? How do the author's ideas and writing style support the purposes?

- What visual images does the author use to help you understand the text?

- What does the author mean when he or she compares the_____to the _____?

Literary Analysis Guide

1. **Authors use many techniques to introduce the reader to a story. In this book, the author uses a prologue to set the scene. Is this an effective way to capture the reader's attention?**

   The prologue helps the reader think about what would happen in order to connect three important events: Mae meets her sons only once in ten years; Winnie Foster wants to run away; and there is a stranger at the Foster's gate. The prologue gets the reader interested in the story and points out some important events.

2. **The author uses images in the story to foreshadow coming events. When the author writes in Chapter 24 "…a low mumble, still far away, announced at last the coming storm," what event is foreshadowed?**

   The author uses that description just before Winnie helps Moe escape. The image describes the escape and the trouble that is to follow.

3. **In Chapter 12, the author uses the image of a wheel to describe life. Does the author use a good example to explain his message?**

   Yes, the author uses the wheel to show how everything is growing, changing, and moving on. You can't pick out parts of life that you like and ignore those that you don't like.

4. **How does Winnie change from the beginning of the book to the end?**

   In the beginning, Winnie is unhappy but has no plan to change her life. At the end, Winnie takes a stand for something she believes in.

5. **Would you have drunk the water if you were Winnie?**

   No, I think everyone must grow old in order to enjoy all things in life. For example, you can't be a grandparent if you don't grow old.

6. **What is the theme of the book?**

   It is best not to change the circle of life.

7. **In Chapter 16, what does the constable mean when he asks, "Did you get a gander at that suit of clothes?"**

   The man in yellow had unusual clothes and looked suspicious.

8. **Who would you tell to read this book?**

   I would tell my friend Marie because she likes mysteries, and this is a different kind of mystery.

Literary Analysis Guide for *Tuck Everlasting*

Writing Extension

If your students are keeping reading response journals while they discuss the story in groups, you have a built-in writing component. The application/extension strategy for this menu, Journal Response, is described next. Also, you might ask students to write a letter to a friend in which they recommend the text based upon their responses to the Literary Analysis Guide.

Assessment

It would be inappropriate and unnecessary to implement a separate assessment strategy for Personal Response since there are usually no right answers to the questions or prompts used for this strategy. The Journal Response strategy, whether completed

Literary Analysis Guide

1. **William Wordsworth uses several forms of figurative language in the poem "I Wandered Lonely as a Cloud." Identify the type of figurative language used in the following lines and explain your interpretation of their meaning.**

   a. "I wandered lonely as a cloud

      That floats on high o'er vales and hills"

      Type of figurative language: simile

      Interpretation: The person felt alone walking about just like a cloud floating around in the sky.

   b. "Tossing their heads in sprightly dance"

      Type of figurative language: personification

      Interpretation: The flowers were tossing about just like someone dancing.

2. **What do you think Wordsworth means when he writes**

   "In vacant or in pensive mood,

   They flash upon that inward eye

   Which is the bliss of solitude"?

   He sees daffodils when he is alone and closes his eyes.

3. **Use the context of the poem to define the meaning of the word jocund.**

   Jolly

4. **Do you think that Wordsworth chooses appropriate language to describe the daffodils? Explain your answer and use examples from the poem to support your response.**

   Yes—daffodils look happy because they are gold and have a bouncy fan frame for their heads.

5. **Choose a flower that you would like to describe. Write a metaphor or simile that expresses your view of that flower.**

   A lily as lovely and quiet as a sunset

   A daisy as bright as a sunny day

6. **Identify an example of personification that Wordsworth uses in the third stanza of the poem.**

   Waves dancing

7. **What kind of wealth do you think the daffodil show brought to Wordsworth?**

   He can often picture the daffodil show in his mind and that will make his heart dance.

8. **To whom would you recommend this poem? Why?**

   To my mom and dad when we are in the middle of winter and it is cold and gray and they have been working hard.

A Literary Analysis Guide for "I Wandered Lonely as a Cloud"

during the discussion groups or after, would serve to indicate the effectiveness of the strategy for helping students respond personally to the text. Since the purpose of the Literary Analysis Guide is to develop your students' critical thinking skills, you should evaluate this strategy on the basis of whether it accomplished its purpose. One way you can do that is by listening to students' responses during small-group discussion to determine if students are able to support and justify their answers. You can also include critical thinking questions based upon those used in the guide in a test that students have to take after they've read and discussed the story or poem.

APPLICATION/EXTENSION STRATEGY:

Journal Response

Journals (Fulweiler, 1982) are notebooks in which students keep written responses to their reading. By linking reading with writing, journals help students become fluent and confident in their writing as they either construct their personal meanings of text or engage in literary analysis. The Journal Response strategy provides you with two ways of differentiating instruction to meet your students' needs. First, you can use different prompts to guide students' thinking. For example, some students may need to respond to questions about character development. Other students may need to focus on identifying and interpreting an author's use of literary devices such as similes and metaphors. Still others might need to focus on expressing their personal reactions to a text. Second, you can provide different levels of support for students depending on the type of journal they are completing. For example a dialogue journal allows you to respond to students' writing and perhaps encourage them to probe text for deeper meaning. Figure 4H presents different types of journals; examples are presented in Figures 4I–4L.

Four Types of Journals

FIGURE 4H

DIARY: A private record of personal observations and thoughts shared only at the student's request.

RESPONSE JOURNALS: Students note predictions, reflections, reactions, and questions about reading; may be used to keep track of independent reading (personal or shared with others). For younger students, you may want to create a class response journal, in which individual students contribute to the journal with the support from their peers and you.

DIALOGUE JOURNALS: Similar to a response journal except that the teacher or a classmate or parent carries on a written conversation with the student about what was written; helps the student construct and clarify text meaning.

DOUBLE-ENTRY JOURNALS: A split page for students to write predictions and ideas; student makes notes before and during reading on the left side and writes reactions after reading on the right side. (Teachers may also make comments on the right side of the page.)

Teaching Procedure

- Describe the idea of journal writing to the class as a way for students to think about what they read and how they share their thoughts with others. Discuss the different types of journal entries. Show examples on an overhead transparency.

- Have the students work in groups to write journal entries.

- Use prompts to help students get started if they need help. (Refer to the suggestions for open-ended and structured prompts described in the discussion of the Literary Analysis Guide, page 95.)

Dialogue Journal

Teacher: If you were Bright Morning, what would you say was your worst time and best time in the two-year exile?

Student: I think the worst time was when Tall Boy got shot trying to save me. Because of me, he was unable to be a warrior or hunt anymore. Many people in the tribe believed that he was useless and would not be a good husband.

The best time was when I returned to the canyon with my son and Tall Boy. It would now be a home for us again. My son would grow up to be free to live with nature.

A portion of a fifth-grade student's dialogue journal for the story *Sing Down the Moon*

- Develop a system with the students to use and store their journals, for example, file alphabetically in a crate or file drawer.

- When responding to journal entries, write comments that encourage students, and guide and refocus their responses when necessary.

Assessment

The evaluation of Journal Response as an effective writing strategy is built into the strategy itself, that is, if students are willing and able to write journal entries, then the strategy has accomplished its purpose. Journals also give insight into students' use of the thought processes of analyzing, synthesizing, creating, and evaluating.

Portions of Class Response Journal

Contributions of three kindergarten students to a class response journal for the story *Froggy Goes to School* (London, 1996)

Excerpts from a Response Journal

What was the author's purpose in not naming all the characters in the story?
Armstrong did not name all the characters so the story could represent every family, not just one family. Armstrong named Sounder because of the role he plays in this book. Sounder plays a dog that barks loud and long.

What is the mood of the story?
The mood of the story is happy for the first chapter when they are eating ham for dinner. When the boy's dad is taken away, the mood changes to sad and confused. The mood also changes when Sounder is shot. The story get ever sadder then.

Excerpts from a sixth-grade student's response journal for the book *Sounder* (Armstrong, 1969)

Double-Entry Journal

I think Grandfather will get better when Willy completes the harvest.	I was wrong. The harvest wasn't the problem. Grandfather is still sick and upset.
The owner of the house may be a friend of Grandfather's who can help Willy solve the problem.	The visitor wasn't a friend, but he told Willy what the problem was. I wonder if Willy can get five hundred dollars to pay taxes. He only had fifty dollars in savings. Josh: Do you have any ideas about how Willy could gather enough money to pay the taxes? 　　　　　　　　　　Mrs. Bayler

Excerpts from a fourth-grade student's double-entry journal for the book *Stone Fox*

Alternative Comprehension and Application/ Extension Strategies for Responding to Narrative Text

The goal of this chapter is to present a coherent lesson plan for helping students respond to narrative text, both personally and critically. In addition to the strategies presented in the previous section, we offer four others to choose from, based on your students' needs and lesson objectives. The two comprehension strategies are Prediction and Prediction Chart and the application/extension strategies are Literary Poster and Pictorial Outline. All are designed to help students respond meaningfully to narrative text.

COMPREHENSION STRATEGY:
Prediction

Prediction is a strategy that asks students to think about what is going to happen in the story. Students examine the title, cover, back cover, chapter titles, illustrations, photographs, or other text features and then use this information and their prior knowledge to make predictions. Then they read to confirm, adjust, or reject their predictions. After reading, students compare their personal predictions with what actually happened in the text (Fitzgerald, 1983). See Figure 4M for a fourth grader's prediction for *Hatchet*. Before you implement this strategy with the students, you need to review with them how to use clues in the text along with their background knowledge to help them infer information necessary for making predictions.

Before the Lesson

- Select predictable books to provide readily apparent text clues for students to identify and use to infer. For younger students, you might use books such as *The Doorbell Rang* (Hutchins, 1986), *One Monday Morning* (Shulevitz, 1967), and *The Something* (Babbitt, 1970). For older students, appropriate books include *Knee-Knock Rise* (Babbitt, 1970), *From the Mixed-Up Files of Mrs. Basil E. Frankweiler* (Konigsburg, 1967), and *Tuck Everlasting* (Babbitt, 1975).

FIGURE 4M

Prediction

I think the story is about a boy and his dad going on a hunting trip. The plane crashes and his dad gets hurt. He has to find his way through the wilderness to get help.

Chapter 2: The plane will crash and Brian will have to survive alone in the wilderness.

Chapter 3: Brian will crash land near an open space.

This fourth grader made several predictions for the intermediate-level book *Hatchet* (Paulson, 1987). The first prediction was made after the title and cover of the book were examined. The other two predictions were made before chapters 2 and 3 of the book were read.

Teaching the Lesson

- Discuss with the students the purposes for making predictions: it gives them a purpose for reading, keeps them engaged in the text, and encourages them to use their background knowledge and make connections to the text.

- Model or use explicit instructional talk to describe how you make predictions. You can begin by modeling for the whole class the thought processes that are involved. For example, you could say to students, "When we predict, we must think about the knowledge and experience we have, as well as clues that are in the text, all of which help us infer or predict what might happen. For example, when I read *The Talking Eggs* (San Souci, 1989), I predicted that Blanche would be rewarded for her kindness because I know from reading fairy tales that goodness is rewarded. I also used the text clues that Blanche is kind to the Old Woman and helps her get the eggs to predict that the Old Woman would help Blanche."

- Have students make their first prediction about a text after having examined the title and cover of the book. They can continue to make predictions while reading, using their background knowledge and clues in the text. When students are first learning to make predictions, you can do this in a whole-class setting. Several students can share their predictions with the class and discuss why they made the predictions.

- In time, students can work in small groups or pairs to predict what is going to happen and to model, though think-alouds, the thinking that helped them develop their predictions. Working in small groups or pairs allows students to make more individual predictions than they could in a large-group situation.

COMPREHENSION STRATEGY:
Prediction Chart

A Prediction Chart can extend the Prediction strategy described above (Hammond, 1991). It helps students monitor their understanding of text, builds a purpose for reading, and involves students in writing. With this strategy, students record their predictions in writing before they read a section of text. After reading, they note what really happened. In this way, they keep track of their predictions as they read, and you can review their thinking. The Prediction Chart allows students to work independently; however, they need to have practiced prediction before they can use the chart. (See the examples in Figures 4N–4P.)

Before the Lesson

- Create a Prediction Chart template on chart paper or the overhead to serve as a model for students; you'll find a template on the CD.

- Prepare questions that will spur students to make predictions at key points in the text. You can ask young children to make three or four predictions at appropriate places in a picture book. You can ask older students to predict before each chapter of a book.

Teaching the Strategy

- Help the students make a Prediction Chart in their reading response journals that has two columns, one labeled "Prediction" and the other "What Happened."

- Ask the students a question requiring them to make a prediction before reading that is based on an examination of the text, including the title and illustrations.

- Continue to pose prediction questions at intervals throughout the reading of the text. Show students how to use their Prediction Chart in their reading response journal to compare their predictions with what actually occurs in the story.

- After students have finished reading the text, help them review what occurred in the story. Have them complete their Prediction Charts.

Prediction Chart

Prediction	What Happened
Chapters 3–7 He's going to need food and shelter. I bet he uses a hatchet to kill a bear and get food. He'll find a cave to live in and take clothes and medicine from the plane.	Brian finds berries to eat. He builds a lean-to under a stone ledge for a shelter. The plane sank in the lake and he could only save his hatchet.
Chapters 8–12 I think he'll live in the cave and learn to catch fish. He'll make a trap to catch small animals like rabbits.	He lived in the lean-to and learned to live in the forest. He made a fire using his hatchet and tree bark. He carved a spear and bow and arrow to catch fish. He also ate raw turtle eggs.
Chapters 13–18 Animals would be a danger. Probably bears are in the woods.	A moose attacked him and Brian almost drowned. A tornado came through and wrecked his lean-to. But the tornado also helped him because it turned the plane around in the lake so the tail stuck up and Brian could reach it.
Chapter 19 Brian escapes by using the plane radio to call for help. A search party comes and rescues him.	Brian finds supplies in the plane. He takes the radio transmitter and leaves it on, even though he thinks it's broken. A fur buyer, flying in the area, heard the transmitter and saw the plane. He rescues Brian.

A Prediction Chart for *Hatchet*

Prediction Chart

Prediction	What Happened
Chapters 1–5 1. A girl gets a pet pig. 2. Fern takes good care of the pig. 3. Wilbur runs away from the farm. 4. Wilbur is happy to stay at the farm but is lonely for Fern. 5. Wilber meets his friend.	Mr. Arable was going to kill the runt before breakfast, but Fern stopped him. Fern took care of Wilbur and is forced to sell him to Mr. Zuckerman. Wilbur escaped and got caught about a 1/2 hour later. Then Wilbur meets Templeton. He then sees Charlotte and thinks she's beautiful.
Chapters 6–12 6. Charlotte helps Wilbur make more friends. 7. The goose egg breaks. 8. Charlotte thinks of a way to save Wilbur. 9. Mrs. Arable has the doctor check Fern. 10. Fern tells her parents about Charlotte's plan to save Wilbur. 11. Charlotte will do something special in her web to help Wilbur. 12. Wilber is famous and will stay a pet.	The goose hatched her eggs. One was rotten so Templeton took it. Templeton told Wilbur that they were making him fat so that they could eat him on Christmas. Fern told her parents about the animals talking, so they wanted to take her to the doctor. Wilbur bragged about making a web. Charlotte weaved the words, "some pig," in her web. The animals had another meeting and decided that Charlotte should weave "terrific."
Chapters 13–16 13. More people come to see Wilbur. 14. Fern's mom takes her to the Doctor because she thinks that she is crazy. 15. Fern is allowed to keep going to the barn. 16. Wilbur goes to the fair without Charlotte.	Charlotte sends Templeton to look for words. Fern's mother went to see Dr. Darian. Summer ends and Charlotte writes "radiant" in the web. Wilbur gets ready for the fair.
Chapters 17–22 17. Everyone wants to see Wilbur. 18. Charlotte is sick and can't help Wilbur. 19. Charlotte weaves a surprise for herself. 20. The family doesn't kill Wilbur because he wins a special prize. 21. Wilbur returns to the farm and spends happy days with his friends. 22. Wilbur takes care of Charlotte's babies.	At the fair Wilbur and Charlotte talk about the plump pig. Wilbur is worried about Charlotte because she's not feeling well. Charlotte told Templeton to go out and find a new word. He found "humble" so she weaved it in her web. Charlotte laid her egg sac and got sick. Wilbur is sad because he thinks Henry is stealing Fern from him. Then Wilbur won first place! Charlotte died and Wilbur took her egg sac with him. Charlotte's eggs hatched. Three babies stayed with Wilbur. People visited him from time to time and he was happy. Wilbur kept Charlotte in his heart.

A Prediction Chart completed by a fourth-grade student for *Charlotte's Web* (White, 1952). Predictions were made for sets of chapters as the book was read.

108 Teaching Comprehension: A Systematic and Practical Framework

Prediction Chart

Prediction **CHART**

"Rosie's Mouse"

pg	What do you think will happen?	What did happen?
15	the mouse is in the fishbowl.	the mouse pop out, find ab
17	tiered to chas the mouss.	she get angry moves still making messes.
27	She plant be nice to the moves in be. If taped in she well not be angry no more.	to get Freed the cat,
31	the cat in the moves is mane it eathove.	the cat in the moves is mane it eathe
43	can you be my faird,	there was a fire

A Prediction Chart for *Rosie's Mouse* (Mayer, 1992), completed by a second-grade student

APPLICATION/EXTENSION STRATEGY:

Literary Poster

A Literary Poster (Johnson & Louis, 1987) is a postreading strategy that gives students an opportunity to interpret text and write a creative personal response to it. It is a strategy that students like to use because it allows for lots of creativity. They can choose to create a Wanted Poster, a Reward Poster, or any poster that is appropriate for the story. When students are designing their posters, encourage them to use newly learned vocabulary words to increase their understanding of the words. Figure 4Q is an example of a Wanted Poster completed by a first-grade student after reading the story *The Librarian from the Black Lagoon* (Thaler, 1997).

Before the Lesson

• Gather or prepare samples of several different kinds of posters including a Reward Poster, an ad, and a Wanted Poster.

Teaching the Strategy

• After students have completed their Personal Response or other comprehension activity, tell them they have the opportunity for another personal response, this time in the format of a poster.

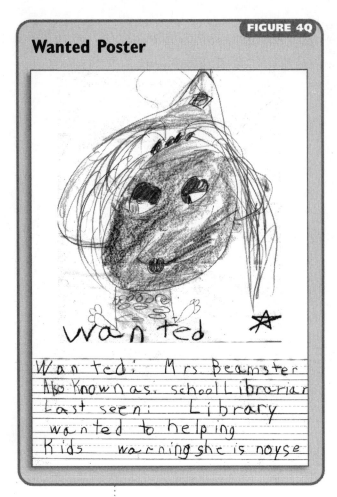

Wanted Poster

FIGURE 4Q

Wanted: Mrs Beamster
Also Known as: school Librarian
Last seen: Library
wanted to helping
Kids warning she is noyse

A first-grader's Wanted Poster
created in response to
The Librarian from the Black Lagoon

• Show students the examples of different kinds of posters. Tell them that they can design any kind of poster they wish as long as it depicts their personal interpretation of the story and includes the vocabulary words they learned. For example, if students choose to do a Reward Poster, it should include a description of a character, the reason for offering a reward (e.g., the problem the character caused or contributed to), and perhaps details about places the character might be hiding.

• Allow students to work together on this project, either in pairs or in small groups.

• Have a sharing time when students can tell about their posters. Display their work around the room.

APPLICATION/EXTENSION STRATEGY:
Pictorial Outline

A Pictorial Outline (Carr & Wixson, 1986) is a free-form illustration constructed by students to organize text concepts and vocabulary words in a visual way. A Pictorial Outline gives students the opportunity to integrate information in a creative response while encouraging vocabulary development. Students love this creative way of showing their learning. See Figure 4R for a sample done by a fifth-grade student.

Before the Lesson

• Prepare a sample Pictorial Outline to use as a model (or show student work from a previous year). Your example should include a brief description of what the picture represents, using vocabulary words the students have learned.

Pictorial Outline

The class was up on the mesa and Caro wandered away. She walked cautiously down the steep slope and discovered a cave with the skeleton of an Indian girl and her doll.

A Pictorial Outline created by a fifth-grade student after she read *The Secret Among the Stones* (Mayhar, 1997)

Teaching the Strategy

- Elicit the theme of the story or poem you've discussed earlier. This strategy is most effective after students have read the story and completed at least one comprehension activity, such as Personal Response or Literary Analysis (see page 95).

- Pair up students and ask them to brainstorm some ideas central to the theme of the story or poem (Think-Pair-Share; see page 34).

- Have students illustrate the ideas they brainstorm and write an accompanying description. Encourage them to use key vocabulary words from the story or poem in their writing.

- Have a sharing time when students can present their Pictorial Outlines. Display their creations around the room.

ThinkingWorks Lesson Planning Guide

A number of strategies have been introduced in this chapter that will enable you to teach a complete lesson for narrative text with an emphasis on personal response and literary analysis. Figure 4S shows two completed ThinkingWorks Lesson Planning Guides using the strategies introduced in this chapter.

ThinkingWorks Lesson Planning Guides

	STRATEGIES			
	Background Knowledge	Vocabulary	Comprehension	Application/ Extension
COGNITIVE PROCESSES	ETR	Possible Sentences	Personal Response/ Literary Analysis	Journal Response
Develop Background Knowledge	✔			
Expand Vocabulary Knowledge		✔		
Use Text Structure				
Set a Purpose for Learning	✔			
Infer/Select Information			✔	
Create Images			✔	
Relate/Connect Ideas			✔	
Clarify/Monitor Understanding			✔	
Analyze			✔	✔
Synthesize			✔	✔
Evaluate/Justify			✔	✔
Create/Invent			✔	✔
LANGUAGE PROCESSES				
Read			✔	
Write				✔
Listen/View	✔	✔	✔	
Communicate Orally	✔	✔	✔	

COGNITIVE PROCESSES	ETR	Possible Sentences	Prediction Chart	Literary Poster
Develop Background Knowledge	✔		✔	
Expand Vocabulary Knowledge		✔		
Use Text Structure				
Set a Purpose for Learning	✔		✔	
Infer/Select Information			✔	
Create Images			✔	
Relate/Connect Ideas			✔	
Clarify/Monitor Understanding			✔	
Analyze				✔
Synthesize				✔
Evaluate/Justify				
Create/Invent				✔
LANGUAGE PROCESSES				
Read			✔	
Write		✔	✔	✔
Listen/View	✔	✔	✔	
Communicate Orally	✔	✔	✔	

CHAPTER 5

Understanding
Expository Text

In This Chapter:

BACKGROUND KNOWLEDGE:	Anticipation Guide
VOCABULARY:	Concept of a Definition Adapted for Technical Vocabulary
COMPREHENSION:	KWL
APPLICATION/EXTENSION:	RAFT
ALTERNATIVE COMPREHENSION STRATEGIES:	KWL Plus, I-Chart, About Point, About Point Notetaking
ALTERNATIVE APPLICATION/EXTENSION STRATEGIES:	SCAMPER Expository

I n this chapter, we turn our attention to expository text. Here, and in the next two chapters, we share strategies that help students comprehend and remember expository text.

In contrast to narrative, which follows a consistent structure that is familiar to students from early home and school experiences, expository text has a number of different structures with which children are often not familiar. Moreover, since there is no prototypical structure for expository text, past reading experiences do not necessarily provide clues to the structure of future texts. Since we rely on expository texts to teach information we want students to learn and retain, and since much of the reading they will do as adults will be expository, we must teach strategies that help students comprehend expository texts (Graves et al., 1998). Toward that end, we have developed the lesson sequence in this chapter. Chapter 6 provides strategies for analyzing expository texts and Chapter 7 addresses strategies for helping students interpret and respond to these texts.

ThinkingWorks Lesson Plan Sequence for Understanding Expository Text

To introduce students to expository text and develop their understanding of it, we have designed the following lesson sequence:

BACKGROUND KNOWLEDGE: . . . . .Anticipation Guide

VOCABULARY: . . . . .Concept of a Definition Adapted for Technical Vocabulary

COMPREHENSION: . . . . .KWL

APPLICATION/EXTENSION: . . . . .RAFT

In this chapter, the application/extension strategy, RAFT, is a writing activity, so this component fulfills the writing recommendation for the lesson. We also encourage students to write summaries of what they've read at various points of the lesson to enhance their comprehension.

In addition, we include four alternative strategies: KWL Plus, I-Chart, About Point with About Point Notetaking for comprehension, and SCAMPER (Expository) for application/extension. Choose the strategies that are most appropriate for your students and learning objectives.

BACKGROUND KNOWLEDGE:
Anticipation Guide

An Anticipation Guide (Vacca & Vacca, 1999) activates students' background knowledge by asking them to respond to a series of statements on a topic. Students draw on what they already know to agree or disagree with the statements. The guide can pique students' interest in a topic and helps them set a purpose for reading; they actively search the text for information that confirms or refutes the statements.

The key to using this strategy effectively is developing statements that address key concepts and get students thinking critically about them. For instance, in an anticipation guide developed for a class studying pioneers and the westward movement, the teacher created statements such as *Pioneers usually made the journey west in about one month*. Before reading, most students thought this sounded reasonable, and it got them thinking about traveling across the country and wondering how long it really took, before there were such things as airplanes and automobiles. In effect, it gave them a purpose for reading and built their motivation. (See Figure 5A for the complete Anticipation Guide.)

FIGURE 5A

Anticipation Guide

Before reading please check whether you agree or disagree with the statements. Do the same after reading and change any statements that are incorrect.

Before Reading		Statement	After Reading	
Agree	Disagree		Agree	Disagree
✔	_____	Pioneers usually made the journey west in about one month. **They made the journey in 4–5 months.**	_____	✔
✔	_____	Settlers traveled together in wagon trains so their trip was not too dangerous.	✔	_____
✔	_____	Many people left their heirlooms behind because there was not a way to travel with them. **People took their heirlooms with them.**	_____	✔
✔	_____	Pioneers carried all their food and provisions with them. **Pioneers also hunted.**	_____	✔

An Anticipation Guide created for students to complete and discuss before they read about the pioneers and the Westward Movement

Anticipation Guide

Directions: Write Agree (A) or Disagree (D) for each statement.
After reading, change any statement that is inaccurate.

Before Reading	After Reading	Statement
D	A	More kinds of plants and animals are found in a rain forest than anywhere else on earth.
D	D	Most rain forests have very cool temperatures all year. *Rain forests are usually hot and humid.*
A	A	Rain forests get rain almost every day.
A	A	The canopy is the top layer of trees' branches in a rain forest.
D	D	Scientists are familiar with all the plants and animals that live in rain forests. *Scientists are still learning about rain forests. There are thousands of plant species to be identified.*
D	D	Rain forests serve no purpose to humans. They just take up space, so people are cutting them down. *Rain forests have many good effects for humans. Trees supply oxygen. Plants produce cures for diseases.*
A	D	The understory is the underground part of the rain forest. *The understory is beneath the forest canopy.*
A	A	Rain forests have been around for a long, long time.
D	A	Some people live in rain forests.
A	D	The greenhouse effect happens when lots of rain causes trees and grass to turn very green. *It happens when sunlight passes through the atmosphere and reflects off the earth's surface.*

Another format of an Anticipation Guide
for the science topic rain forests

We recommend including some accurate and inaccurate statements in Anticipation Guides. Invite students to discuss the statements before reading, giving them the opportunity to agree or disagree and explain their responses. After reading, have students use their Anticipation Guide to determine if the beliefs they held before reading changed as a result of new information from the text. In the Anticipation Guide for pioneers, students changed their mind about how long it took pioneers to cross the country; they noted that it really took 4 to 5 months.

Before the Lesson

- Analyze the reading assignment to identify the important ideas.

- Develop 5 to 8 short, clear statements about those ideas that will spark students' interest. Include statements that express an opinion different from those that might exist in your students' background knowledge (i.e., opinions that are controversial). Include both accurate and inaccurate statements.

- Create a three-column chart with the statements in the middle column. In the first and third column, add lines labeled Agree and Disagree before and after each statement (see the examples in Figures 5A and 5B; there's also a template on the CD).

- Write directions for the students, telling them to place a check in the Agree column if they agree with the statement and in the Disagree column if they disagree.

- Make copies of the handout for students.

Teaching the Strategy

- Tell students that you have created an Anticipation Guide to get them ready for their upcoming reading. By considering what they know about the statements in the guide, they will activate their background knowledge, make predictions, and set a purpose for reading.

- Model responding to the first statement by thinking aloud about your prior knowledge and then agreeing or disagreeing. The science teacher who prepared the Anticipation Guide in Figure 5B thought aloud this way: "This says that more kinds of plants and animals are found in a rain forest than anywhere else on earth. That's a pretty broad statement. I can think of other environments that have many different kinds of animals, such as the regular forests. I'm not sure why a rain forest would have more types of plants and animals than a regular forest. So I think I will disagree with this statement for now, but I am curious to know what the text has to say about this. I'll be thinking about this statement as I read."

- Distribute the Anticipation Guides and have students complete the prereading section. Have students discuss their responses to the statements in small groups.

- Gather the class together and invite groups to summarize their results for the whole class. Continue to encourage discussion among all students. Wrap up the discussion by asking students to look for information in the text that will confirm or negate their positions on the statements. This helps them set a purpose for reading.

- Have the students read the text in class or assign it as homework.

- After reading, tell students to work in their groups, or independently, and follow the same procedure for the post-reading section, agreeing and disagreeing with the statements on the Anticipation Guide. Encourage students to correct statements or add details to them based on their reading.

• Call the class together to share the results.

According to Alvermann and Phelps (1994), teachers need to be careful not to make the statements on the Anticipation Guide too text-dependent, because when the statements are too far removed from the students' background knowledge, students make wild guesses about whether or not they are true. For example, this statement is too text-dependent: "The Oregon Trail passed through the states of Missouri, Kansas, Colorado, Utah, Wyoming, California, and Oregon." Instead, use a more general statement, such as "Pioneers usually made the journey west in about one month."

Writing Extension

Students can choose one statement from the Anticipation Guide and explain why they agreed or disagreed with it. They can do this before reading, to expand their thinking about the topic. Or they can write about a statement on which they changed their position after the reading. In this case, they would discuss the information that led to the change in their thinking.

Assessment

Listen carefully to the group summaries and discussions before the reading to assess whether or not students drew upon their prior knowledge to make predictions and set a purpose for reading. After reading, listen to the discussion to make sure there are no misconceptions about the statements, and be sure that students cite evidence from the text to support their responses. Another means of evaluating the strategy is through the writing students would do at the end of the lesson (see the RAFT application/extension strategy on page 122).

 VOCABULARY STRATEGY:
Concept of a Definition Adapted for Technical Vocabulary

In Chapter 3 we discussed Concept of a Definition (Schwartz & Raphael, 1985), a strategy for helping students develop full definitions for vocabulary words by considering the category in which the word falls ("What is it?"), its properties ("What is it like?" or "What is its purpose?"), and illustrations of the term ("What are some examples?"). You can adapt this strategy into a format that will help students learn and remember the complex technical vocabulary that they encounter in their expository reading assignments. The difference between the adapted version and the original Concept of a Definition strategy is that the adapted version visually depicts the complete definition without the questions (e.g., "What is it?"), which helps students see how different aspects of the definition are related. In most cases, you would implement this strategy after the students have read the text.

Before the Lesson

• Select two or three words from the reading assignment that represent or describe important concepts in the text.

Teaching the Strategy

• Have students read the definition of the word that is given in the text or provide the definition for them. Write the definition on the board.

• Help students pick out the important kernels of information in the definition. Write these on the board in outline form so that they answer the three questions: "What is it?," "What is it like?," and "What are some examples?" However, do not write those questions (see Figures 5C and 5D for two examples).

• Have the students write their completed definition for the word in notebooks or on index cards for easy access and studying.

• Tell the students to complete the definitions for the remaining word or words using the same procedure. Check their work the first few times to make sure their definition outlines are completed correctly.

Figure 5C shows how students used the streamlined version of Concept of a Definition to help them retain the definition of the word *pioneer* from the unit on Westward Expansion. In Figure 5D, the strategy is applied to the vocabulary word *camouflage* encountered in a science text.

Writing Extension

Students can write a "word paragraph" using the About Point Writing Response strategy. The topic sentence consisting of the word itself (About) and a statement about what it is (Point) would be followed by three or four sentences explaining the word and providing examples. The closing statement of the paragraph could express an opinion about the concept defined by the vocabulary word.

FIGURE 5C

Concept of a Definition Adapted for Technical Vocabulary

Pioneer
- Person
    - Settles a new region.
    - Prepares the land for development by others
        - Wilder (Little House)
        - Daniel Boone

FIGURE 5D

Concept of a Definition Adapted for Technical Vocabulary

Camouflage
- Method of survival
    - Blend into environment
    - Coloration
    - Pattern or markings
        - Chameleon
        - Cobra

Younger students who are not proficient writers can write a sentence that answers just one of the three questions in the Concept of a Definition strategy. Following are examples for the word *whale* created by first graders.

> A whale is a *mammal* (What is it?)
>
> A whale lives in the water and feeds its babies. (What is it like?)
>
> An orca is a type of whale. (What is an example?)

Very young students may use invented spelling to express their ideas or combine their writing with a dictated sentence written by the teacher. Students also can accompany their ideas with illustrations.

Assessment

There are two ways to successfully evaluate this strategy. First, use the students' paragraphs to determine if they learned the meaning of the vocabulary words. Second, give them a quiz in which they have to write down or say the complete definitions of the words.

COMPREHENSION STRATEGY:
KWL

KWL (Ogle, 1986) takes students through the entire comprehension process, including preparation for reading and processing of text during reading. A natural complement to KWL is KWL Plus (Carr & Ogle, 1987), which includes all of the KWL steps for comprehension, while adding steps that help students organize and summarize information; this strategy is discussed on page 125.

KWL is an acronym for "Know," "Want to know," and "Learned." It emphasizes a number of cognitive processes that students need to use in order to comprehend and learn from expository text. Students brainstorm and write down information they know about the topic (K). They then write down information they want to learn and anticipate learning about the topic (W). Finally, they read the text and write down what they learned (L). Figure 5E shows a completed KWL chart. With KWL, students activate background knowledge, set a purpose for reading, infer information, select and retain information, and monitor understandings. Because this strategy is particularly well-suited for group oral discussion, it encourages students to use their listening and speaking skills. After much practice with KWL, students also will be able to use the strategy independently.

Before the Lesson

• Create a KWL chart on chart paper or the overhead to use as a model. Also make copies for student use (see Figure 5E for an example). A template can be found on the CD.

KWL Chart

Know	Want to Know	Learned	
fix wheels	What did they do if they ran out of food?	decide how to cross rivers	hot coals
horse die, oxen	How did they survive the weather?	2,000 miles	abandoned wagons
dirt, stone road	Did they stop and help others?	only brought needs/heirlooms	fire
many decisions	How was it named?	4 months	hunt, gather
bugs	What dangers awaited?	15–20 miles a day	wagon stuck
wild berries	Where was it?	Missouri, Oregon, California	bad weather
covered wagons	What did they do if supplies were lost?	Kansas, Colorado, Utah	robbers, run away
hunt	What did trails lead to?	Wyoming, Idaho	cook, wash, set up camp
trade	What did they do if animals died?	1 out of 17 died	build homes, crops, animals
groups	Who would help with accidents?	cholera	oxen—strong, horses, mules cows
town far	How many rivers?	20 miles wide—flat areas	flour, cornmeal, sugar, meat
water	What were the trails like?	erosion—rain, tracks, wind, ruts	rough, grassy, no trees
hides	Wagon fires?	leave certain times	Platte River
fish		push carts up mountains	steep mountain passes
long trip		water barrels	captains—decisions
tree/bush		travel groups—trains	guidebook
danger		broken wheels/axles	animals and humans—born
look for food			
forts			
nature			
no toilets			

A KWL chart completed by a fourth-grade student during a lesson on the Oregon Trail

Teaching the Strategy

- Tell students what they are going to be reading about and explain how the KWL chart will help them.

- Divide them into groups and give each group a KWL chart.

- Have students brainstorm what they know about the topic and list the information in the first column of the group's chart.

- Have the groups share what they know; list their ideas in the K column of your KWL chart.

- Ask students to develop questions about what they want to know about the topic. Have them write the questions down in the second column on their group chart.

- Have the groups share their questions and list some of them on your chart. Add questions of your own if something important was not mentioned by students.

- Have students read the text in segments, encouraging them to look for answers to their questions. After each segment, groups should list in the third column important information they learned, including answers to their questions. Ask students to share some of their information after each segment; add it to your KWL chart.

- When the entire text is read and groups have completed their charts, discuss with students what they learned from reading. (Note: KWL can be used with one or more texts to encourage students to link information.)

- Review questions students recorded in the second column on their charts and discuss ways to find information about those that were not answered.

Writing Extension

If you would like to have your students write at this point in the lesson, continue with KWL Plus (page 125), which has a writing component built into the strategy.

Assessment

To determine whether the KWL strategy has been effective, test students on important pieces of information from the text after they finish the lesson and again several weeks later.

APPLICATION/EXTENSION STRATEGY:

RAFT

RAFT (Santa, 1988) is a prewriting strategy that gives students the opportunity to apply and extend in a new way what they have learned in their reading assignment. Students prepare to write by determining the following:

R: THE ROLE OF THE WRITER *Who are you? What perspective do you have— that of yourself? A scientist? A character in the text?*

A: AUDIENCE *To whom is the writing addressed—a political body? Readers of the local newspaper? A friend?*

F: FORMAT *What format will you use—a business letter? An editorial? A journal? A report?*

T: TOPIC AND STRONG VERB *What topic will be addressed? Which strong verb will convey your intent—**persuade** a legislator to vote affirmatively on an* *issue? **Inform** a group of colleagues about important data? **Invite** a character in a book to dinner with other notable guests?*

Students can use RAFT independently or in a group. When worked on as a group, students discuss possibilities for each of the four components. Figures 5F and 5G show examples of the RAFT strategy.

Teaching the Strategy

- Ask students whether the reading assignment and comprehension strategy make them think about any relevant writing topics. That is, did the reading assignment spark any ideas for writing? Write their ideas on the board.

- Present the four components of RAFT and discuss the value of using them as a prewriting strategy for extending the reading assignment.

- Select three or four of the writing topics on the board and model the procedure for using RAFT with each topic. List possible roles, audiences, formats, and strong verbs appropriate for each topic. For example, if students studying the Oregon Trail suggest writing a letter back home describing their travels, you could extend their thinking this way: "What an interesting topic. Let's flesh it out using our RAFT strategy. First, we'll think about the role of the writer. In this case, it's someone who has left their home to travel west. We need to decide on how old this

---

FIGURE 5F

RAFT: Friendly Letter

Assignment: Pretend you are a pioneer traveling on the Oregon Trail. You need to write a letter to your cousin Clara back in Boston. Convince Clara why her family should pack up and move to this new land near you. Be sure your letter contains the five letter parts (heading, greeting, body, closing, and signature). When writing the letter use the information you read about in class to convince Clara.

R = Relative

A = Cousin Clara

F = Friendly letter

T = Should move

April 28, 1872

Dear Clara,

I think you should move to Oregon. If you lived in Oregon, you could live in a cabin. We all miss you especially me. Out West there is a lot of room. You can run around and have fun. There are a lot of flowers. You know how your mom loves flowers. There is a lot of grass. You know how you always wanted a dog. Now you can have one. That's why I think you should move to Oregon.

Your cousin,
Carrie Lynn

A fourth-grade student wrote a friendly letter using RAFT to extend a reading assignment on the topic of the Oregon Trail.

person is, where they're from, and why they've decided to make such a long journey. Let's see. Since we read several diary excerpts from children, why don't we imagine a ten-year old girl from New York who's traveling west with her family in search of a better way of life?" Continue thinking aloud through the other components of RAFT.

- Have students create a RAFT assignment in groups using one of the topics mentioned or one of their own choosing. Have them then complete the assignments.

- Encourage the groups to share their completed assignments with the whole class.

Writing Exercise

The RAFT activity is the recommended writing activity for this lesson sequence. It is also a meaningful way to incorporate writing across the curriculum and a good preparation activity for many different writing formats, including reports, essays, friendly and business letters, and invitations. Since students are already familiar with the About Point Writing Response strategy, you can show them how to apply that strategy when they are using RAFT to write reports and essays.

Assessment

If RAFT helps students successfully write an editorial, a report, a journal entry, or a letter, then it can be deemed a valid and effective strategy.

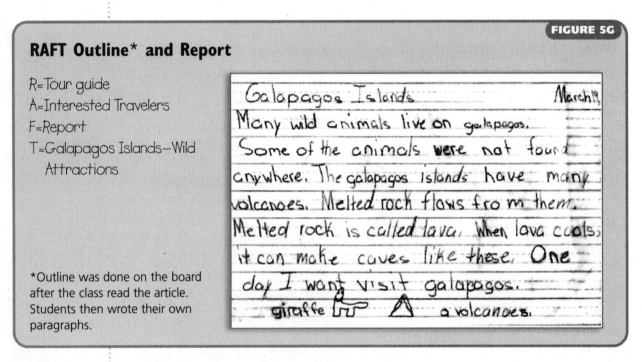

FIGURE 5G

RAFT Outline* and Report

R=Tour guide
A=Interested Travelers
F=Report
T=Galapagos Islands—Wild
   Attractions

*Outline was done on the board after the class read the article. Students then wrote their own paragraphs.

> Galapagos Islands   March 19
> Many wild animals live on galapagos.
> Some of the animals were not found
> anywhere. The galapagos islands have many
> volcanoes. Melted rock flows from them.
> Melted rock is called lava. When lava cools,
> it can make caves like these. One
> day I want visit galapagos.
> giraffe   a volcanoes.

A RAFT outline that a second-grade student used as a basis
for writing a science report about the Galapagos Islands

Alternative Comprehension and Application/Extension Strategies for Understanding Expository Text

The goal of this chapter is to present a coherent lesson plan for helping students understand expository texts. In addition to the strategies presented in the previous section, we offer four others you may wish to use based on your students' needs and your lesson objectives. The comprehension strategies are KWL Plus, I-Chart, and About Point With About Point Notetaking. The application/extension strategy is SCAMPER (Expository).

COMPREHENSION STRATEGY:

KWL Plus

KWL Plus (Carr & Ogle, 1987) is a strategy that helps students organize information they recall from text. Students complete all of the steps of KWL (see page 120) and then carry out the additional steps of categorizing, mapping, and summarizing what they've learned. Research indicates that these additional steps increase text comprehension, especially of unfamiliar and difficult concepts, and improve writing ability (Carr & Ogle, 1987). KWL Plus provides enough guidance for students to independently comprehend and summarize complex and difficult expository text.

Before the Lesson

- Have students complete all of the steps in KWL for the topic, as described on page 120. Allow them to work in small groups, if possible.

Teaching the Strategy

- Tell students you are going to teach them a way to organize the information from their KWL charts to help them comprehend the material even better and learn to write a summary.

- Have students categorize the information in the third column of the chart (Learned). You might give them categories and have them plug in the information. In the Oregon Trail example shown in Figure 5H, for instance, the teacher provided four categories: Hardships, Physical Characteristics, What Pioneers Brought, What Pioneers Did. Alternatively, you might want to ask students to create their own categories based on the information.

- Have students color code the information in the third column to make mapping easier. Every statement that falls into the same category would be highlighted with the same color. See the Learned column in Figure 5H for how students categorized what they learned about pioneers into four headings.

KWL Plus

K (Know)	W (Want to Know)	L (Learned)*
fix wheels	What did they do if they ran out of food?	H—decide how to cross rivers
horse die, oxen	How did they survive the weather?	P—2,000 miles
dirt, stone road	Did they stop and help others?	B—only brought needs/heirlooms
many decisions	How was it named?	P—4 months
bugs	What dangers awaited?	P—15–20 miles a day
wild berries	Where was it?	P—Missouri, Oregon, California
covered wagons	What did they do if supplies were lost?	P—Kansas, Colorado, Utah
hunt	What did trails lead to?	P—Wyoming, Idaho
trade	What did they do if animals died?	H—1 out of 17 died
groups	Who would help with accidents?	H—cholera
town far	How many rivers?	P—20 miles wide—flat areas
water	What were the trails like?	H—erosion—rain, tracks, wind, ruts
hides	Wagon fires?	D—leave certain times
fish		H—push carts up mountains
long trip		B—water barrels
tree/bush		D—travel groups—trains
danger		H—broken wheels/axles
look for food		B—hot coals
forts		H—abandoned wagons
nature		H—fire
no toilets		D—hunt, gather

Right column of L (Learned):

B—hot coals
H—abandoned wagons
H—fire
D—hunt, gather
H—wagon stuck
H—bad weather
H—robbers, run away
D—cook, wash, set up camp
D—build homes, crops, animals
B—oxen—strong, horses, mules cows
B—flour, cornmeal, sugar, meat
P—rough, grassy, no trees
P—Platte River
P—steep mountain passes
D—captains—decisions
B—guidebook
D—animals and humans—born

*Legend
H=Hardships
P=Physical Characteristics
B=What They Brought
D=What They Did

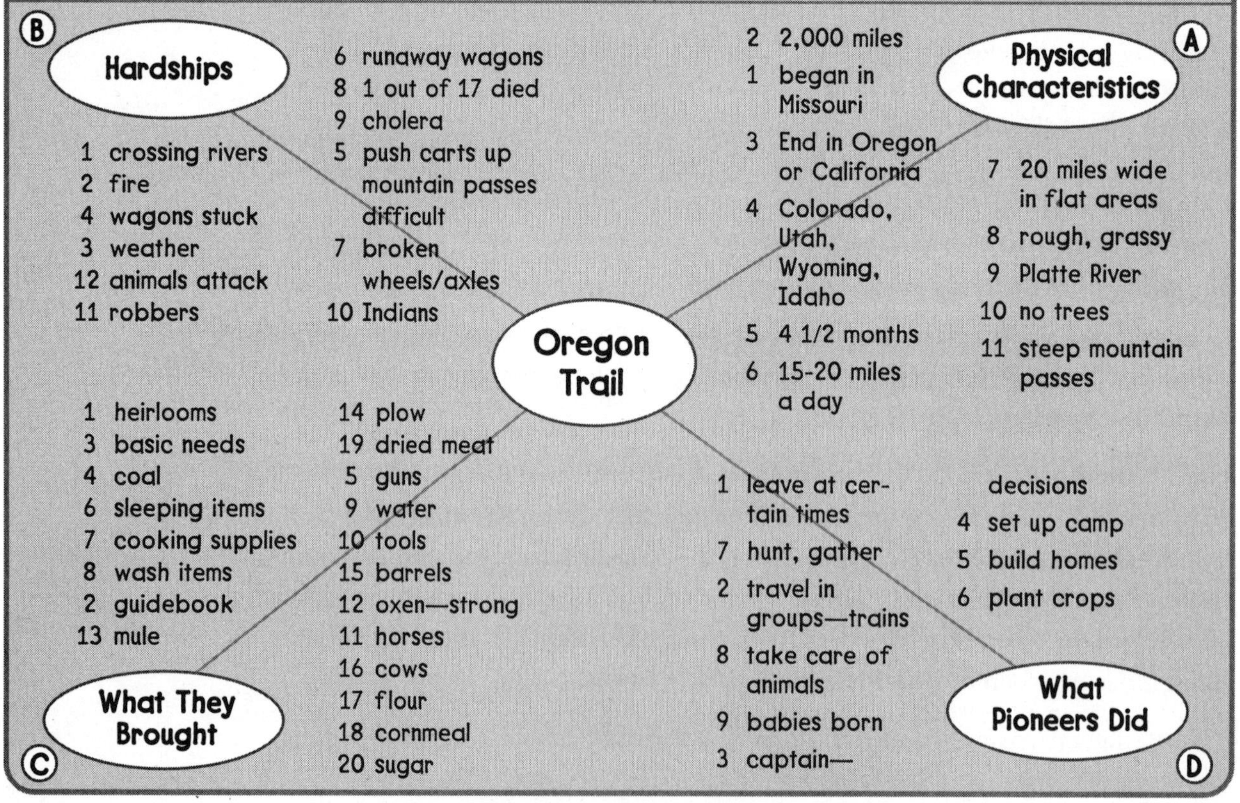

Hardships (B)
6 runaway wagons
8 1 out of 17 died
9 cholera
5 push carts up mountain passes difficult
1 crossing rivers
2 fire
4 wagons stuck
3 weather
12 animals attack
11 robbers
7 broken wheels/axles
10 Indians

Physical Characteristics (A)
2 2,000 miles
1 began in Missouri
3 End in Oregon or California
4 Colorado, Utah, Wyoming, Idaho
5 4 1/2 months
6 15-20 miles a day
7 20 miles wide in flat areas
8 rough, grassy
9 Platte River
10 no trees
11 steep mountain passes

Oregon Trail

What They Brought (C)
1 heirlooms
3 basic needs
4 coal
6 sleeping items
7 cooking supplies
8 wash items
2 guidebook
13 mule
14 plow
19 dried meat
5 guns
9 water
10 tools
15 barrels
12 oxen—strong
11 horses
16 cows
17 flour
18 cornmeal
20 sugar

What Pioneers Did (D)
1 leave at certain times
7 hunt, gather
2 travel in groups—trains
8 take care of animals
9 babies born
3 captain—decisions
4 set up camp
5 build homes
6 plant crops

A student's KWL Plus for a lesson on the Oregon Trail. Note that the capital letters in the L column of the KWL chart designate the categories in the map.

- Show students how to create a map from the color-coded KWL chart. The topic should be written in the center of the map. Major categories (concepts) should be written in their own space, with details (i.e., statements from the L column) included beneath each category. Students can draw lines to show the connection between the main topic and the categories (see the map in Figure 5H). Instruct students to work with their group to create a map.

- Have students use the map as an outline for writing a summary. Instruct them to use letters to organize the categories on the map in the order that makes the most sense to them for writing purposes. Then have them check to make sure that the important details are listed under each category in a logical order. If not, have students number the details according to the sequence they wish to follow when writing. The map in Figure 5H shows how students sequenced the topics for their summaries in this manner. (Students can work in groups at first; after they have enough practice, they can write the summaries independently.)

KWL Plus: Summary

Summary The Oregon Trail

Most people traveled the Oregon Trail out west. Many people said it starts in Missouri. It is two thousand miles long. It ended in Oregon or California. There are four different states the trail goes through: Colorado, Utah, Wyoming, and Idaho. It usually takes four to five months. They always traveled fifteen to twenty miles a day. Sometimes on flat areas the trail would be twenty miles wide. Most of the trail is really rough and grassy. One of the rivers that runs a long ways is the Platte River. Very often there are trees. They had to go through very steep mountain passes. That is what the Oregon Trail looks like.

Many people had many hardships. Pioneers say it is really hard crossing rivers. There were really bad fires along the trail. Weather was often bad. If they left too early the wagon would get stuck. They would have to push the wagons up the mountains. If there was one little mistake the wagon ran away down the hill. Broken wheels and axles caused problems. One out of seventeen died. Many people died of the disease cholera. Abandoned wagons meant dead people. Those who lived were attacked by Indians, robbers, and animals.

Many people brought their heirlooms, a guidebook and also things for their needs. Coal, guns, sleeping stuff, and cooking supplies were needed for the trip. Wash items, water and tools were also needed. Tow horses, strong oxen, mules, a plow, barrels and cows were needed. Flour, cornmeal, dried meat and sugar were used for cooking and eating. When they left the wagon would be full.

Pioneers did a lot of things. They left at certain times and had to travel in groups which is called a train. There was a captain who had to make decisions, and if someone did not agree they would have to split up. When they got to where they wanted to settle they would have to make camp. Then they would have to build their home. Now the boys and the men would have to plant crops. Men hunted a lot. Everybody needed to help take care of the farm animals. Men also had to deliver baby animals and humans. That is all about the Oregon Trail.

The summary is a natural outgrowth of the KWL columns and the map.

- Have students write summaries based on their outlines. Students should use the About Point Writing Response strategy for writing a one-paragraph summary or a summary consisting of a series of paragraphs. If they're writing one-paragraph summaries, the name or concept in the center of the map answers the question of what the paragraph is about—e.g., *the Oregon Trail*. Students should select one of the categories to answer the question of what the point is—e.g., *It had many hardships for the pioneers*. By combining the two pieces of information, students have their topic sentence: *The Oregon Trail had many hardships for pioneers*. They should then write three or four sentences using the details listed under the "Hardships" category to support the topic sentence. Finally, they should close the paragraph with a sentence that restates the idea in the topic sentence.

- If students are writing a summary that consists of several paragraphs, they should write one paragraph for each category on the map. Tell them to write an About Point for each category, which then becomes the topic sentence for the paragraph. (See the summaries in Figures 5I and 5J. Additionally, see pages 48 and 166 for more discussion of summary writing.)

- Students also can write group reports and class books using this strategy.

As an alternative, students can write the information they've learned on individual cards rather than on the chart. They can then categorize the cards and place them on a map in appropriate categories. Students can easily sequence cards in the appropriate order to write a summary.

After students have become proficient at completing the entire KWL Plus strategy, they can use a short cut and omit the mapping step by using the following procedure:

1. categorize and color code information in the "L" column;

2. use numbers to order the information in each category into a logical sequence for writing; and

3. write the summary, including a paragraph for each category.

Although this modification may save time, it can be confusing for students if there is a lot of information in the "L" column. Additionally, it is important for students to see the visual regrouping of information so that the logic and the procedures for structuring information become clear to them. Figure 5K is an example of a modified KWL Plus chart on which a fifth-grade student has categorized and numbered the "L" column information as an aid to summary writing. He then used each of the categories to write a paragraph. The first paragraph follows the About Point Writing Response strategy (e.g., topic sentence, details, and closing), while the other two paragraphs do not.

KWL Plus

K (Know)	W (Want to Learn)	L (Learned)
William: It is hot.	Archie: Are there a lot of people living in the desert?	1—The desert is sandy.
Marissa: It is dry.	William: Are there houses in the desert?	1—The desert is hot and dry.
Kyle J.: It has lots of animals.	Ray: So people wear shoes?	1—At night, the air is cool.
Archie: It doesn't have water.	Darius: Are there a lot of people and animals in the desert?	2—Very few people live in the desert, they are called nomads.
Ali: It doesn't have houses.	Dustin: Are there many trees in the desert?	5—There are very few animals because there is little food and water.
Darius: It is beautiful and you can see a mirage.	Corey: How do you survive in the desert?	1—There is little rain in the desert.
Amanda: It has cactus.	Charlene: Are there dangerous animals in the desert?	5—Some of the animals in the desert are lizards, camels, birds, snakes, desert skunks, sidewinders, and jackrabbits.
Dustin: It has camels.	Nikitia: Are there cactus in the desert?	
Charlene: It has a lot of dirt.	Elizabeth: Is it windy in the desert?	5—Spadefoot toads burrow into the ground to sleep.
Elizabeth: It doesn't have food.	Sheila: Does it rain in the desert?	3—Hundreds of different kinds of insects live in the desert.
Corey: It has lizards.	Desmond: Does the cactus hurt you?	4—There are cactus plants, yucca plants, and spring flowers. Cactus have thorns.
Ray: The desert has snakes.	Ali: Is there sand in the desert?	
Kyle S.: The desert has quicksand.	Sierra: What do animals do because it is so hot?	2—People wear sandals.
Demarco: You can die.		2—Nomads live in tents.
Nikitia: There are mountains.		

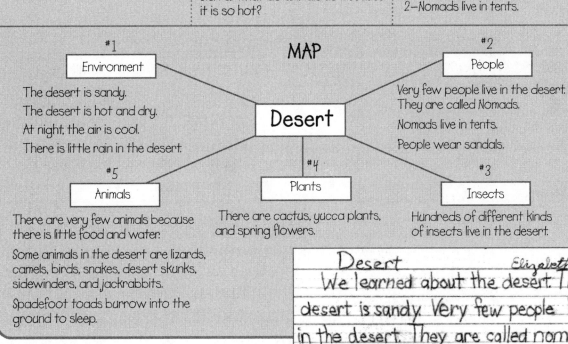

MAP

#1 Environment
The desert is sandy.
The desert is hot and dry.
At night, the air is cool.
There is little rain in the desert.

Desert

#2 People
Very few people live in the desert. They are called Nomads.
Nomads live in tents.
People wear sandals.

#5 Animals
There are very few animals because there is little food and water.
Some animals in the desert are lizards, camels, birds, snakes, desert skunks, sidewinders, and jackrabbits.
Spadefoot toads burrow into the ground to sleep.

#4 Plants
There are cactus, yucca plants, and spring flowers.

#3 Insects
Hundreds of different kinds of insects live in the desert.

Desert   Elizabeth
We learned about the desert. The desert is sandy. Very few people live in the desert. They are called nomads. Hundreds of diffenrent Kind of insects live in the desert. There are cactus, yucca plant, and spring fowes. There are very few animals because there is very little water.

This is a KWL Plus completed by second-grade, Title I students on the topic of the desert. The students completed both class and individual worksheets. Students' names were included on the class worksheet as they contributed information, a procedure that encourages students to participate. After they completed the mapping, students wrote individual summaries that included one idea from each category in the map.

Modified KWL Plus Chart and Summary

K (Know)	W (Want to Learn)	L (Learned)
Early people in Australian grasslands hunted for their food. Houses are made of wood and straw.	What kind of food did the people eat? Did the people move to find food? What kinds of clothing did they wear? How did they celebrate holidays and special occasions? **Categories** P=People H=Hunting S=Shelter	P-1—The people to first live in the grasslands of Australia were Aborigines. P-4—They did not have many belongings. P-2—The early Australians were nomads. H-1—They used spears to hunt. H-2—They would throw a spear by using a woomera or spear thrower. S-1—The Australian Aborigines sometimes made houses called wurleys. H-3—They hunted animals and fish. P-3—Tribes were divided into smaller groups called bands. S-2—Some Aborigines build shelters called lean-tos build with twigs and bark. P-5—The Aborigines still lead a way of life somewhat like people many years ago. S-3—Many Aborigines live on government owned land.

Summary The Aborigines of Australia

The people to first live in the grasslands of Australia were Aborigines. The early Australians were nomads. Tribes of nomads were divided into smaller groups called bands. They did not have many belongings and moved a lot. Aborigines still lead a way of life somewhat like people did many years ago.

Aborigines used spears to hunt. They would throw a spear by using a woomera or spear thrower. They hunted animals and fish.

The Australian Aborigines sometimes made houses called wurleys. Some Aborigines built shelters called lean-tos. Now Aborigines live on government-owned land.

This figure shows a modified KWL Plus chart on which a fifth grader has categorized and numbered the "L" column information as an aid to summary writing. He then used each of the categories to write a paragraph.

Assessment

Evaluate student responses on the KWL chart to determine if the strategy helped students activate background knowledge and set a purpose for reading. Examine the map to see if the strategy helped students organize information. Finally, assess students' summaries to determine whether the KWL Plus strategy helped them to accurately record the most important pieces of information about the topic.

I-Chart

The I-Chart (Hoffman, 1992) is an excellent strategy for guiding students in a research project. It involves many of the same components as KWL and KWL Plus, capitalizing on students' background knowledge. Once students become familiar with the strategy, I-Charts can be the basis for whole-class, small-group, or individual inquiry. I-Charts include headings for topic, background knowledge, sources of information, and summaries. Once a topic has been selected, three or four core questions are developed that will guide the research process. The questions are listed at the top of the chart; see Figure 5L for a sample. There is a template on the CD. When the chart is complete, students are ready to write a report.

Before the Lesson

- To introduce the strategy, prepare an I-Chart template for a whole-class demonstration. You can use an overhead or a large piece of chart paper. Also have blank I-Charts for students to complete as you demonstrate the strategy.

I-CHART TEMPLATE

Topic:	Q1:	Q2:	Q3:	Q4:	Other Interesting Facts	New Questions
What We Know:						
Source:						
Source:						
Source:						
Summaries:						

Teaching the Strategy

- Introduce the idea of doing research to students, highlighting that it's a process that allows them to discover information on any topic they want to know about.

- Introduce the I-Chart strategy as a way of helping students focus their research and organize the information they find. Show them a blank template and discuss each part and how students will use it. Tell them that this time, the class will work through the I-Chart together; in the future, students will choose their own research topics (related to units of study) and complete the charts independently or in small groups.

- Select a topic for a research report in an area that students are studying. With students, develop three or four key questions that will guide them in researching the topic. Write the topic and questions in the appropriate columns on the demonstration I-Chart. Ask students to do the same on their charts.

- Discuss what students already know about the various questions and record their information on the I-Chart in the second row called "What We Know." You can record some of your students' background knowledge on the demonstration chart.

- Discuss several sources of information, including encyclopedias, books, magazines, the Internet, and interviews. Determine how many and what types of information you want students to consult during their research. Younger students may look only at books, while older students might conduct interviews and consult the Internet as well as read books and encyclopedias.

- Show students how to write the names of the sources they use on the left-hand column of the I-Chart.

- Tell students that as they read a source, they should record relevant information from that source in the box under the question it answers.

- Model how to read each kind of source students will use. Record relevant information in the corresponding boxes on the I-Chart.

- At this point, students can conduct their own research, using in-class resources you have collected or visiting the library.

- Complete your demonstration chart with information from various sources.

- When students have completed their research, gather the class together and show them your completed I-Chart. Model how to summarize the information for each question in the last row of the chart. Compare information from different sources to information they listed as background knowledge before the inquiry.

- Ask students to do the same for the information recorded on their individual charts.

- Tell students that they can use the chart as a basis for an oral or written report. Each summary statement at the bottom of the chart can be the basis of a paragraph in their report. They should follow the About Point Writing Response format.

- When the students have sufficiently practiced this method of organizing information for a research report with your help, they should be able to take a blank I-Chart and conduct their own independent inquiries.

For younger students, you can model the completion of the I-Chart, acting as a scribe for the whole class. Choose a topic and help students construct several "class" questions that you write on the chart along with any questions that you have developed. Then, read aloud one or two texts about the topic. Your reading of the books will provide students with "research" that they can use to construct answers to their questions. After reading, students can work in small groups, with each student in the group writing a one- or two-sentence answer to one of the questions or several sentences about an interesting fact that they learned. Each group's writings can be put together to form a "group" book or report. When needed, you can reread aloud parts of the books and help students with their writing.

I-Chart

Topic: Cobras	Question 1: Do experts consider the cobra the most dangerous animal?	Question 2: What are characteristics of the cobra?	Question 3: Do humans and cobras live together without fear?	Question 4: What are cobras capable of doing in nature?
What We Know	Yes. Many wildlife experts believe the cobra is one of the deadliest snakes.	The characteristics of the cobra are probably vicious, dangerous and sneaky.	No, I do not think that humans and cobras live together without fear because cobras hunt humans.	Cobras are capable of blending in and creeping very slowly. In camouflage with dead leaves, tree bark, grass and dusty places on earth.
Source/Book #1 Animals of Africa	Yes, because they're strong and quick killers. They don't even fear man.	Some characteristics of the cobra are strong, quick, different and fearless.	Cobras live with humans without fear but I couldn't live with a cobra without fear.	Cobras are capable of surviving in nature because they are aggressive and afraid of nothing.
Source/Book #2 The Marvels of Animal Behavior	Yes, the cobra is considered extremely dangerous.	Some characteristics of the cobra are fast, mobile, sleek, and great hunters.	In some places yes because humans worship cobras. To me no.	Cobras are capable of moving fast and destroying anything in their paths.
Source/Book #3 Illustrated Encyclopedia of Animals	Yes, experts consider the Indian cobra to be the most dangerous snake of all.	Some characteristics of the cobra are smart, dangerous, and poisonous.	No because it kills people but also it lives outside homes.	Cobras are capable of playing dead or going limp when danger is near and it has an inflated hood to protect from neck bites.
Summary	Yes, all the answers and sources agree that cobras are one of the most dangerous animals. They are strong and quick killers that don't fear anything at all including man.	The characteristics of a snake are dangerous, poisonous, smart, quick, hunters, fearless, quick, sleek, fast, and mobile.	In some places yes but in most places no because the cobra can kill a man and even make them go blind.	One of the main things a cobra can do in nature is survive. Some of the other things are destroying anything that gets in their way, going limp when danger is near and protecting themselves from neck bites.

Other Interesting Facts
Deadlier than the rattlesnake.
Cobras will chase and hunt man to death.
Cobras have markings on their backs that looks like a second head.

New Questions
What are other deadly snakes?

An I-Chart completed by a sixth-grade student for the topic, Cobras

About Point with About Point Notetaking

About Point (Martin, Lorton, Blanc, & Evans, 1977) is a key strategy that helps students determine the main idea of a text. It is described fully on page 16; here we present a lesson outline for teaching the strategy.

Before the Lesson

- Prepare copies of graphic organizers for students. The organizer has two columns: one for writing down the About Points and the other for writing down the statements; see page 16 in Chapter 1 for an example.

Teaching the Strategy

- After students have completed an Anticipation Guide (or another prereading strategy), tell them that you're going to introduce a strategy that will help them understand the main ideas in their reading.

- Tell students to read the first paragraph in their assignment for the purpose of understanding the main idea.

- Discuss with them what the paragraph is about. Tell them to write their response on the About line of their guide. Discuss what point the author is making about the topic, and have students write their response on the Point line.

- Tell students to combine the About and the Point to make a statement which they should write on their guide.

- Repeat these steps, modeling them when necessary, until students understand the process.

- Have them finish the reading assignment in pairs, writing down the About Points and statements reflecting the main ideas.

- Remind students that they should use this strategy whenever it's important for them to understand the main ideas of an expository reading assignment.

ABOUT POINT TEMPLATE

About: Statement:

Point:

An extension of About Point (see page 16) is a strategy called About Point Notetaking (Carr, January 2000), which is used to help students study; see Figure 5M for an example. Using a guide prepared beforehand, students take notes on a reading assignment by writing down for each paragraph or section the About, the Point, and supporting details. When students finish taking notes on the assignment, they can use the guide for studying by folding it over and covering everything except the Abouts. They test themselves by seeing if they can remember the Point and the details for each About. A variation on this procedure is to divide students into groups and instruct each group to take notes and summarize a section. You can make copies of each group's notes and summaries and distribute them to the students for studying before a test.

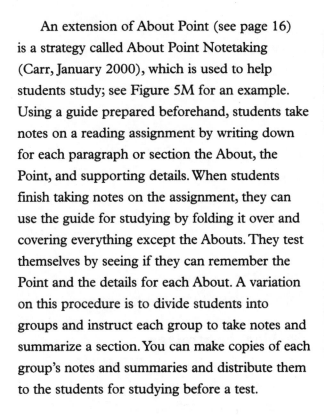

About Point Notetaking

About: Immigrants	**Point:** Came from all over the world to live here.

Details:
1. A large number of immigrants came to America between 1900–1920.

2. Most immigrants came to America from Europe.

3. The immigrants brought with them their own culture and customs.

Summary: Immigrants came from all over the world to live here. A large number of immigrants came to America between 1900–1920. Most immigrants came to American from Europe. The immigrants brought with them their own cultures and customs.

An About Point Notetaking guide completed with information about the topic, immigrants

APPLICATION/EXTENSION STRATEGY:

SCAMPER: Expository

SCAMPER is a strategy that can be used to encourage students to problem solve by thinking critically and creatively. It was introduced in Chapter 3 as a strategy to be used with narrative text for the purpose of encouraging students to view situations in an innovative way. It is equally effective with expository text or content information (Manzo & Manzo, 1990). You can use the SCAMPER strategy to develop challenges for your students in all subject areas. Following are suggestions for implementing each of the SCAMPER "challenges" with expository text.

SUBSTITUTE . . . another ingredient, step in the procedure, place, time, or event

COMBINE . . . ingredients, actions, or purposes

ADAPT . . . an event, situation, or idea

MODIFY . . . by adding a new twist, change, or addition

PUT TO OTHER USES . . . an item, procedure, or audience

ELIMINATE . . . or streamline an event, step, place, or tool

REVERSE . . . the arrangement of events, steps, components, or patterns

Make a Parachute

1. Cut a 30 cm square from a plastic grocery bag or use a tissue.

2. Cut lengths of thread about 30 cm long.

3. Tape 1 piece of thread to each corner of the square and tie the loose ends together.

4. Attach 3 paper clips to the thread.

5. Drop the parachute and observe its fall.

6. Choose a partner and have one partner cut a 50 cm wide hole in one parachute.

7. Drop the parachutes and observe what happens.

Substitute: Use a heavier material than plastic or tissue.

Combine: Cut holes throughout the parachute.

Adapt: Fold the parachute and drop it.

Modify: Add additional weight to the strings.

Put to use: Pull one string as the parachute falls.

Eliminate: Eliminate the clips from the parachute.

Reverse: Let the strings fall freely. Do not tie them.

SCAMPER challenge for a science lesson

If your students have applied the SCAMPER strategy to narrative text, they are already familiar with the procedure (see Chapter 3). Having worked with KWL or KWL Plus on the text at hand, they are also knowledgeable about the ideas and information in the text. Familiarity with both the strategy and the material facilitates the use of SCAMPER with a piece of expository text. Figure 5N shows how SCAMPER could be applied to a science experiment in which students make and test a parachute.

Before the Lesson

• Prepare SCAMPER challenges.

Teaching the Strategy

• After you've reviewed the SCAMPER strategy with your students and they understand what actions each of the terms in the acronym require them to perform, have them break into small groups.

• Tell the students that their group assignment is to rewrite a portion of the text incorporating one or more of the SCAMPER "challenges."

• Give the students an opportunity to read their changes to one another.

ThinkingWorks Lesson Planning Guide

A number of strategies have been introduced in this chapter that will enable you to teach a complete lesson for expository text. Figure 5O shows two completed ThinkingWorks Lesson Planning Guides using strategies introduced in this chapter.

ThinkingWorks Lesson Planning Guides

FIGURE 50

	STRATEGIES			
	Background Knowledge	Vocabulary	Comprehension	Application/ Extension
COGNITIVE PROCESSES	Anticipation Guide	Concept of a Definition	KWL Plus	RAFT/Letters, Response
Develop Background Knowledge	✔		✔	
Expand Vocabulary Knowledge		✔		
Use Text Structure				
Set a Purpose for Learning	✔		✔	
Infer/Select Information			✔	
Create Images				
Relate/Connect Ideas			✔	
Clarify/Monitor Understanding			✔	
Analyze			✔	✔
Synthesize			✔	✔
Evaluate/Justify				
Create/Invent				✔
LANGUAGE PROCESSES				
Read			✔	
Write			✔	/✔
Listen/View	✔	✔	✔	
Communicate Orally	✔	✔	✔	
COGNITIVE PROCESSES	Anticipation Guide	Concept of a Definition	I-Chart	SCAMPER
Develop Background Knowledge	✔		✔	
Expand Vocabulary Knowledge		✔		
Use Text Structure				
Set a Purpose for Learning	✔		✔	
Infer/Select Information			✔	
Create Images				
Relate/Connect Ideas			✔	
Clarify/Monitor Understanding			✔	
Analyze			✔	✔
Synthesize			✔	✔
Evaluate/Justify				
Create/Invent				✔
LANGUAGE PROCESSES				
Read			✔	
Write			✔	✔
Listen/View	✔	✔	✔	
Communicate Orally	✔	✔	✔	

CHAPTER 6

Analyzing
Expository Text

In This Chapter:

BACKGROUND KNOWLEDGE:	Structured Overview
VOCABULARY:	Personal Clues
COMPREHENSION:	Frames
APPLICATION/EXTENSION:	Discussion Web
ALTERNATIVE APPLICATION/EXTENSION STRATEGIES:	Proposition/Support Outline, Editorial

O nce students have been introduced to expository texts, they will be eager to read more. From discovering how a star is formed, to how food is transported around the globe, to how animals survive in the jungle, a wealth of fascinating information awaits students. To capitalize on their motivation to read these texts, however, we must teach them strategies that will make it easier for them to approach the vast array of nonfiction.

In addition to reading expository texts to students and making them available for independent reading, we must show students the different structures and organizational patterns that authors use with expository text. One way to help them is by teaching them Frames, which is the comprehension strategy for this lesson.

ThinkingWorks Lesson Plan Sequence for Analyzing Expository Text

To extend students' ability to analyze expository text, we have designed the following lesson sequence that focuses on the structure of these texts:

BACKGROUND KNOWLEDGE: . . . . Structured Overview

VOCABULARY: . . . . Personal Clues

COMPREHENSION: . . . . Frames

APPLICATION/EXTENSION: . . . . Discussion Web

The heart of this lesson is using frames to help students recognize and understand the five main organizational patterns used in expository text: description, sequence/time order, compare/contrast, cause/effect, and problem/solution. Frames can also be used to teach writing strategies. While many students can do personal and creative writing, they have more difficulty with expository writing such as a summary or an essay. Therefore, the frames serve a dual purpose: they help students identify patterns of organization in texts, which facilitates their understanding, and they provide structures for students to use as they compose their own texts.

Writing summaries is an excellent way for students to demonstrate their comprehension of a piece. Summaries also help teachers assess students' compre-hension. We have recommended summary writing in earlier chapters, but here we turn our attention to the process more fully. An additional section to this chapter describes step-by-step procedures for using the information from frames to write one-paragraph summaries and multiple-paragraph essays. You can teach your students these writing procedures simultaneously with your teaching of frames, or you can wait until a later time when you want to focus on writing. In either case, you will need to have taught your students to do the About Point Writing Response strategy (see page 17).

Structured Overview

A Structured Overview (Vacca & Vacca, 1999) is a visual outline that resembles the Semantic Map presented in Chapter 2 (see page 39). However, it differs from a Semantic Map in two ways. First, the teacher develops the Structured Overview independently, instead of with students, in order to provide a framework for the lesson. Second, unlike a map that categorizes related concepts, a Structured Overview presents a hierarchical outline of information with the most inclusive concepts subsuming subordinate ones. Relationships among concepts are shown by connecting lines (see Figures 6A and 6B for examples).

The Structured Overview provides a "big picture" of the concepts being studied and their relationships to one another. When students view the visual outline, they have a good idea of the information they will encounter and how all the pieces are related. You build students' background knowledge and vocabulary as you lead a discussion of the graphic organizer you have prepared in advance. In addition, the strategy integrates the language processes of reading, listening/viewing, and oral communication.

Figure 6A shows a Structured Overview on recycling, completed by a fourth-grade teacher. Figure 6B presents a Structured Overview that a sixth-grade teacher completed to help her students understand a science chapter on biomes.

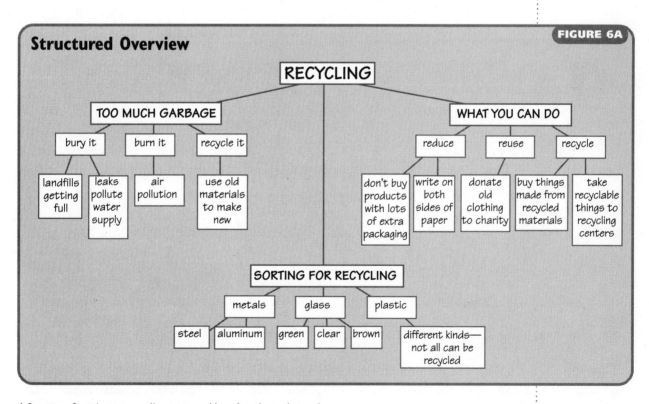

Structured Overview

FIGURE 6A

A Structure Overview on recycling, prepared by a fourth-grade teacher

Structured Overview

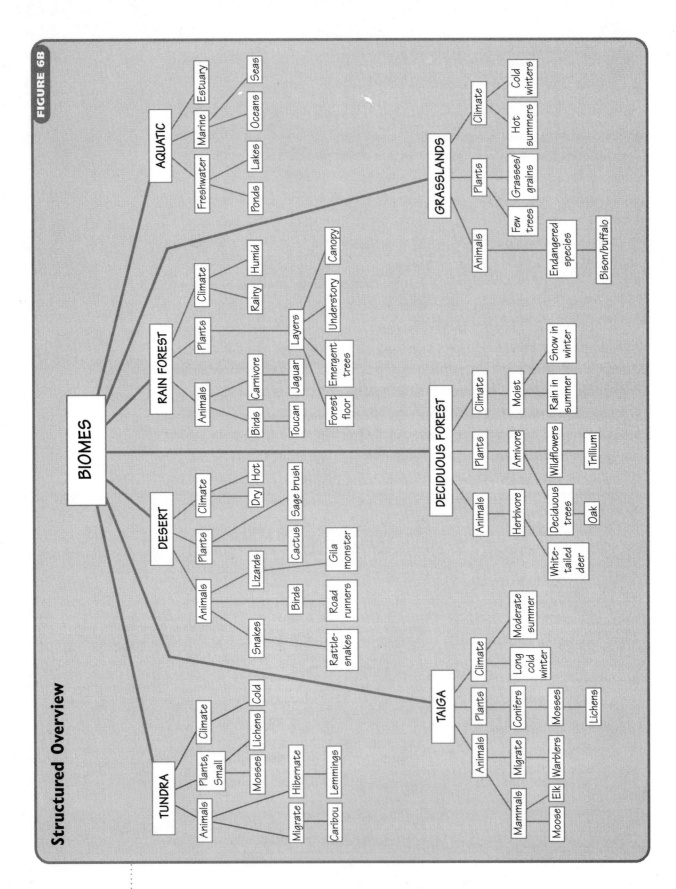

A sixth-grade teacher prepared this Structured Overview on biomes

Before the Lesson

• Analyze the text and select the concepts and vocabulary words that are critical to understanding it. Write down the concepts and vocabulary words. For a reading on biomes, the teacher selected the seven biomes covered in the text along with important information about the plants, animals, and climate found in each.

• On chart paper or an overhead, arrange the words in hierarchical order depicting the relationships among the concepts. The most inclusive concepts include subordinate ones. In the biome example, the teacher made the seven biomes the major categories, with the plants, animals, and climate information as subcategories.

• Draw connecting lines between concepts to show relationships (see Figures 6A and 6B for examples of complete Structured Overviews).

Teaching the Strategy

• Use the Structured Overview to introduce the content of an expository reading assignment to students. Tell them why you arranged the words the way you did, and encourage them to discuss the concepts.

• Keep the Structured Overview displayed in the classroom and encourage students to use it to help them understand the relationships among concepts as they read. In class discussions about a reading assignment, you and your students can use the overview to clarify information students have encountered while reading the text. If you are reading aloud to students, you can stop at various places and discuss how information in the text fits with what is shown on the overview.

• After the students have read the material, show them how they can use the overview for study and review of critical concepts.

• When students have become familiar with the purpose and components of the overview, encourage them to develop their own overviews as a culminating activity to a lesson. They can do this either individually or in groups.

Assessment

Evaluating the effectiveness of the Structured Overview takes place when you test students on the information in the chapter. If the strategy was successful in helping students understand the concepts in the chapter and their relationship to one another, the students should do well on questions regarding the main ideas and important details.

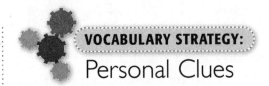

VOCABULARY STRATEGY:

Personal Clues

Personal Clues (Carr, 1985) is a vocabulary strategy that helps readers know and remember the meanings of difficult words that have been selected from the text because of their importance to comprehension. With this strategy, students link the definition of a word to personal experiences or clues that act as a hook to help them retrieve meaning. Personal Clues reinforces for students the meanings of words. In addition, the strategy motivates students to learn vocabulary because, as they reach a deeper understanding of the word through discussion and study, students are able to use it outside of the particular context in which the word was introduced.

After you and your students have completed the Structured Overview, begin the Personal Clues strategy by introducing vocabulary words selected from the text and having the students participate in actively defining the words through a discussion of their meanings. Elaborate on the definitions by discussing the attributes of the words and by examining examples and non-examples of the words. For example, the word *extraordinary* means "exceptional" or "unusual." Attributes of the word might include "being able to do things ordinary people cannot do" or "being talented in a particular area." Examples might include "an Olympic swimmer" or "the artist, Monet." Non-examples could be "a novice swimmer" or "an art student."

Once students understand a definition, they can then link the meaning to a personal experience or clue that helps them remember it. A student's clue for *extraordinary*, for example, might be "Superman" or "Michael Jordan." It is important to emphasize to students that personal clues are individual choices; no two students are likely to have the same clue. As students encounter difficult words in the reading, they will remember the meanings of the words, and comprehension will not be interrupted.

Before the Lesson

• Select words from the reading; prepare definitions to share with students.

• Make copies of Personal Clues handouts (template on CD) if desired.

Teaching the Strategy

• Introduce the vocabulary words, providing student-friendly definitions with examples and non-examples.

• Encourage students to participate in the discussion of each word.

• Have students make a personal clue card for each of the words by drawing three lines, one underneath the other (see the examples in Figure 6C).

• Direct your students to write the vocabulary word on the first line and the definition or synonym on the third line.

- Tell the students to think of a word or a phrase that they associate with the vocabulary word and that will help them remember the word. Note: Clues can be in the native language of nonnative learners or can be drawings.

- Have students write their personal clues on the second line beneath the vocabulary word.

- Give students the opportunity to study the words by covering the clue and the definition (lines two and three). If they cannot recall the definition, have them uncover the personal clue. If they still cannot recall the meaning, have them uncover the definition.

- Provide students with many opportunities to practice making personal clue cards until they can transfer the skill to new material they are reading independently.

If students have difficulty coming up with personal clues that will help them remember the words, model the process for them. Begin by saying, "If I want to think of something that will truly help me to remember the vocabulary word, I ask myself what I immediately associate the word with, what first comes to mind when I hear the word..."

FIGURE 6C

Personal Clues

Grade 6 Unit on Biomes

WORD: biome
CLUE: | grasslands/rain forest
DEFINITION: major geographic region with
      unique plants and animals

WORD: plankton
CLUE: | algae
DEFINITION: organisms in water

WORD: food chain
CLUE: | snake/mouse
DEFINITION: organisms with interrelated feeding
      patterns, larger eats smaller

Grade 4 Unit on Conservation

WORD: predator
CLUE: | lion
DEFINITION: animal that feeds on another animal

Personal Clues created for vocabulary words from a sixth-grade unit on biomes and a fourth-grade unit on Conservation

Writing Extension

An added benefit of the Personal Clues strategy is that the vocabulary words learned "deeply" can be incorporated in writing activities. For example, have students write a paragraph using the vocabulary words.

Assessment

An obvious method of evaluating the effectiveness of Personal Clues instruction is to test students on the meanings of the vocabulary words. Another suggestion is to combine assessment with writing; if students are successful in writing a story using the vocabulary words, you can be certain that the Personal Clues strategy taught them the meaning of the words.

COMPREHENSION STRATEGY:

Frames

Frames are graphic outlines representing different types of text structures authors use to present information (Jones, Pierce, & Hunter, 1988-89). Frames help students discover different text patterns, and students use them to understand, organize, and think about information in a particular way—for example, comparing and contrasting information versus listing information. Frames can also help students improve their writing when they use them to organize information for summaries and essays. What follows is an explanation of the most predominant structures in expository text—*description, sequence/time order, compare/contrast, cause/effect* and *problem/solution*. We provide graphic organizers (frames) and key questions to help students recognize the different structures. We have also added a frame that can be used for science experiments, called an *exploration frame*.

DESCRIPTION

The text structure of *description* provides information about a topic by presenting its attributes, such as describing the characteristics of tornados as shown in Figure 6D. It is also referred to as a *listing* of information because the attributes may be described in any order. Figure 6E shows a more detailed Descriptive Web.

To help students understand description, we use a frame that takes the form of a web. The main topic goes in the center, and the characteristics or attributes are written on spokes coming out of the center. This frame is effective for description because the order of the information is not important. When reading a text that uses description, students can ask these key questions to identify the topic and important details.

Key Questions

- *What is being described?* (The topic goes in the center of the web.)

- *What are its attributes?* (These go in spokes emanating from the center.)

- *Might there be situations in which one attribute would be more important than another?* (In this case, the descriptive frame may not be the best choice to represent the text structure.)

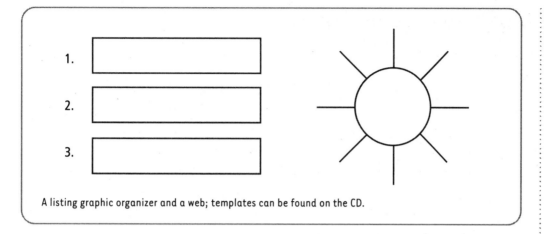

A listing graphic organizer and a web; templates can be found on the CD.

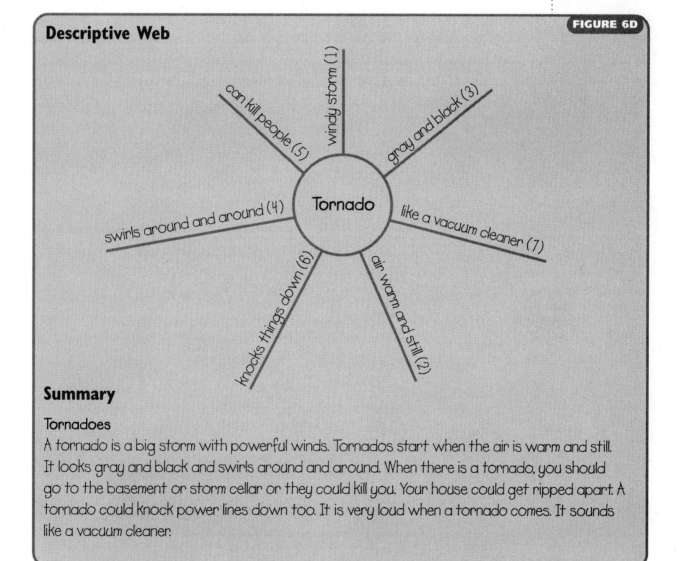

Descriptive Web

Tornado

- windy storm (1)
- can kill people (5)
- gray and black (3)
- swirls around and around (4)
- like a vacuum cleaner (7)
- knocks things down (6)
- air warm and still (2)

Summary

Tornadoes

A tornado is a big storm with powerful winds. Tornados start when the air is warm and still. It looks gray and black and swirls around and around. When there is a tornado, you should go to the basement or storm cellar or they could kill you. Your house could get ripped apart. A tornado could knock power lines down too. It is very loud when a tornado comes. It sounds like a vacuum cleaner.

Figure 6D shows a web and summary on the topic tornadoes, completed by a second-grade student. The student has numbered each characteristic in preparation for writing a summary of the information on the web.

Descriptive Web

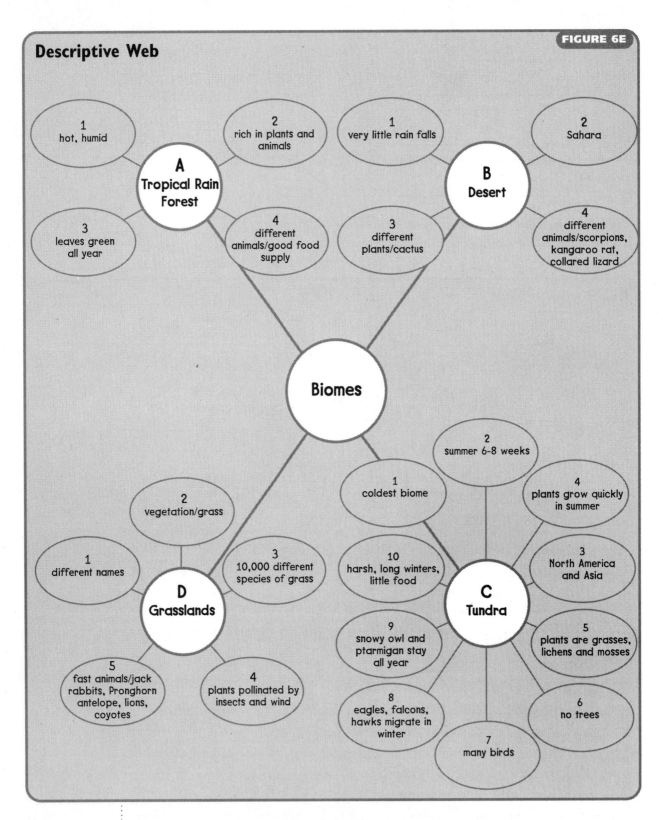

This more detailed Descriptive Web was completed by a sixth-grade student for the topic biomes. The student identified four sub-categories and included descriptive details for each on the web. The categories and supporting details are marked to indicate the order the student plans to use when summarizing the information on the web.

SEQUENCE/TIME ORDER

Information presented using the sequence text structure is written in a prescribed or chronological order. This structure is often used to describe steps in a procedure, such as solving a math problem, or stages of development, such as the metamorphosis of a butterfly. To help students identify this structure, we use a frame that consists of a series of boxes connected by arrows to reinforce the idea that the events must occur in order, as shown at right. However, a sequence frame can be as simple as numbering the steps (see Figure 6F) or a bit more creative, as shown in Figure 6G.

When reading a text that presents information in sequence, students can ask these key questions to understand the process being described.

Key Questions

- *What is the procedure being described?*

- *What are the steps or stages?*

- *How do the stages lead to one another?*

- *What is the final outcome?*

- *What would be the outcome if the steps were reversed?*

- *Is this procedure similar to others that you know?*

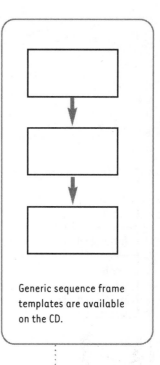

Generic sequence frame templates are available on the CD.

FIGURE 6G

Sequence Frame

This frame on how to make a mask was done by a primary student with a developmental disability.

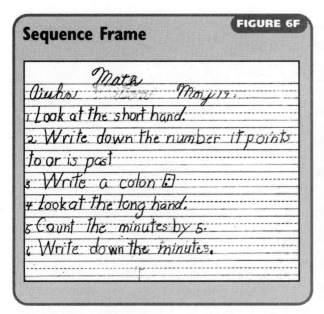

FIGURE 6F

Sequence Frame

This simple frame about telling time was done by a second grader.

COMPARE/CONTRAST

Writers use the compare/contrast text structure to highlight similarities and differences between and among concepts or topics. Different frames can be used to show similarities and differences separately or to make point-by-point comparisons. For example, the differences between World War I and World War II can be analyzed point by point by examining alliances of countries involved, causes, effects, weapons, and so forth. The Venn Diagram is a well-known frame for showing similarities and differences. Figure 6H shows a Venn Diagram a second-grade Title 1 student completed to compare and contrast two types of energy. We use a grid to detail point-by-point comparisons; the attributes are listed down the left-hand side and the two (or more) topics being compared are listed as the column headers; see Figure 6I.

When reading a text that compares and contrasts topics, students can ask these key questions to understand the similarities and differences between them.

Key Questions

- *What is the author comparing and contrasting?*
- *How are they alike and different?*
- *What are the advantages and disadvantages of each?*
- *What choice would you make in a specific situation?*

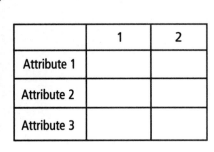
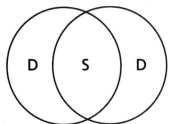

Generic compare/contrast frames;
templates are available on the CD.

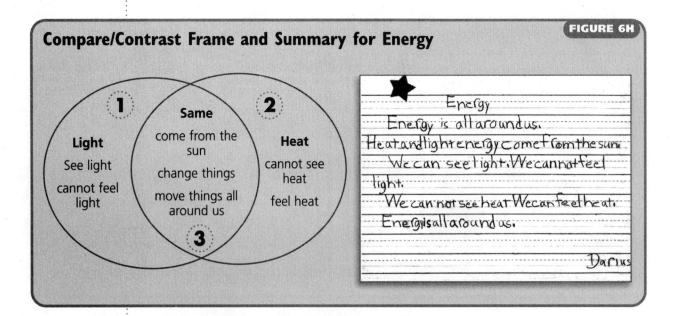

Compare/Contrast Frame and Summary for Energy

Light
See light
cannot feel light

Same
come from the sun
change things
move things all around us

Heat
cannot see heat
feel heat

Energy
Energy is all around us.
Heat and light energy come from the sun.
We can see light. We cannot feel light.
We cannot see heat. We can feel heat.
Energy is all around us.

Darius

A compare/contrast frame and summary on energy completed by a second-grade Title 1 student

Compare/Contrast Frame

	Wind Caves	Sea Caves	Ice Caves	Limestone Caves
Formation	Wind blows sand across rock. Deep holes form over time.	Waves breaking against rocks for hundreds of years form caves.	Cold temperatures cause ice formations over everything.	Water drips through cracks and rocks and makes large holes until a cave is formed.
Location	Mountains	Underwater	—	Land
Temperature	Constant	Constant	Constant	Constant

A compare/contrast frame on the topic caves using a chart format

CAUSE/EFFECT

The cause/effect text structure shows causal relationships among ideas, events, or pieces of information. Sometimes a text begins with effects and then discusses the causes. Often, a single cause will have more than one effect, and a single event may have more than one cause. Cause-and-effect relationships would be exemplified in science experiments, in a discussion of the effects of different nutrients on the body, or in an analysis of historical events.

Cause and effect is a difficult relationship for many students to grasp, so the cause/effect frame is especially useful in helping students identify these important relationships. A simple frame relates one cause to one effect. A more sophisticated frame allows students to list multiple effects from one cause. (See Figures 6J and 6K for examples.)

When reading a text that depicts causal relationships, students can ask these key questions to understand the impact one idea or event has on another.

Key Questions

- *What is the effect?*
- *What are the causes?*
- *How are the causes related?*
- *What would be the effects if one or more causes were changed in a specific situation?*

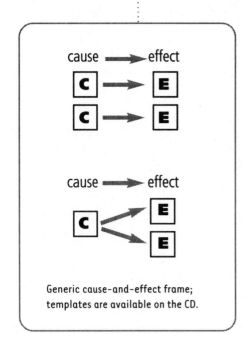

Generic cause-and-effect frame; templates are available on the CD.

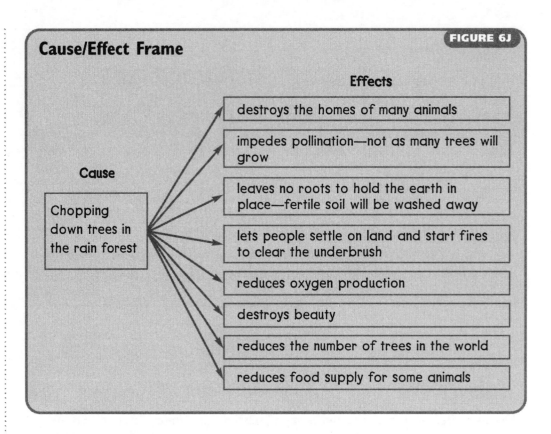

Cause/Effect Frame

FIGURE 6J

Cause

Chopping down trees in the rain forest

Effects

destroys the homes of many animals

impedes pollination—not as many trees will grow

leaves no roots to hold the earth in place—fertile soil will be washed away

lets people settle on land and start fires to clear the underbrush

reduces oxygen production

destroys beauty

reduces the number of trees in the world

reduces food supply for some animals

A cause/effect frame about conservation
completed by a fourth-grade student

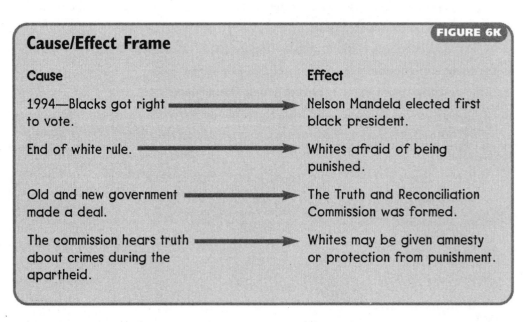

Cause/Effect Frame

FIGURE 6K

Cause	Effect
1994—Blacks got right to vote.	Nelson Mandela elected first black president.
End of white rule.	Whites afraid of being punished.
Old and new government made a deal.	The Truth and Reconciliation Commission was formed.
The commission hears truth about crimes during the apartheid.	Whites may be given amnesty or protection from punishment.

A cause/effect frame on apartheid
completed by a fourth-grade student

PROBLEM/SOLUTION

The problem/solution organizational pattern identifies a problem and presents one or more solutions. Sometimes these structures contain elements of decision making, such as defining options and discussing the consequences of each option. An example would be a text that addresses the problem of the Great Depression.

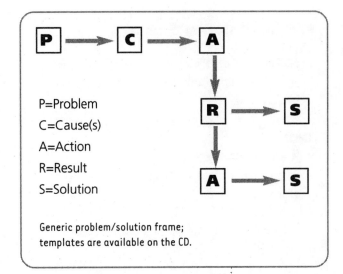

P=Problem
C=Cause(s)
A=Action
R=Result
S=Solution

Generic problem/solution frame; templates are available on the CD.

The frame we use to help students understand texts written using the problem/solution pattern asks them to first identify the main problem and its causes. Then students list examples of the problem. In Figure 6L, a student identified the main problem as "The depression of the 1930s was economically devastating to many Americans." The causes of the problem were "weakness in the economy" and "spectacular rises in prices on the stock market." The examples include "coal mining and railroads were depressed" and "banks and businesses failed." The final section of the frame asks students to record the solutions to the problem. In Figure 6L, the student recorded three solutions, which addressed the details given in the examples, including "Civilian Conservation Corps (CCC) sent men to plant trees and drain swamps."

When reading a text that describes problems and solutions, students can ask these key questions to understand the text more fully.

Key Questions

- *What is the problem?*
- *Who is involved in the problem?*
- *What caused this problem?*
- *What actions have been taken to solve the problem?*
- *What are the results of these actions?*
- *Has the problem been solved?*
- *Which actions would you take in a similar situation?*

Students can use frames in a variety of ways. For example, they can use a frame to develop questions that will guide them in their studying. They can also use frames as an outline for summaries of the text. Finally, they can analyze materials from different texts, incorporating the material into the original frame. As you will see later in this chapter, frames are especially effective for integrating reading and writing.

Problem/Solution Frame

Problem: The depression of the 1930's was economically devastating to many Americans.

Causes:
- Weakness in the economy
- Spectacular rises in prices on the stock market

Examples:
- One in four Americans out of a job
- A depression in farming
- Coal mining and railroads were depressed
- Banks and businesses failed
- High stock market prices did not reflect economic conditions

Attempted Solutions:
- National Recovery Administration (NRA) established minimum wages and fair competition in industries to spread jobs and stabilize production
- NRA declared unconstitutional by Supreme Court

Solution: New Deal put people back to work

Examples:
- Civilian Conservation Corps (CCC) sent men to plant trees and drain swamps
- Works Progress Administration (WPA) employed people in many occupations
- Public Works Administration (PWA) paid millions to build highways and public buildings

A problem/solution frame completed by a sixth-grade student on the Great Depression

Before the Lesson

- Examine the reading assignment and determine which text structure is used to present the most important concepts.

- Develop a graphic organizer, or frame, to help students see the relationships among the ideas and information. Prepare a large copy for display on chart paper or the overhead; make handouts for students. You'll find template for each kind of frame on the CD.

Teaching the Strategy

- Explain that writers use different organizational patterns in their work. Review the story structure for narrative, and explain that while narrative texts typically follow the same pattern, expository texts may have one of about five different structures (description, sequence, compare/contrast, cause/effect, and problem/solution). Discuss how understanding a text's organizational pattern can give readers insight into the text.

- Explain the organizational pattern that the writer uses in the piece students will read. Show them the frame you've developed to help them identify important information and relationships in the text.

Signal Words

Description	Sequence/ Time Order	Compare/ Contrast	Cause/Effect	Problem/ Solution
also furthermore however but moreover in addition	first then immediately soon finally	*Comparison:* similarly likewise furthermore moreover in addition *Contrast:* but yet however on the contrary while	because the reason that as a result of another	causes of the problem solutions programs for solving the problem

A chart of signal words commonly used in each of the five expository text patterns

- Present the Key Questions for the frame and discuss how asking them will help students identify important information and relationships, which they will record on the frame.

- Show students how to look for cue words or signals that typically occur with a particular text structure. For example, the words *first*, *then* and *finally*, signal that a text is written using the sequence structure. See Figure 6M for a list of common signal words for the five most frequently used text structures. These words can give students clues about the structure of a text and about relationships between the ideas presented.

- Guide students through the reading assignment by asking them Key Questions and modeling how to complete the frame on your enlarged example.

- Once students understand a particular organizational pattern and have had practice using the corresponding frame and Key Questions, they can use the frame independently to aid their comprehension of text, to review information for tests, and to prepare for writing summaries or essays.

Some organizational patterns are more difficult for students to understand than others. For example, cause/effect is often more difficult to understand than compare/contrast. Both of those are generally more difficult than sequence or description. Easier organizational patterns should be introduced to students first, with corresponding frames. When students are comfortable using these frames, other, more difficult structures and frames can be introduced to provide students with practice in thinking about information in different ways. After sufficient practice, give the students opportunities to construct their own frames for the different text structures.

Writing Extension

Students can write summaries, using the frame as an outline. See pages 48 and 166 for more details on writing summaries.

Assessment

If your students can write paragraphs and summaries for each of the predominant organizational patterns in expository text, the strategy was successful in first teaching students to identify the patterns and second, helping them to use the patterns to relate and integrate text information. In addition, examine students' chapter and unit tests; the use of frames to understand text information should result in higher scores.

A FRAME FOR SCIENCE

The frames we have just described can be used across the curriculum. However, in some subject areas, you may want to introduce a frame that models a text structure frequently encountered in that subject area. For example, science books often use the inquiry process to guide students through experiments. This type of text has its own specialized structure, and we have developed an *exploration frame* (Carr, March 2000) to help students understand and apply information presented in this way.

Although some science materials or kits provide graphic organizers which students can record observations, students often need a more comprehensive organizer where they can relate additional information covered in the lesson to see a big picture of the inquiry process. Students can use the exploration frame as they proceed through a science lesson. The frame encourages them to make a prediction, collect and interpret data, and write a conclusion about what has occurred in an experiment. If you have data forms in your kits, you may want to use only parts of the exploration frame (e.g., the parts that encourage students to interpret, reflect on, and write about what they have learned and still want to learn).

Exploration Question:	Prediction/Hypothesis:
Data Collection	Interpretation About: Point: Why (Conclusion)?
Prediction/Hypothesis Confirmed? Yes ❑ No ❑	New Question(s):

Generic exploration frame; template is available on the CD.

To guide students through an experiment, teach them to ask the following questions and record their answers on the exploration frame.

Key Questions

- *What question or problem is being investigated in the experiment?*

- *What is your prediction?*

- *What did you observe happen (data)?*

- *Did you hear, smell, or feel anything?*

- *How do you interpret the data?*

- *Was your prediction confirmed?*

- *What new questions would you like to have answered?*

Figure 6N presents a completed exploration frame for a science experiment investigating the effects of blubber on the survival of polar bears. Note how the About is derived from the Exploration Question, the Point from the Data Collection, and the Conclusion from the answer to the Why question. The materials and method for the experiment are as follows.

Materials
- thermos of hot water
- 1 plastic cup
- 2 thermometers
- 2 plastic cups (blubber cup) joined with electrical tape and lard spread between them before taping (serves the same function as blubber)
- 1 pan of ice water (acts like arctic cold)

Method
- Fill the blubber cup and the regular cup with hot water.
- Put a thermometer in each cup.
- Record the starting temperature for each cup of hot water.
- Immerse both cups of hot water (blubber cup and regular cup) in the pan of ice water.
- Record the temperature of each cup every 30 seconds for two minutes.
- Compare the temperatures of the water in the regular cup and the blubber cup.

Before the Lesson

- Prepare materials for the experiment, and make copies of the exploration frame for all students; there is a template on the CD.

Exploration Frame

Exploration Question:
How does the blubber help polar bears survive?

Prediction/Hypothesis:
Blubber warms the polar bears.

Data Collection:
Starting Temperatures of Hot Water:
A. Regular cup: 118° F
B. Blubber cup: 118° F

Cold Water Temperatures:
A. Regular cup: 114° F (30 sec.)
                   110° F (1 min.)
                   106° F (1½ min.)
                   100° F (2 min.)
B. Blubber Cup   118° F (30 sec.)
                   117° F (1 min.)
                   116° F (1½ min.)
                   116° F (2 min.)

Interpretation:
About: Blubber

Point: It maintains temperature longer than no blubber.

Why (conclusion)? Blubber serves as an insulator from the cold and maintains body heat.

Prediction/Hypothesis Confirmed?
    Yes [✔]   No [ ]
Blubber keeps polar bears warm.

New Question(s):
Does fat protect all animals this way?

NOTE: If you would like to have your students "feel" the difference in temperatures between the two conditions (regular and blubber), put two zip lock bags together with lard between them. Wrap the bags around a student's hand and have the student plunge his hand into a pan of ice water. Wrap a clean bag around his other hand and have him plunge that hand into ice water.

An Exploration Frame completed for a science experiment on blubber

Teaching the Strategy

• Introduce the experiment and the exploration frame. Students will work on the frame before, during, and after the experiment. You will need to walk them through each section of the frame the first few times they use it.

• Ask students, "What is the question to be answered through the experiment, collection of data, and interpretation of data?" Have students write the question to be resolved on the frame.

• Explain the materials and procedures for the experiment.

• Engage students in a discussion that answers the question: "What is your best estimate of what the results of the experiment will be based on your background knowledge of the topic, including information learned from previous science lessons?" Have students write their prediction/hypothesis on the frame.

- Have students perform the experiment in small groups, pairs, or individually. As students conduct the experiment, they should record the data they collect on the frame.

- Have each pair or group discuss the data they collected. Circulate among the students to answer questions and correct any misunderstandings.

- Have students complete the About, the Point, and the Why sections of the frame. Show them how they can derive the About from the Exploration Question and the Point from the Data Collection. The Why is a conclusion they draw to explain their About Point. By completing the Interpretation part of the frame, students are learning to express clearly what they have learned.

- Ask students to decide if their Prediction/Hypothesis was confirmed and to check the Yes or No box on the frame.

- As a class, discuss new questions for investigation. Tell students to write down one or two questions that they now have, based on the results of the experiment and the class discussion.

Assessment

You can assess students' understanding of the science concepts explored in the lesson by evaluating their exploration charts. You may also want to supplement your "hands-on" science lesson with ThinkingWorks strategies that activate students' background knowledge, help them understand new vocabulary, and apply and transfer what they have learned to new situations. By having your science lesson cover the four components of background knowledge, vocabulary, comprehension, and application/extension, as well as all four language processes, you will be including those facets of thinking and language use that help students understand and process information effectively.

APPLICATION/EXTENSION STRATEGY:
Discussion Web

A Discussion Web (Alvermann, 1991) is a graphic aid that helps students analyze information by looking at both sides of an issue before drawing a conclusion. The Discussion Web presents a controversial question or a central issue and provides space where students can write down evidence to support opposing points of view. Implement this strategy when you want students to consider competing ideas or different points of view. Using this graphic as a guide, have students work first in pairs and then in groups of four to reach a consensus about the question. We do not recommend using a whole-class setting where a few of the more verbal students may monopolize the discussion. The Discussion Web offers opportunities for all students to discuss and reflect on the reading assignment (see the examples in Figures 6O and 6P).

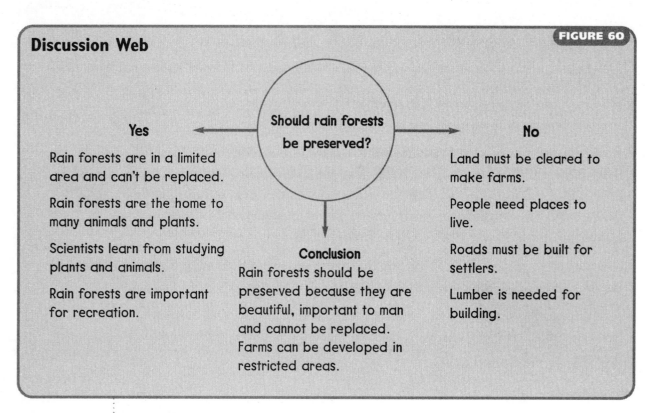

Discussion Web

FIGURE 6O

Yes

Rain forests are in a limited area and can't be replaced.

Rain forests are the home to many animals and plants.

Scientists learn from studying plants and animals.

Rain forests are important for recreation.

Should rain forests be preserved?

No

Land must be cleared to make farms.

People need places to live.

Roads must be built for settlers.

Lumber is needed for building.

Conclusion

Rain forests should be preserved because they are beautiful, important to man and cannot be replaced. Farms can be developed in restricted areas.

A Discussion Web completed by sixth-grade students on the topic of rain forests from the unit on biomes.

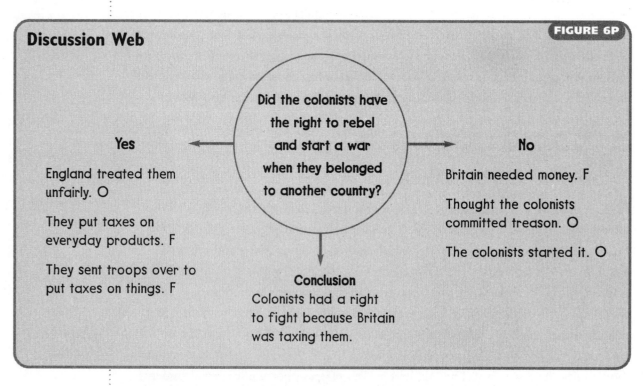

Discussion Web

FIGURE 6P

Yes

England treated them unfairly. O

They put taxes on everyday products. F

They sent troops over to put taxes on things. F

Did the colonists have the right to rebel and start a war when they belonged to another country?

No

Britain needed money. F

Thought the colonists committed treason. O

The colonists started it. O

Conclusion

Colonists had a right to fight because Britain was taxing them.

A Discussion Web completed by fourth-grade students for the American Revolution. Note that opinions are distinguished from facts by the letters F and O.

Before the Lesson

- Prepare the central question and Discussion Web; there is a template on the CD. Make copies of the web for students.

Teaching the Strategy

- After students have read the assignment, introduce the central question for discussion and distribute the Discussion Web you prepared ahead of time.

- Have students pair up and discuss the two points of view defined by the web (Think-Pair-Share; see page 34). Tell them to take turns writing down an equal number of supports for each point of view. This would be an appropriate time to discuss the difference between facts and opinions in a text. As students work on their web, you may want to illustrate for the whole class examples of the author's opinion (e.g., point of view) and examples of facts (e.g., can be proved or are universally accepted).

- After students have written down their supports, tell each set of partners to pair up with another. Instruct the new groups of four to compare their webs and reach a group conclusion. If there is no consensus in the group, have each side present its opinion.

- Give each group three minutes to discuss its conclusion, its best reason, and any opposite opinion.

- Follow the small group discussions with a whole-class discussion.

According to Alvermann, you can vary the basic Discussion Web simply by changing column headings. For example, you can use the strategy for eliciting students' predictions; to do so, label the columns "Prediction 1" and "Prediction 2." You can use the Discussion Web structure for comparing events in social studies, setting hypotheses in science, analyzing characters in English, and determining the relevance of information in math word problems.

An adaptation of the Discussion Web is Conflict Identification and Resolution (Frager & Thompson, 1985), a strategy that extends students' critical thinking ability. With this strategy, students integrate information for oral and written presentation by reviewing it from different perspectives. This activity spans several class periods. First, divide students into groups of four and then pair them within those groups (Think-Pair-Share). The two pairs then take opposing sides on an idea or issue from the reading assignment. The pairs prepare arguments or defend their positions. Each pair presents its position and both perspectives are discussed within the group. Students then reverse roles and argue the opposite position so they understand both views. Group members must resolve the conflict by reaching a consensus. Finally, students in each group write and then present a collaborative report, which explains their position and includes a rationale for the position.

Writing Extension

Students can write a paragraph or summary answering the Discussion Web question. Using the About Point Writing Response strategy, students write a topic sentence with an About (topic of discussion) and an opinion about the topic (Point) that reflects the group's consensus. The body of the paragraph consists of the reasons for their opinion, and the closing statement summarizes the information. Display individual responses in the classroom and/or have the students share them.

Assessment

If students have the opportunity to respond in writing to the Discussion Web question, their individual responses not only bring closure to the strategy but allow you to evaluate its effectiveness. Were your students able to write a paragraph in which they stated their opinion and justified their own reasons and the ideas of others? If so, the strategy worked.

Alternative Application/Extension Strategies for Analyzing Expository Text

The goal of this chapter is to present a coherent lesson plan for helping students analyze and understand the structural patterns typical of expository texts. Frames are the most effective comprehension strategy for teaching these patterns. To develop students' understanding further, we have provided two additional application/extension strategies here: Proposition/Support Outline and Editorial.

APPLICATION/EXTENSION STRATEGY:

Proposition/Support Outline

Proposition/Support Outlines (Santa, 1988) are organizational frameworks that teach students to select and relate information from the text to support an argument with evidence. This strategy focuses on the cognitive process of analysis and can be used by students to analyze information for either discussion or writing in any content area. You can use Proposition/Support Outlines to help students support or refute arguments from the text or develop their own opinions from the reading. See Figure 6Q for a sample Proposition/Support Outline and two student summaries written based on it.

Proposition/Support Outline and Summaries

Proposition	Support	Refute
Capital punishment is a good way of punishing people for the crime of murder.	Do unto others—an eye for an eye. Person could get out—kill again. Revenge Punishment should fit the crime. Teaches that murder is wrong.	Think about a prisoner's family. Wrong to kill Prison might be worse. People can change—second chance What if a person is innocent? Money factor—rich people get good lawyers.

Student Summary: Support

I believe that capital punishment should exist in the United States.

The most popular reason why capital punishment should exist is prisoners could escape and kill again. Several alleged murderers have escaped from prison while on Death Row in the past three decades because he or she was afraid to die.

I believe the second most popular reason why capital punishment should exist is revenge. When a person kills someone's family member, they are to most likely want revenge. When the person is executed, the family feels they've gotten revenge.

I believe that the third most popular reason capital punishment should exist is if someone kills a person, they should be killed the same way, because they want to show how much pain and agony that person went through before he died.

This is why I believe capital punishment should exist.

Student Summary: Refute

I believe that capital punishment is wrong.

I think capital punishment is wrong because what if the person is innocent? What if the person was put on trial and sentenced to death, and then a year later the real killer said it was him who did the crime? Then what would you do about the innocent person who is dead? You also have to think about that person's family. What if that person had a child? That person's child will have to go through the rest of its life know his father or mother was killed and he or she was innocent. That could also put their family in misery. You wouldn't want that to happen, would you?

I think people could change. I mean if a person is in prison for a long period of time, they probably would say prison is a bad place to be. But if you give them capital punishment then they won't have a second chance to live. If the person is not killed and they get out of prison, they are a changed person. I mean that person has changed their whole life around. They probably will be able to see their kids and be part of their lives. Now that won't happen if that person is dead. Now would it?

I think it is wrong to kill period. I think everyone deserves to live. You could put them in prison but don't kill them. At least they are alive. Think about if they had kids. Their kids would have to go the rest of their lies without their parent. I think no matter how bad the crime was, everybody needs a second chance. Everybody needs to live no matter what.

I believe that capital punishment is wrong.

A Proposition/Support Outline completed by sixth-grade students on capital punishment.
Two student summaries that support and refute the proposition are included in the figure.

Teaching the Strategy

- Divide students into small groups. Have the students in each group divide a sheet of paper into two columns and label them "Proposition" and "Support," or distribute copies of the template found on the CD.

- Through a discussion of the reading assignment, help each group come up with a statement that reflects a main idea in the text. This becomes their proposition statement. Tell students to write the statement in the first column.

- Show students how to find facts in the text that support the proposition statement and tell them to write these facts in the second column for support.

- If there are facts in the text that refute the proposition statement, have students add a third column, label it "Refute," and write down those facts.

- Model for students how they can write a summary using the information in the support and refute columns. If students are young or inexperienced writers, they may write a summary for one position; if they are older, they can include a synopsis of both positions in their summaries. Students can use the About Point Writing Response strategy (see page 17). See the further discussion on summary writing later in this chapter on page 166.

- When students are adept at implementing this strategy with a reading assignment from one text, have them apply it using information from several texts, thereby encouraging them to look at information from different perspectives.

 APPLICATION/EXTENSION STRATEGY:

Editorial

An editorial is a short, persuasive essay that presents the writer's opinion about or reaction to an event or idea. The purpose of an editorial is to convince others to adopt the writer's point of view. To accomplish this goal, the writer uses one or more persuasive tactics, including logical arguments, compelling details and examples, and the endorsements or opinions of others.

Students can write editorials following the implementation of strategies that help them to make judgments about or evaluate characters in a story (narrative text) or ideas in a content text (expository). They must then justify their opinions. Two strategies we have described in this lesson, Discussion Web and Proposition/Support Outline, lend themselves nicely to student-written editorials because both provide students with an opportunity to arrive at a point of view and then justify it. A natural extension of those strategies would be for students to attempt to convince others of their point of view. The teaching procedure below assumes that students have previously completed either the Discussion Web or the Proposition/Support Outline. Use an Editorial Planning Guide to help students organize their thoughts before they begin writing. The guide helps students identify their audience, clarify their purpose, and develop their supporting arguments (see sample in Figure 6R and the template on the CD).

Before the Lesson

- Prepare the Editorial Planning Guide (see the template on the CD).

Teaching Procedure

- Give your students an Editorial Planning Guide to help them write their editorials. Explain the purpose of an editorial and the fun they will have writing one. You might say something like, "We've done a lot of reading and thinking about rain forests and how humans' actions are affecting this biome. Many of you have voiced strong opinions about what should be done to protect rain forests. In this extension activity, you will get your chance to persuade others to your point of view by writing an editorial. I've prepared a guide to help you organize your ideas. Let's go over it."

- Go over the parts of the guide. For instance, you might discuss the audience this way, "It's important to think about who you're trying to persuade. This is your audience, and you'll need to keep their point of view in mind as you write. You want to appeal to them, not offend them. For instance, if you're writing to persuade a government agency to stop cutting down trees to clear the way for roads, you'll need to consider why they're doing so. Then you'll need to give them strong reasons to stop." Continue discussing the guide in detail.

- Instruct the students to fill in the parts of the guide with information from their Proposition/Support Outline or Discussion Web, whichever strategy you implemented in class. They can do this individually or in groups.

> **FIGURE 6R**
>
> ## Editorial Planning Guide and Editorial
>
> ### Editorial Planning Guide
>
> **Author:** Latisha
>
> **Audience:** Readers/newspaper
>
> **Opinion:**
>
>   About: Tropical Rain Forests
>
>   Point: are being destroyed by humans
>
> **Reasons:** Humans cut down trees.
> Humans clear farmland.
> Roads are built.
> Farmers use land.
>
> **Closing:** Government should do something to stop destruction of the rain forest.
>
> ### Editorial
>
> The tropical rain forests are being destroyed because of humans. Humans have been cutting down the beautiful trees and burning them when they're dead. They clear the land to make farmland. After the trees are cut down, roads are being built. Settlers start moving in and farm the entire area. Now it's getting worse. Pretty soon the forest will be completely destroyed if this doesn't stop! The government should stop the destruction of the rain forest.

A completed Editorial Planning Guide and editorial written by a sixth-grade student following the implementation of a Discussion Web for the topic, rain forests, from the unit on biomes.

- Go around the room, checking to make sure that the students are completing the Editorial Planning Guide correctly.

- When students have completed the guide, show them how they can use the information on the guide to help them write their editorial. The topic sentence should reflect their point of view, and the body of the editorial, divided into paragraphs, should consist of supports that justify that point of view. The closing paragraph should restate the point of view and summarize the justification.

- Since this is a strategy that promotes creative as well as critical thinking, you should prominently display students' editorials and provide opportunities for sharing.

Combining Writing with the Reading of Expository Text

ThinkingWorks strategies provide a framework for different kinds of writing for both narrative and expository text. In our chapters on narrative text (Chapters 2, 3, and 4), writing opportunities are described in detail. For example, students write summaries from Story Grammars. They write Character Sketches for the Literary Report Card and Character Rating Scale strategies and editorials for the Story Map from Characters' Perspectives strategy. With expository text, students write summaries in conjunction with strategies such as KWL Plus and Frames. With both types of text they may write editorials, letters, essays, and journal entries.

While writing in conjunction with narrative text is relatively easy for students, because they've had so much exposure to stories, writing about expository text is more difficult. Because students have not had the exposure to expository text that they've had with narrative and because expository text structures tend to be more complex, students need instruction and practice in writing summaries and essays as extensions of their reading of nonfiction. For these reasons, we present here strategies for helping students write summaries and essays in conjunction with expository text only.

WRITING A ONE-PARAGRAPH SUMMARY

In this section, we describe how to teach students the steps in a procedure based on the About Point Writing Response strategy described in Chapter 1. We then present a completed planning guide and an example of a one-paragraph, cause/effect summary. Since our goal is to demonstrate how to help students write summaries and essays in conjunction with expository text, our example summary and essay follow the procedures that we outline here, and you can use them as writing models for your students. In Chapters 2 through 7 of this book, the emphasis is on reading and critical thinking strategies and student summaries appear as extensions of those strategies. The student summaries may not include all of the parts that we suggest for a summary. Since writing is a developmental process, requiring practice and feedback, you may want to think of the student summaries as being in various stages of development. You can work toward the goal of having your students write summaries and essays like the ones we present in this section.

Before the Lesson

- Create and make copies of a planning guide (see template at right and on the CD).

- Choose a short selection to use as a model; complete an appropriate frame (see page 146) to use in your example.

Teaching the Strategy

- Introduce summaries as a way of solidifying one's understanding of text. You might say, "Today we're going to work on writing summaries. Summaries present the main ideas from a passage, or chapter, or book. They are much shorter than the piece you read. In a summary, you have to capture only the most important ideas, details, and relationships. To do this well, you really have to understand what you've read. So going through the process of writing a summary is a great way to make sure you understand a text. And, by reading your summaries, I have a sense of how well you understood the material."

- Distribute copies of the planning guide to students. Say something like, "To help you write your summaries, I've prepared this planning guide, based on the About Point Response strategy that you're all familiar with. Let's go through it together."

- Review the components of the planning guide.

- Model completing a sample guide with a short paragraph or passage everyone has read. First, write down what the piece was about after the About heading. Then think aloud about how you determine the point of the piece; record the point in the appropriate place. Then show how you can combine these two to create a topic sentence.

- Show students the frame you completed for the model passage. (Students should already be familiar with the type of frame.) Demonstrate how to use the frame to complete the planning guide by recording key details in the information section.

- Review your guide and think aloud about how to create a closing statement that rephrases the topic sentence.

- Ask students to work through the same process for a piece they have just read, preferably one for which they have completed a frame as part of their comprehension strategy. You may want to have students work in groups the first few times.

PLANNING GUIDE FOR ONE-PARAGRAPH SUMMARY

About:

Point:

Topic Sentence:

Details:

Closing:

- Model how to use your planning guide to write the actual summary. Say something like, "Wow, we've done a lot of work here. But this will make our job of writing the summary much easier. We already know everything we want to say! Begin with the topic sentence you've already written on your planning guide. Then write several sentences about the key information you've recorded from your frame. Finally, write down the closing sentence."

- Ask students to write their summaries based on their planning guides.

Figure 6S shows a completed planning guide and a one-paragraph, cause/effect summary using information from the cause/effect frame on conservation that appeared earlier in this chapter in Figure 6J. You can see how the completed summary follows the About Point Writing Response strategy used in the planning guide. Because this is a cause/effect summary, all the information in it should explain either the causes for something that has happened or the results (effects) of something that has happened

Planning and Writing a Cause/Effect Summary

Planning Guide

About: Chopping down trees in the rain forest

Point: It has many negative effects.

Topic Sentence: Chopping down trees in the rain forest has many negative effects.

Details:

It reduces the number of trees and destroys the homes of many animals.

It leaves no roots to hold the earth in place so fertile soil will be washed away.

It reduces oxygen production and impairs pollination.

It reduces the food supplies for some animals.

It destroys beauty.

Closing: Chopping down trees in the rain forest has so many negative effects that we should convince people and organizations not to do it.

Summary

Chopping down trees in the rain forest has many negative effects. First of all, as a result of reducing the number of trees, the homes and food supplies of many animals are destroyed. Another negative effect is the washing away of fertile soil because there are no roots to hold the earth in place. Oxygen production is reduced, pollination impaired, and a lot of beauty destroyed. Chopping down trees in the rain forest has so many negative effects that we should convince people and organizations not to do it.

A fourth grader's Cause/Effect Summary based on the frame in Figure 6J.

(e.g., in our example, the information is about the effects of chopping down trees in the rain forest). Remind students about the signal words common to each frame (see chart on page 155); students may want to use these in their summaries.

WRITING AN ESSAY

When students have had practice in writing one-paragraph summaries, you will want them to engage in more sophisticated forms of writing, especially if they are reading increasingly long and complex material. This is a good time to teach them how to write an essay, which consists of several paragraphs including an introduction and a conclusion. In this section, we present step-by-step procedures for planning the three parts of an essay (introduction, body, conclusion) and then show a completed planning guide and an example of an essay based on information from a problem/solution frame. As is the case with the writing of one-paragraph summaries, you will need to give your students copies of the planning guide, which they will use to fill in the information needed to write the different parts of an essay.

Before the Lesson

- Create and make copies of a planning guide (see template at right or on the CD).

- Choose a text everyone is familiar with to use as a model for your demonstration essay.

Teaching the Strategy

- Introduce essays as a way of discussing the content of a text in more detail than a summary allows. You might say, "You've all gotten very good at writing one-paragraph summaries. Now we're reading longer and longer texts, and it's getting hard to keep our summaries to one paragraph. There's so much information. Today I'm going to show you how to write an essay, which will give us more room to write and think about what we've read."

- Distribute copies of the planning guide to students. Say something like, "As with summaries, I've prepared a planning guide to help us write our essays. You'll notice that an essay is similar to a summary. It has a beginning, which states the main idea of the reading. It has a middle, which provides key details from the reading. And it has an end, a conclusion. While we did all this in one paragraph for summaries, for essays, we break each part into paragraphs. Now,

PLANNING GUIDE FOR AN ESSAY

Introduction
   About:
   Point:
   Attention-Getter:
   Transition Sentence:
   Thesis Statement:

Body Paragraph
   About:
   Point:
   Topic Sentence:
   Supporting Details:
   Closing Statement:

Conclusion
   Rephrase thesis statement:
   Topic Sentences:
   Ending Sentence:

the introduction becomes its own paragraph. Each main supporting idea becomes its own paragraph. And the conclusion becomes its own paragraph. Let's go over each part of an essay more closely."

Teaching the Introduction of an Essay

• Tell students that the introduction to an essay has three purposes: (1) to get the attention of the reader; (2) to connect the "attention-getter" with the thesis statement (the About Point for the whole essay); and (3) to state the thesis.

• Have the students write down the About Point for their essay by asking themselves what the essay will be about and what point they want to make; they should write this on their planning guide. Then they can use their About Point to create the thesis statement for their essay. Model how to do this with a sample text.

• Encourage students to think of an interesting way to begin their essay. They can ask a question, quote an expert, tell a brief story, or write an amazing fact about the topic. This beginning is called an "attention-getter." You may want to read aloud several samples of effective beginnings to give students ideas. Tell students to write down their attention-getter on their planning guide.

• Now have them write down on their planning guide one or two sentences that connect their attention-getter with their thesis statement. Explain to students that these sentences form a transition and make their writing smooth. Model how to do this with your example.

Teaching the Body of an Essay

• Tell students that the body of an essay consists of two or more paragraphs that provide information to support the thesis statement. Each paragraph will have three parts: (1) a topic sentence (About Point); (2) supporting details; and (3) a closing statement.

• Help students determine how many paragraphs will make up the body of their essay. The easiest way to do this is to assign paragraphs on the basis of categories of information included in the graphic organizer students completed during the comprehension portion of the lesson. At first, students can select two or three categories and write a paragraph for each. Model how you determine the number of paragraphs and the topic of each one for your demonstration essay.

• Demonstrate how to write an About Point for your first paragraph. Then turn it into a topic sentence; write these both on the planning guide. Have students do the same.

• Show students how to gather pieces of information from the text to justify the topic sentence. These are called supporting details. Have students write three or four sentences that contain supporting details.

- Have students write on their planning guide a closing statement that repeats the idea expressed in their topic sentence. The closing statement should use different words and should summarize the supporting details.

- Instruct students to repeat the last three steps for each paragraph in the body of their essay.

Teaching the Conclusion of an Essay

- Tell students that a conclusion for an essay should (1) refer to the thesis statement; (2) summarize the information; and (3) end the essay.

- Instruct students to write on their planning guide a statement that repeats the idea in their thesis statement but uses different words. Model this with your example.

- Have them summarize the information by writing down a restatement of each of the topic sentences on their planning guide. Model this with your example.

- Tell students they need to write on their planning guide an ending sentence that refers to their attention-getter. Model this with your example.

Figure 6T shows a completed planning guide and essay on the Great Depression using information from the problem/solution frame depicted in Figure 6L.

Throughout this book, you have been encouraged to have students write in conjunction with all of the strategies as a way of helping them comprehend and apply what they have learned. In this chapter, we have demonstrated how frames can be used to help students write summaries or essays for expository text. The steps for writing are the same regardless of the type of frame. For example, the steps in writing an introduction are basically the same for a descriptive essay as they are for a compare/contrast essay. Whenever possible, assign students one-paragraph summaries and essays as extensions of the reading assignment. Once students have learned a text structure, by using frames and writing summaries of texts, they can incorporate that text structure into their own writing.

ThinkingWorks Lesson Planning Guide

A number of strategies have been introduced in this chapter that will enable you to teach a complete lesson that focuses on analyzing expository text. Figure 6U shows two completed ThinkingWorks Lesson Planning Guides using strategies introduced in this chapter.

Planning and Writing a Problem/Solution Essay

Planning Guide for Introduction

About: The Depression of the 1930s

Point: It was the most devastating the United States has ever known.

Attention-getter: You probably have heard your parents or your grandparents tell stories about the Great Depression that took place in the 1930s.

Transition Sentence: It lasted for more than ten years and drove Americans to poverty, despair, and feelings of insecurity about our economy.

Thesis Statement: The Depression of the 1930s was the most devastating the United States has ever known.

Planning Guide for Body
First Paragraph

About: The causes of the Depression

Point: There were serious weaknesses in our economy and spectacular rises in prices on the stock market.

Topic sentence: Two major causes of the Depression were serious weaknesses in the economy and the spectacular rise in prices on the stock market.

Supporting Details: One American worker out of four was out of a job.

One weak spot in our economy was a depression in farming.

Industries such as coal mining and railroads were also depressed. Banks and other businesses failed at a rapid and unstoppable rate.

The high stock market prices did not reflect the economic conditions (information from text and discussion).

Closing Statement: The weak economy and over-inflated stock prices marked the beginning of the Great Depression.

Second Paragraph

About: President Roosevelt

Point: He tried to give hope and stimulate the economy.

Topic sentence: President Roosevelt tried to give people hope and stimulate the economy.

Supporting Details: In his inaugural address he said "the only thing we have to fear is fear itself."

Roosevelt tried different programs to save the economy, but many were unsuccessful.

The National Recovery Administration established minimum wages and fair competition in industries.

It was set up to spread jobs and stabilize production.

The NRA was declared unconstitutional by the Supreme Court.

Closing Statement: Closing Statement: President Roosevelt's plan to stimulate the economy and end the Depression were at first unsuccessful.

Third Paragraph

About: Roosevelt's New Deal

Point: It put people back to work

Topic Sentence: President Roosevelt's New Deal put people back to work.

Supporting Details: The New Deal gave people who couldn't find jobs federal relief.

The Civilian Conservation Corps (CCC) sent young men out to plant trees and drain swamps.

The Works Progress Administration (WPA) employed people in every kind of occupation.

The Public Works Administration (PWA) spent billions so that men could build highways and public buildings.

Closing Statement: President Roosevelt's New Deal succeeded in putting people back to work and helped to end the Depression.

A Problem/Solution Planning Guide and Essay written by a sixth grader using the Problem/Solution Frame in Figure 6L

Planning Guide for Conclusion

Repeat of Thesis Statement: It would be hard to find a period in time in the history of the United States that affected so many people as did the Depression of the 1930s.

Topic Sentences: Two major causes of the Depression were serious weak spots in our economy and high prices on the stock market.

President Roosevelt's attempts to stimulate the economy and end the Depression were unsuccessful at first.

He implemented his New Deal, which put people back to work and helped end the Depression

Ending Sentence: The 1930s Depression was devastating and left millions of Americans feeling insecure about their country.

Complete Essay

You probably have heard your parents or your grandparents tell stories about the Great Depression that took place in the 1930s. It lasted for more than ten years and drove Americans to poverty, despair, and feelings of insecurity about our economy. The Depression of the 1930s was the most devastating the United States has ever known.

Two major causes of the Depression were serious weaknesses in the economy and the spectacular rise in prices on the stock market. The job situation was so bad that one American out of four could not find employment. One weak spot in the economy was a depression in farming. Industries such as coal mining and railroads were also depressed. Banks and other business failed at a rapid and unstoppable rate, while stocks rose higher. Unfortunately, the high stock market prices did not reflect the poor economic conditions. The weak economy and over-inflated stock prices marked the beginning of the Great Depression.

President Roosevelt tried to give people hope and stimulate the economy. In his first inaugural address he said that the "only thing we have to fear is fear itself." Roosevelt tried different programs for saving the economy, many of which failed. One such program was the National Recovery Administration, which established minimum wages and fair competition in industries. It was set up to spread jobs and stabilize production. The NRA was declared unconstitutional by the Supreme Court. Many of President Roosevelt's plans to end the Depression were at first unsuccessful.

President Roosevelt's New Deal was successful in putting people back to work. It gave people who couldn't find jobs federal relief. One program that was part of the New Deal was the Civilian Conservation Corps (CCC) which sent young men out to plant trees and drain swamps. Another was the Works Progress Administration (WPA) which employed people in every kind of occupation. A third, the Public Works Administration (PWA), spent billions so that men could build highways and public buildings. Roosevelt's New Deal succeeded in putting people back to work and helped to end the Depression.

It would be hard to find a period in time in the history of the United States that affected so many people as did the Depression of the 1930s. Two major causes of the Depression were serious weak spots in our economy and high prices on the stock market. President Roosevelt tried unsuccessfully at first to end the Depression. Then he implemented his New Deal, which was successful in putting people back to work and helped to end the Depression. The 1930s Depression was devastating and left millions of Americans feeling insecure about their country.

ThinkingWorks Lesson Planning Guides

	STRATEGIES			
	Background Knowledge	Vocabulary	Comprehension	Application/ Extension
COGNITIVE PROCESSES	Structured Overview	Personal Clues	Frames/ Summaries	Discussion Web/ Summary or Editorial
Develop Background Knowledge	✔			
Expand Vocabulary Knowledge	✔	✔		
Use Text Structure	✔		✔	
Set a Purpose for Learning	✔		✔	
Infer/Select Information			✔	
Create Images		✔	✔	
Relate/Connect Ideas			✔	
Clarify/Monitor Understanding			✔	
Analyze			✔	✔/✔
Synthesize				✔/✔
Evaluate/Justify				✔/✔
Create/Invent				
LANGUAGE PROCESSES				
Read			✔	
Write			/✔	/✔
Listen/View	✔	✔	✔/✔	✔
Communicate Orally	✔	✔	✔/✔	✔
COGNITIVE PROCESSES	Structured Overview	Personal Clues	Frames/ Summaries	Proposition/Support Outline/Editorial
Develop Background Knowledge	✔			
Expand Vocabulary Knowledge	✔	✔		
Use Text Structure	✔		✔	
Set a Purpose for Learning	✔		✔	
Infer/Select Information			✔	
Create Images			✔	
Relate/Connect Ideas			✔	
Clarify/Monitor Understanding			✔	
Analyze			✔	✔/✔
Synthesize				✔/✔
Evaluate/Justify				✔/✔
Create/Invent				/✔
LANGUAGE PROCESSES				
Read			✔	
Write			/✔	✔/✔
Listen/View	✔	✔	✔/✔	✔
Communicate Orally	✔	✔	✔/✔	✔

CHAPTER 7

Interpreting
Expository Text

In This Chapter:

BACKGROUND KNOWLEDGE:	Quickwriting with Knowledge Rating Scale
VOCABULARY:	Semantic Feature Analysis
COMPREHENSION:	QAR; Question, Clues, Response; Questions for Quality Thinking; Thinking Minds
APPLICATION/EXTENSION:	Four-Step Summary
ALTERNATIVE COMPREHENSION STRATEGY:	Reciprocal Teaching
ALTERNATIVE APPLICATION/EXTENSION STRATEGY:	Learning Logs

The previous two chapters presented strategies for helping students understand and analyze expository text and its various structures. This chapter emphasizes questioning strategies that encourage readers to think about and react, either orally or in writing, to the material they have read. Asking and answering questions, on the part of both the students and the teacher, is a natural outgrowth of reading and serves as the final link in the comprehension chain (Graves et al., 1998). Questions are valuable teaching tools because they promote thinking at different levels—from recalling and interpreting information to analyzing, synthesizing, and evaluating.

In addition to questioning strategies, we introduce two writing strategies. The Four-Step Summary helps students synthesize information from a reading passage. It is particularly helpful after students have participated in discussions about the reading because it provides them with an outline for organizing ideas brought out in the discussion. We also show how one of the questioning strategies in the chapter, Question, Clues, Response, can be used to guide students through the process of responding to an inferential question in the form of an essay.

ThinkingWorks Lesson Plan Sequence for Interpreting Expository Text

To help students interpret expository text, we have designed the following lesson sequence:

BACKGROUND KNOWLEDGE:	Quickwriting with Knowledge Rating Scale
VOCABULARY:	Semantic Feature Analysis
COMPREHENSION:	QAR; Question, Clues, Response; Questions for Quality Thinking; Thinking Minds
APPLICATION/EXTENSION:	Four-Step Summary

The questioning strategies are the key to getting students to think critically about expository text (or any text for that matter). Activating background knowledge and exploring vocabulary help students prepare to ask questions about their reading. The summary strategy helps them clarify and integrate concepts in a passage they've read so they can begin to question it critically; it is the recommended writing activity for this lesson.

We also present an alternative comprehension strategy, Reciprocal Teaching, and an alternative application/extension strategy that incorporates writing, Learning Logs.

Quickwriting With Knowledge Rating Scale

Quickwriting (Elbow, 1973) is a brainstorming strategy that is used before and after reading a text. Using a stream of consciousness format, students write about a topic, or words that are central to the topic, to demonstrate their current level of knowledge and understanding. During the five- to ten-minute activity, students write about anything that they associate with the topic or the designated words without worrying about spelling or grammar.

Quickwriting helps students access what they know about a topic, which will help them make connections to new information they encounter in their reading. As students write, they become aware of the breadth of their knowledge and can identify gaps in it, which can lead to questions they can use to guide them while reading. If you work with younger students, you can tap their associations orally, and then list their responses on the board. Together, you and your students can categorize the information so your students can see a visual representation of related information before reading. This strategy also gives you insight into the current level of your students' knowledge about a particular topic, so you can plan your instruction accordingly.

After reading and discussing a text, students can review their Quickwriting to elaborate on and extend their thinking, fleshing out their ideas with new information from the text and class discussion. During this process, students assimilate and accommodate new information to reconstruct their previous understandings. Older students can do this in writing, while younger one may do it orally as you lead a discussion.

When students are first learning to do Quickwriting, model the process for them until they get a feel for it. For example, when Christi Hughes' second-grade students were preparing to read *Stellaluna* (Cannon, 1993), a story about bats, she said, "We're going to read a story about bats next called *Stellaluna*. To get ready to read, I'm going to do some Quickwriting so I can see what I know about bats. This will get me thinking about the topic and help me set a purpose for reading; I can ask questions about things I'm not sure of or that I want more information about. So it's a great strategy to use before reading. Okay, here I go." Christi wrote on chart paper, reading aloud as she wrote:

> "There are many different kinds of bats. Most bats have long finger bones that are connected to make wings. Bats live in many different climates around the world."

Christi then asked several students to tell her what they knew about bats. She wrote on chart paper what each student said and told students that these were also examples of Quickwriting. She concluded the Quickwriting like this, "We know a lot about bats! I wonder what new things we'll learn in *Stellaluna*." Christi then did a vocabulary activity before having students read the book.

Quickwriting with Knowledge Rating Scale

Write what you know about the following words in your journal:

Cells

Muscles

Nerves

Bones

Oxygen

Arteries

Student response:

Muscles help us move our bodies. You can pull a muscle.

Bones are in our body. They can break.

We breathe oxygen to live.

	Have No Idea	Have Seen	Can Define	Use in Sentence
Cells	✔			
Arteries		✔		
Nerves			✔	✔
Muscles		✔	✔	✔
Bones		✔	✔	✔
Oxygen		✔	✔	✔

An example of Quickwriting for a second-grade assignment on the body. Also included is a Knowledge Rating Scale that complements the Quickwriting strategy.

Teaching the Strategy

- Explain to students the topic for their reading assignment. If students are young or have difficulty writing without prompts, write a few of the important vocabulary words on the board.

- Explain that the purpose of this activity is to find out what they already know about the topic. This will help you plan your instruction, and it will help students set a purpose for reading.

- Tell the students to write down anything that comes to mind when they think of the topic or when they see the words you've written on the board. Ask them to write continuously for five to ten minutes without worrying about grammar or spelling.

- If you use vocabulary words from the lesson to prompt their Quickwriting, you may include the Knowledge Rating Scale (Blachowicz, 1986), a strategy in which students rate their understanding of the presented words on a scale ranging from no understanding ("Have no idea") to strong competence ("Can use in a sentence"). Intermediate levels include "Have seen" and "Can define." After students complete the Knowledge Rating Scale, you can judge the type of vocabulary instruction that is necessary for them to understand the lesson. For students with limited knowledge of words, you can discuss word meanings and use vocabulary learning strategies as appropriate. See Figure 7A for an example of Quickwriting and the Knowledge Rating Scale used together by a second grader; Figure 7B shows an example of Quickwriting done by a fourth grader.

FIGURE 7B

Quickwriting

Recycling helps the environment. It keeps pollution down by reducing trash in landfills. Recycling also saves money because it is cheaper to reuse items. Companies can make new products out of old ones.

An example of Quickwriting for a fourth-grade assignment on recycling

- Collect the Quickwritings and review them in order to plan your instruction.

- After the unit, return the Quickwritings to students and ask them to review their Quickwriting to see how much they've learned. Students can prepare Semantic Maps (see page 39) in small groups, using both the information from their Quickwriting and new knowledge gained from their reading and class discussion.

Assessment

The purpose of Quickwriting is to activate background knowledge. If your students write for five to ten minutes on a topic, the strategy was successful in accomplishing its purpose. If your students do not write, determine whether they lack information or are unable to write. When the writing itself is a problem, you have to find another way to activate background knowledge before your students read the assignment, probably by doing an oral version of Quickwriting.

VOCABULARY STRATEGY:
Semantic Feature Analysis

Semantic Feature Analysis or SFA (Johnson & Pearson, 1984) is a strategy that develops students' vocabulary knowledge and builds their background knowledge of concepts related to the topic being studied. The strategy requires that you develop a grid or matrix to help students analyze similarities and differences among related concepts. On the matrix, list important words related to the topic horizontally and list features common to some of the words vertically (see Figures 7C and 7D for examples). Students analyze each word in relation to each feature, using check marks or plus and minus signs to indicate if the feature is associated with the word.

In Figure 7C, the vocabulary words for a second-grade study of the body are listed across the top: *brain*, *heart*, *nerves*, and *muscles*. The features include "helps us think" and "helps us move." In this example, students checked off that the brain helps people

Semantic Feature Analysis

Topic: The Body

	Brain	Heart	Nerves	Muscles
Help(s) us think	✔		✔	
Help(s) us move	✔		✔	✔
Keep(s) heart working	✔		✔	✔
Keep(s) blood flowing		✔		✔

A completed SFA grid using concepts from a second-grade unit on the body

think and move; they left these rows blank under the heart. If students are unsure about a word having a particular feature, they can use a question mark to indicate their uncertainty. The visual organizer and related discussion about word meanings make distinctions among words concrete for students.

Before the Lesson

• Select a topic or category from the reading assignment.

• On chart paper or the board, create a grid on which students can compare and contrast concepts (see Figure 7D for an example in which students compare words that describe ways of walking; there is a template on the CD). Write the vocabulary words across the top of the grid. In the left column, list features or properties that are shared by some of the words.

Teaching the Strategy

• Display the grid. Explain to students that it will help them understand how related words from their assignment are similar to or different from one another.

• Lead a discussion in which students analyze each word, feature by feature. Have the students take turns going to the board and placing a + or - in each cell of the grid to indicate whether the word has the feature or not. If they are uncertain, tell them to place a question mark in the cell.

Semantic Feature Analysis for Ways of Walking

Topic: Ways of Walking

	Stride	Strut	Amble	Saunter	Promenade
Fast	+	+	−	−	−
Dignified	+	−	−	−	+
Relaxed	−	+	+	+	+

A completed SFA grid for older students using words that describe different ways of walking

- Brainstorm with the students additional words and features that can be added to the grid and complete the procedure with the additional words. The words can be those that appear in the text students are reading or related to concepts that are critical to understanding the text.

- Have the students refer to the SFA after they have read the material to clarify and change some of their initial responses on the grid.

Writing Extension

You may have students choose one or more vocabulary words and write a descriptive paragraph using as many of the features as are appropriate for the word or words. Since this activity may be difficult for some students, having them complete it in pairs (Think-Pair-Share; see page 34) or in groups would provide the necessary instructional support.

Assessment

You can determine the effectiveness of the SFA strategy for teaching vocabulary by examining your students' writing for evidence that they have learned the words. If you do not implement a writing component at this point of the lesson, a simple vocabulary test will tell you whether the students learned the words. Regardless of which method you choose—paragraph writing or a vocabulary test—you should test your students on the words a couple of weeks later to determine if the SFA strategy resulted in vocabulary retention. You can also evaluate your students' writing by applying the holistic scoring criteria described in Chapter 8.

COMPREHENSION STRATEGY:

Questioning

We present four questioning strategies in this chapter: QAR; Question, Clues, Response; Questions for Quality Thinking; and Thinking Minds. Students use many cognitive processes when they answer questions, including inferring, selecting information, creating visual images, relating and connecting ideas, and clarifying and monitoring understanding. The first strategy presented, Question Answer Relationship (QAR), is the foundation strategy. It helps students identify sources of information to use to answer questions. The second strategy, Question, Clues, Response, helps students construct an answer to an inferential question by combining information from their background knowledge and text clues. The third strategy, Questions for Quality Thinking, consists of different levels of questions that prompt students to engage in many facets of thinking including higher-order thinking. The fourth strategy, Thinking Minds, helps students think critically and creatively about persuasive text.

QUESTION ANSWER RELATIONSHIP (QAR)

QAR (Raphael, 1982) is a strategy that helps students identify the kind of question they're being asked, such as literal or inferential, so they know where to look for the answer, either in the text, in their own knowledge, or a combination of the two. The three types of questions Raphael describes are "right there" (explicitly stated in the text), "think and search" (put together from different parts of the text), and "on my own" (gathered from the reader's own knowledge). Three different types of questions can be asked depending on the source of information:

- Literal questions for "right there" information

- Inferential questions for "think and search" information

- Scriptal (i.e., drawing from students' background knowledge) questions for "on my own" information

Students who need mental modeling or have learning difficulties can benefit from the way QAR mirrors different thinking processes involved in asking questions and constructing answers. You can provide students with practice in this strategy by developing questions to guide them as they read. The questions should include the three QAR categories of "right there," "think and search," and "on your own" (see the example in Figure 7E). After you have done this, you can encourage students to develop their own questions based on the QAR categories.

FIGURE 7E

QAR

What are the three parts of your brain? (Right There)

Which part of your brain helps you understand schoolwork? (Think and Search)

How would you rate the importance of the function of each part of the brain? (On Your Own)

How does blood travel? (Right There)

What similar function does the blood perform for the kidneys and lungs? (Think and Search)

How would you describe the functions of the blood? (On Your Own)

An example of how QAR was used to help second-grade students understand a health unit on the body

Before the Lesson

- Prepare questions for each kind of QAR—literal, inferential, and scriptal—from the reading assignment.

Teaching the Strategy

- Tell students you're going to teach them a strategy that will improve their ability to answer questions about their reading assignments. Explain the three question-answer relationships and give students examples of each based on their actual textbook reading assignments (see examples in Figures 7E, 7F, and 7G).

QAR

What rights did slaves have? (literal)

Slaves had no rights at all.

How were slaves purchased? (literal)

Slaves were bought at auctions and sold to the highest bidder like cattle.

What was the life of a slave like? (inferential)

Slaves' lives were very bad. They worked hard for no pay. They had small spaces to live in, and didn't have good food. They weren't treated very well.

Why did sickness spread so easily throughout the slave ships? (inferential)

The slave ships were so crowded. If someone got sick there probably wasn't anywhere for him to go so he would spread his germs to other slaves.

What could a slave owner have done to improve the quality of a slave's life? (scriptal)

He could have let them live in the big house. He could have made sure they had good food to eat. He could buy a whole family of slaves so they wouldn't be separated.

If you were a slave, how would you learn to read? (scriptal)

I would try to make friends with my master's children and ask them to help me learn. I would ask for all their old books. I also might try to have a school started for slaves.

An example of QAR applied to a fifth-grade unit on the Civil War

QAR

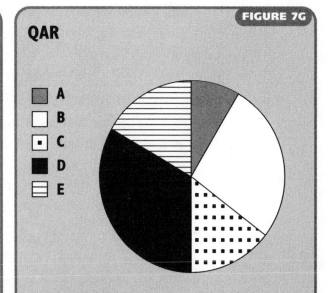

- A
- B
- C
- D
- E

The sections represented on the circle graph represent areas of a city that sell the most cases of cola. Use the graph to answer the following questions:

1. **Which section sells the fewest cans of cola?** (Think and Search) Answer: **A**

2. **Which two sections together sell as many cans of colas as the other sections?** (Think and Search) Answer: **D and E**

3. **Which two sections make the least profit?** (Think and Search) Answer: **A and C**

4. **Which section is most likely to make the most profit from selling cans of cola?** (On Your Own) Answer: **C**

5. **How can graphs help you?** (On Your Own) Answer: **Graphs can help you see information so you can answer questions.**

An example of how QAR can be used to help students understand information presented in graphs

- Show students how each relationship works, using the material for their reading assignment. Begin with the "right there" QAR. Tell students that the answer is in the text. The words to make the questions and the words to make the answer are "right there." "What are the three parts of the brain?" is a "right there" question. Model the process of answering a "right there" QAR with the text.

- Now explain the "think and search" QAR. Tell students that clues to the answer are in the text but are a little hard to find. They must act like detectives and search for the clues in different parts of the text. Model the process of finding "think and search" QARs. "Which part of your brain helps you understand school work?" is a "think and search" question.

- Finally, explain the "on my own" QAR. Tell students that the answer won't be told by words in the text. They must construct the answer in their heads by connecting what they've read to their background knowledge. "How would you rate the importance of the function of each part of this brain?" is an example of an "on my own" question. Once again, model the process of constructing "on my own" QARs.

- When the students seem to understand the relationships, give them questions labeled "Right There," "Think and Search," and "On My Own" and tell the students to come up with the answers.

- Direct students' attention to the questions at the end of a chapter in their text or to those that you've prepared for the reading assignment. Tell them to answer the questions and write down the question-answer relationship for each. Have students use a Think-Pair-Share format for developing and checking responses.

- Make a study guide or a QAR bookmark for students to refer to before reading and after reading a text on their own.

QUESTION, CLUES, RESPONSE

Question, Clues, Response (Carr, January 2000) is a strategy that helps students answer questions on the basis of clues from the text or lesson *and* their background knowledge. It is an adaptation of the Inferential Training Technique or ITT (Carr, Dewitz, & Patberg, 1989) that explicitly teaches inferential thinking by having students make connections between background knowledge and new information from a text or lesson. With this strategy, students use a guide (in essence a visual model of the inferential process) to record clues that are helpful for answering questions (see the sample in Figures 7H).

Before the Lesson

- Prepare a Question, Clues, Response Guide to help students monitor their inferential thinking; there are templates on the CD. In the left column, leave spaces for students to write down questions that you have assigned, either those from the text or those that you have prepared for the lesson. The next two columns are labeled

Question, Clues, Response

Question	Test/Lesson Clues	Background Knowledge Clues	Response
1. How does sandpaper affect the motion of a block?	Sandpaper produces friction and slows the block.	Sandpaper is rough. Rough surfaces slow or stop objects.	Rough surfaces like sandpaper produce friction to slow the motion of an object.
2. How does wax paper affect the motion of a block?	Wax paper produces little friction so objects slide easily.	Wax paper is slippery. Slippery surfaces help objects slide.	Wax paper produces little friction allowing objects to slide easily.

An example of how the Question, Clues, Response strategy can be used to help students answer questions about friction from a science experiment

"Text/Lesson Clues" and "Background Knowledge Clues." In the far right column, leave space so students can write a response to each question.

Teaching the Strategy

• After students have read and discussed the assigned reading, tell them you are going to teach them a strategy that will improve their ability to answer questions about their reading. Explain that in order to answer questions, one often uses different sources of information: previously read text, information from a lesson, and background knowledge.

• Select a question from the text or one you have prepared, and model the process of using various clues to answer the question. Discuss how readers can connect their background knowledge to information in a text or lesson to infer answers to questions. Make sure students understand that they are expected to find clues to the answers themselves, in both the text and their background knowledge (e.g., they should ask themselves, *What do I know about . . . ? and What do I think about . . . ?*) In the example in Figure 7H, students connect their previous experience with sandpaper (it's rough) to clues from the lesson (sandpaper produces friction and slows a block) to develop their response (rough surfaces like sandpaper produce friction to slow the motion of an object).

• Model this process for several questions. When you feel that students understand the strategy, have them apply it in small groups. Tell them to complete the guide for the remaining questions by writing down the clues in the appropriate column(s) and their response to the questions.

• After students have completed the guide in groups, discuss their responses with the class.

The Question, Clues, Response Guide shown in Figure 7H helps students understand text or a lesson and provide relatively short answers to inferential questions. However, Question, Clues, Response can also be used as an application/extension strategy when its purpose is to help students transfer what they have learned to a new situation, something that might be required of them on a classroom test or a state-level examination. You can use the short answer guide or you can modify the guide to encourage longer answers in the form of a paragraph or an essay. The modified guide has just one test or essay question written at the top. Below the question are two columns, one for the text or lesson clues and another for background knowledge clues. Toward the bottom of the page is an outline that students complete prior to writing their summary or essay (see a sample modified guide in Figure 7I). The outline follows the About Point Writing Response format. Students look at their lesson and background knowledge clues. Based on some or all of the information in the clues, they formulate a statement or position with an About and a Point. They then use some or all of their clues to support their statement. Their closing sentence restates their About Point.

FIGURE 7I

Question, Clues, Response Guide with About Point Writing Response

Question: Why is sand used on wet roads in winter?

Clues

Text/Lesson	Background Knowledge
rough surfaces slow objects by increasing friction	wet roads can become slick in the cold slick roads are dangerous sand is rough

Response

Outline	Summary
About: Sand **Point:** is used on wet winter roads to prevent accidents 1. wet roads become slick 2. sand is rough 3. rough surfaces slow object by increasing friction **Closing:** when vehicles are moving slowly, accidents can be avoided	Sand is used on winter roads to prevent accidents. In winter, wet roads can become slick and dangerous. Sand provides a rough surface on the ice. The sandy surface slows cars and other vehicles by increasing friction. Sand slows traffic down and accidents can often be avoided.

A Question, Clues, Response Guide modified for an extended response

QUESTIONS FOR QUALITY THINKING

Questions for Quality Thinking (McTigue & Lyman in Alvermann & Phelps, 1994) is a questioning strategy that promotes thinking, student interaction, and the application of ideas. The questions, which are based on Bloom's Taxonomy of Educational Objectives (Bloom, 1956), can be used as a guide to focus discussion and ensure that students develop the ability to think about content information. The levels and question prompts of Bloom's Taxonomy are in Figure 7J.

The Questions for Quality Thinking strategy can be adapted for various content areas and grade levels. It is also suitable for small-group learning.

FIGURE 7J

Bloom's Taxonomy

LEVELS	QUESTION PROMPTS
Knowledge	• Recalling information • Who, what, when, where, how questions
Comprehension	• Understanding information • Retelling in your own words • Explaining the gist
Application	• Using the information • Providing an example
Analysis	• Separating the whole into parts • Asking how this is different from or similar to_____ • Providing evidence to support
Synthesis	• Combining ideas to form a new whole or picture • Drawing conclusions • Asking how you would respond to the problem or situation
Evaluation	• Forming personal opinions and judgments • Asking yourself what you believe • Developing criteria to judge

Bloom's Taxonomy with question prompts for each level

Before the Lesson

- Use the prompts in the chart to prepare questions for a discussion of the reading assignment. Try to have questions for each of the levels of Bloom's Taxonomy.

- Prepare a thinking matrix (presented in Alvermann & Phelps, 1994) to cross-reference the different kinds of questions with content topics; there is a template on the CD. On the horizontal axis, list the topics or categories that you will be covering in the reading assignment. For instance, in a unit on the body, the teacher chose the topics "cells," "muscles," "nerves," "bones," "arteries," and "oxygen." Assign each one a number, as shown in Figure 7K. On the vertical axis, list the kinds of questions you want to ask from Bloom's Taxonomy. Assign each of those a letter.

- Cross-reference your questions with the content categories and question types. You can use the matrix to analyze your questions, making sure that you have questions that generate high-level thinking (see the sample matrix and related questions in Figure 7K). Alternatively, you can write questions in each box in the matrix, as shown in Figure 7L.

FIGURE 7K

Thinking Matrix

	(1) Cells	(2) Muscles	(3) Nerves	(4) Bones	(5) Arteries	(6) Oxygen
(A) Knowledge	A1			A4		
(B) Comprehension			B3			B6
(C) Application		C2			C5	
(D) Analysis	D1		D3			
(E) Synthesis	E1	E2				
(F) Evaluation	F1	F2				

A1 What do the cells need besides food?
A4 How does our skeleton protect us?

B6 Explain how oxygen helps you breath?
B3 Describe how the nerves work to protect us from injury.

C2 Why are muscles important?
C5 Why are arteries important?

D1 How are cells different?
D3 How are nerve cells like a messenger?

E2 Why is it important to exercise?
E1 What would happen if cells didn't divide?

F2 Do you think it more important for the development of your muscles to eat or to exercise?
F1 Choose a food that would help you develop healthy cells in your body. Explain your choice.

A Thinking Matrix designed for a
second-grade health unit on the body

Thinking Matrix

	Lever	Pulley	Wheel & Axle	Inclined Plane	Wedge	Screw
Knowledge	Which class of lever has the effort in the middle?	In a single-fixed pulley system, in which direction is the effort applied?				
Comprehension	Explain each of the three lever systems.	Explain each of the four pulley systems.			Tell how a wedge is used to accomplish work.	Explain how a screw provides a mechanical advantage.
Application	Give an example of each class of lever.	Where are pulley systems used in real life to provide a mechanical advantage?	Create a situation showing how a wheel and axle are used to get the job done.		Think of how a wedge and the screw provide a mechanical advantage. How are these two machines similar?	
Analysis		How does a single-fixed pulley differ from a single-moveable pulley?				
Synthesis		How could you use a pulley system to rescue a car stuck in the mud?		Suppose you are moving. How can a simple machine be used to move the family's piano?		
Evaluation	Which simple machine do you feel is the most important? Why?					

A Thinking Matrix for a sixth-grade science unit

Tips to Encourage Successful Student Responses to Questions

- Provide at least three seconds of thinking time after a question and after a response.

- Allow individual thinking time, discussion with a partner (Think-Pair-Share), and class discussion.

- Ask follow-up questions—for example, "Tell me more."

- Respond to student answers in a non-evaluative fashion, such as "I appreciate your thinking."

- Ask for a summary to promote active listening.

- Ask students if they agree with the author's point of view.

- Have students call on other students.

- Encourage students to defend their reasoning against different points of view.

- Ask students to describe how they arrived at their answer.

- Call on students randomly.

- Let the students develop their own questions.

- Assure the students that there is not a single correct answer for this question.

Teaching the Strategy

- Tell students that you're going to guide them in a discussion of the reading assignment, and you really want them to think about the content information.

- Distribute the completed matrix and discuss the different levels of questions you can ask. Explain that the different kinds of questions require different kinds of thinking, some easier and some more challenging. Say that you want them to have practice with all of the different kinds of thinking, so you'll be asking many types of questions.

- Once students are familiar with the different levels of questions, lead a large-group discussion in which students answer questions on the matrix orally. They can also write answers to the questions on notebook paper.

- When the students are familiar with the purpose and the format of the matrix, have them use it to generate their own questions for certain lessons.

- At the end of the unit, you can use the matrix to review the material. Divide your students into small groups and have them take turns leading the discussion using the matrix.

THINKING MINDS

Thinking Minds, based on Questioning the Author (Beck, McKeown, Hamilton, & Kucan, 1997) and Six Thinking Hats (de Bono, 1985), is a strategy that helps students become adept and flexible at thinking critically and creatively about expository text. Thinking Minds teaches students to become independent thinkers and helps them monitor their understanding while reading. With this strategy, you provide students with a set of questions that they can ask themselves whenever they encounter text that attempts to persuade the reader. The questions encourage students to understand the text, evaluate the credibility and appropriateness of the information, support or refute a position, and use the information in a creative way.

While Thinking Minds can be used with students in all grades and with all subject areas, it is especially effective with students in grades 4 and above and with content area text that is persuasive in nature. Younger students may not encounter this type of text frequently. However, in the early grades, some materials can reflect an author's position on a topic. For example, in science, lessons about conservation emphasize the importance of protecting animals and their environment. Or in health lessons (see Figure 7M), young students learn about how to keep their bodies healthy. You can guide younger students to become aware of the author's message and you can discuss with them why that message may be important to them and the community.

> **FIGURE 7M**
>
> ## Thinking Minds
>
> 1. What does the author mean when he says that the brain is a powerful computer?
>   My brain tells each part of my body what to do.
>
> 2. Does the author explain something about breathing that supports information you already know?
>   My mom has allergies. When she breathes, she sneezes to get rid of the dirt and pollen in the air.
>
> 3. What did you learn about the body that would be important to keeping you healthy?
>   It is important to exercise to keep my muscles strong and healthy.

Thinking Minds questions designed for second graders studying a unit on the body

Before the Lesson

• On a large piece of posterboard, write down the following questions:

> • What is the author's message?
>
> • What is the author's viewpoint or purpose in writing the text?
>
> • How does the author support his or her argument?
>
> • Does the author convince me that his or her argument is sound?
>
> • What difference does the information make and of what value is it to me?

- Note that these questions are generic; you can ask them of any persuasive text. The main idea that you want to communicate to students is the importance of reading persuasive text with these kinds of questions in mind.

Teaching the Strategy

- Explain what persuasive text is. You might say, "Often, writers write a piece because they want to persuade us to agree with them about a particular topic. We call this kind of writing *persuasive*. It's important to read this kind of writing carefully so we examine the author's argument and decide whether we agree or not. Today we'll learn a strategy called 'Thinking Minds' that will help us do this."

- Place the poster in a prominent spot in the classroom. Explain to students that these are the kinds of questions you want them to ask whenever they read a persuasive text.

- Discuss each question in detail, explaining the kind of thinking it involves and why it's so important to answer it.

  - For the first question—*What is the author's message?*—tell students they must understand what the author is trying to say. Show them how to determine the main idea and important details. Use the About Point strategy (What is the text about? What point is the author making?).

  - For the second question—*What is the author's viewpoint or purpose in writing the text?*—tell students that, in order to answer the question, they need to examine the author's background and bias, which may entail reading other sources. Show them how to determine if the writing is clear and if the author's viewpoint is easy to recognize. Students have had some experience with using an author's viewpoint or opinion to persuade others if they have written editorials. Both the Discussion Web and Proposition/Support Outline strategies (see Chapter 6) also provide practice in justifying a point of view.

  - For the third question—*How does the author support his/her argument?*—model for students the process involved in evaluating the logic of the author's argument: Why is particular information/evidence important and why is information introduced at specific points? Discuss with them the importance of deciding if the information makes sense in light of what they already know and have read about the topic. Remind students that they know how to analyze information and support an argument with evidence from their use of the Proposition/Support Outline strategy.

  - For the fourth question—*Does the author convince me that his/her argument is sound?*—model for students a three-step procedure: (1) evaluate the positive aspects of the position; (2) evaluate the negative aspects of the position; and

(3) develop a personal viewpoint (e.g., I agree or disagree with the author). Again, students have applied this procedure when they've used the Discussion Web strategy to help them look at both sides of an issue before drawing a conclusion.

- For the fifth question—*What difference does the information make and of what value is it to me?*—show students how they can judge the importance of the argument by asking if it has any value to themselves or their community. Engage them in a creative discussion of how they can use the author's ideas to derive new solutions to the problem—for example, an international science camp would be a new way for astronauts from different nations to cooperate. One way to engage students in a creative discussion is to use the SCAMPER strategy with expository text (see page 135). Discussions based on the Thinking Minds questions or the SCAMPER challenges may extend over several periods.

- When you have discussed with your students how to generate questions that will help them to think critically and creatively about persuasive text and have modeled the thinking processes for each question, have them practice the strategy, first with easy text and then with text that's more challenging. Have the question poster available for them to refer to.

Use the Thinking Minds strategy often enough to convince students that it is good to read persuasive text with a questioning mind, as they can not only understand the author's viewpoint and argument, but can apply it to their own lives. See Figure 7N for an example of how the Thinking Minds questions were used with a sixth-grade class studying Greek Civilization.

Thinking Minds

1. What does the author mean when he states that Athens became the center of the Aegean world?

   The culture of Athens spread to every Greek polis.

2. Does the author explain clearly why the gods were so important to the Greeks?

   The Greeks had many Gods that controlled the world. A chart showed what the gods did but it wasn't easy to understand.

3. Are you able to make any connections between what the author wrote and what you know about the Greeks?

   I know about the Olympics and we have read some myths.

4. What is the author's viewpoint of the Greek civilization?

   That the world is amazed at what they accomplished.

5. Do you agree with the author's viewpoint?

   Yes, the Greeks started the Olympics, wrote poems and plays, and had many famous people like Socrates and Plato.

6. What difference do these contributions make to your life and the world?

   Our country has a democracy like Athens and trial by jury. The world enjoys the Olympics and poetry and theater.

Thinking Minds questions for a sixth-grade unit on Greek civilization

Writing Extension

All four questioning strategies encourage students to think and talk about what they have read and understood about the content, which has the potential to lead to thoughtful writing as well. Later on in this chapter, we describe strategies for expository writing that can be used to extend students' learning. If, however, you would like your students to do additional writing or writing that is specific to the content used for the questioning strategies, have them write paragraphs or essays for parts of the content studied using the About Point Writing Response strategy (see page 17). Since all of the questioning strategies emphasize the importance of higher-level thinking, whatever writing you assign your students should be at the analysis, synthesis, and evaluation levels.

Assessment

The best way of evaluating the effectiveness of the questioning strategies for helping your students learn, think about, and remember information is to test them on the material right after they've studied it and again some time later. The nature of the test is of critical importance. In order for the test to be a valid measure of the effectiveness of these strategies, the questions must evaluate higher-level thinking as well as literal and inferential thinking. If you want to determine whether the strategies aided in the retention of the material, you should include questions at these various levels in a test administered later in the year, such as an end-of-the-unit test.

APPLICATION/EXTENSION STRATEGY:
Four-Step Summary

The Four-Step Summary (Stanfill, 1978) is a writing strategy that has students pull together the most important information in their reading assignments. It provides direction on how to synthesize and summarize several portions of a text. For the first step, students determine the main idea of the piece. Then they provide a gist of the text information by creating a summary that has three parts: a beginning, middle, and end. Figures 7O and 7P show examples of Four-Step Summaries.

Before the Lesson

• Select a short, easy passage that you will use to model the summary strategy.

Teaching the Strategy

• After students have read and discussed the reading assignment, tell them that you are going to teach them a strategy for summarizing passages from the reading, which will help them remember what they've read.

Four-Step Summary

Topic:	Cells
Beginning:	Cells are different shapes—can live a few days or a lifetime.
Middle:	Cells are alike inside and can divide into two cells.
End:	There are billions of cells in the body.
Summary:	Cells are different shapes and live a few days or a lifetime. Cells are alike inside and can divide into two cells. There are billions of cells in the body.

A second grader's Four-Step Summary
of a reading about the body

Four-Step Summary

Topic:	The Spread of Islam
Beginning:	Islam spread quickly through the Middle East and North Africa making it part of the Muslim world.
Middle:	Eventually a battle took place in Tours, Europe. The Muslims were defeated by a frank named Charles Martell who had a grandson named Charlemagne who would soon control Europe.
End:	The Muslims still ruled the Iberian peninsula, North Africa and the Middle East. They controlled more land than the Romans did in one century.
Summary:	Islam spread quickly through the Middle East and North Africa making it part of the Muslim world. Eventually a battle took place in Tours, Europe. The Muslims were defeated by a frank named Charles Martell who had a grandson named Charlemagne who would soon control Europe. The Muslims still ruled the Iberian peninsula, North Africa and the Middle East. They controlled more land than the Romans did in one century.

A sixth-grade student's Four-Step Summary
for a unit on the spread of Islam

- Explain the steps in the Four-Step Summary strategy: (1) Identify the main idea of the reading selection; (2) Tell how the passage begins; (3) Describe what is covered in the middle (or what the passage is about); and (4) Explain how the passage ends. Model the steps for the students using easy material.

- Select a passage from the reading assignment and guide the students in the application of each of the four steps. Do this with several passages until students can implement the strategy and form summaries themselves.

- Divide the students into small groups. Break the reading assignment into sections and give one section to each group for summarizing using the Four-Step Summary strategy. Have the groups share their summaries, which you may want to copy and distribute so that students can use them for review.

Because of the structured, step-by-step nature of the Four-Step Summary, it is particularly helpful for students with learning difficulties.

Assessment

To determine how effective the Four-Step Summary strategy is for teaching summarization, you need only examine your students' summaries to see if they are complete.

Alternative Comprehension and Application Strategies for Interpreting Expository Text

The goal of this chapter is to give students strategies for responding to expository texts, so they can deepen their comprehension. In addition to the strategies presented in the previous section, we offer an additional comprehension strategy, Reciprocal Teaching, and an additional application/extension strategy, Learning Logs. These tools complement questioning and summarizing strategies presented earlier.

COMPREHENSION STRATEGY:

Reciprocal Teaching

Reciprocal Teaching (Palincsar & Brown, 1984) is a powerful teaching strategy consisting of a dialogue between a student leader and classmates as they read segments of a text together. In the dialogue, students use four separate strategies to increase their comprehension. The four strategies are summarizing, question generating, clarifying, and predicting, and they are used in that order.

SUMMARIZING helps student synthesize information, determine the main idea and key details, and infer relationships among concepts.

QUESTION GENERATING helps students identify the key ideas in the text. As they develop questions, they solidify their understanding of the main points.

CLARIFYING is self-monitoring strategy that encourages students to restate what they've read to make sure it makes sense to them. If it doesn't, they stop and reread to figure out why it's not making sense. The process helps students identify text factors that impede their understanding, such as difficult concepts, new vocabulary, and unclear referents. With self-monitoring, students learn to assume responsibility for their understanding and take steps to restore meaning. Note: A way for students to monitor their understanding while reading is to use a modified version of Comprehension Monitoring (Smith & Dauer, 1984). Students note their responses to the material as they read by using the following code: A = Agree; I = Important; Q = Question, D = Don't Understand. They can make notations on sticky notes and attach them to the text margins whenever they want to respond to the material. Comprehension Monitoring is especially helpful for students with learning difficulties.

PREDICTING requires students to recall relevant background knowledge about a topic and form a hypothesis about what the author will discuss in each section of the text. Students then read with a purpose, linking new and prior knowledge as they infer information and refine their predictions.

Tips for Setting Up the Reciprocal Teaching Dialogue

- At the beginning of the dialogue, the student leader makes a prediction based on the title of the text or the chapter.

- Assign students to read silently a segment of the text. The student leader directs the dialogue for that segment once students have finished reading.

- The student leader summarizes the segment, asks questions, and clarifies information if needed.

- Assign another segment of text for students to read and ask a different student to lead the dialogue for that segment. Before reading, the student leader offers a prediction based on what was previously read. After students have read, the student leader summarizes the segment, generates questions about the text, and clarifies information.

- Ask a third student to be the leader who proceeds through the Reciprocal Teaching strategies for the next assigned segment of text.

Before the Lesson

- Teach students each of the four strategies separately and thoroughly. Think aloud to demonstrate how to use each strategy with expository text. Note: Summarizing, predicting, and questioning have been introduced previously in this book.

- Provide enough opportunities for students to practice each strategy before combining it with the other three. Use simple text for practice.

Teaching the Strategy

- Explain to students that Reciprocal Teaching is a powerful strategy that will help them understand and remember what they read, but, before they can use it, they have to know how to summarize, generate questions, clarify information, and predict. Review the procedures briefly.

- Show students how to put the four strategies together in the form of a dialogue between a student leader and the other members of a group (Reciprocal Teaching). Model the strategy for the students and then gradually turn the responsibility for leading the dialogue over to them (see suggestions on page 197).

- Divide students into groups of three or four and tell them to proceed with the dialogue. Every student should have a chance to be the leader.

- Provide guidance for the student leaders whenever they need it in implementing the strategies of Reciprocal Teaching. When guiding students, use Tips for Direct Explanation, below.

Figure 7Q shows a transcript of a Reciprocal Teaching dialogue conducted by fourth graders; the students took turns serving as the student leader. Keep in mind that Comprehension Monitoring (see page 197) can be used to help students learn the clarification portion of Reciprocal Teaching.

Tips for Direct Explanation

- Provide an explanation of a strategy when necessary (e.g., "Remember, a summary is a short version of the text. It does not include too many details, just the main idea.").

- Prompt students when necessary by asking them, "What question do you think a teacher might ask?"

- Allow for modification of the strategy. Tell students, for example, "If you are unable to summarize, think of a question first."

- Ask for peer responses by saying, "Who can help with this one?"

- Encourage group members to add supplemental information.

Reciprocal Teaching

THE STORY OF THE FIRST AMERICANS

Prediction:	Student Leader (Sarah):	My prediction is the first Americans lived long ago.
	All:	(read text)
Summary:	Student Leader (Sarah):	Our country's history tells how the country and the people have changed over time.
Question:	Student Leader:	What tells us about our country's past?
	Student 2:	I'm not sure what you mean.
	Student Leader:	It's a story about the past.
	Student 2:	History
Question:	Student Leader:	True or false: Our country has changed.
	Student 3:	True
Question:	Student Leader:	Does anybody need clarification?
	All:	No
Prediction:	Student Leader (Donal):	My prediction for the next part of the text is: It is a story about the first Americans.
	All:	(read text)
Summary:	Student Leader:	The first Americans were Indians. They lived in groups. One group was the Sioux.
Question:	Student Leader:	Who were the first Americans?
	Student 3:	Indians
Question:	Student Leader:	Were there many Indian groups?
	Student 1:	Yes
Question:	Student Leader:	Where did the Sioux Indians live?
	Student 3:	On the plains.
Clarification:	Student Leader:	Does anybody need clarification?
	Student 1:	Where are the plains?
	Student Leader:	The plains are flat lands out west.
Prediction:	Student Leader (Latrice):	My prediction for the next part of the text is: The Sioux were able to get food from the plains.
	All:	(read text)
Summary:	Student Leader:	The Sioux hunted animals for food and hides. They made clothes out of hides.
Question:	Student Leader:	How did the Sioux get food?
	Student 1:	They hunted buffalo.
Question:	Student Leader:	What did the Sioux make their clothes from?
	Student 2:	Hides
Clarification:	Student Leader:	Does anybody need me to explain?
	All:	No

A fourth-grade Reciprocal Teaching dialogue for a social studies unit

Learning Logs

Reciprocal Teaching gives students practice in a number of learning strategies that they will continue to use whenever they encounter expository text. However, since Reciprocal Teaching focuses on the language processes of reading, listening, and speaking, you might want to select an extension strategy that gives students a chance to integrate writing with the other language processes. Learning Logs (Pappas, Keiffer, & Levstick, 1990) is a strategy that does just that—allows students the opportunity to write about the content they're studying and connect it with information they already know. With Learning Logs, students list ideas that come out of the Reciprocal Teaching experience. They write freely (in the form of brief summaries) about what they've learned, concepts that confused them, and questions that they have developed during the Reciprocal Teaching. It is particularly appropriate to have students use Learning Logs after they have participated in Reciprocal Teaching. However, Learning Logs are a good choice for application/extension after any of the other comprehension strategies presented in this book.

Students can make process entries or reaction entries in their logs. Process entries require students to reflect on how they learned, while reaction entries focus on what they learned (Alvermann & Phelps, 1994). Some examples of the two different kinds of entries are shown in the box on the left.

The Learning Logs strategy provides a quick review of information that students have learned and thus helps them with the process of selecting and retaining information. It also helps them reflect on and synthesize information. Journal comments can be shared with classmates, and questions listed in the logs can be used for discussion.

PROCESS ENTRIES

What did I learn about this topic today?

What didn't I understand?

What questions do I have?

What are my predictions about a new topic?

REACTION ENTRIES

Summarize, analyze, synthesize, compare/contrast, evaluate an idea, topic or person.

Connect information with prior knowledge and experience.

Write letters to people, living or dead, historical or mythical, about the topic.

Respond to higher-order questions posed by the teacher.

Teaching the Strategy

- After students have finished Reciprocal Teaching (or another comprehension strategy), tell them that they are going to have a chance to write about what they learned or questions they have about the reading. Explain that you want them to keep a notebook that will be their journal for the year.

- Tell students they can write about things that demonstrate either how they've learned something or what they've learned from the Reciprocal Teaching experience. Model for the students how you would write a process entry and a reaction entry using a part of the Reciprocal Teaching text. Figure 7R shows two reaction entries.

- After the students finish writing in their logs, invite them to share their journal comments and questions with their classmates. Use their comments and questions as a springboard for discussion.

- Regularly review student logs to have an idea of what is and what isn't working for individual students and the class. You can respond to log entries in a number of ways, ranging from a check mark or a marginal note to an ongoing dialogue with the students. If you use the log to carry on a dialogue, the strategy becomes a reading activity as well as a writing one.

In addition to sharing journal comments and questions with classmates, log entries can be shared with parents to communicate topics that are being covered in school.

FIGURE 7R

Learning Log Entries

> Drugs
> Jacob
> Germs are litle things that can get into your body and make you sick. Vaccines are medicines that keep people from getting sick. If you take to much you mite git sick. Tell someone if your not feeling well.

> Drugs
> Emily
> Medicines
> I learned that some medicines are drugs. If you take the wrong medicines it will change some of your other body parts.

Two second graders' Learning Log entries for content material on the topic of drugs

ThinkingWorks Lesson Planning Guide

A number of strategies have been introduced in this chapter that will enable you to teach a complete lesson for expository text that focuses on the interpretation of text. Figure 7S shows two completed Thinking Works Lesson Planning Guides using strategies introduced in this chapter.

ThinkingWorks Lesson Planning Guides

	STRATEGIES			
	Background Knowledge	Vocabulary	Comprehension	Application/ Extension
COGNITIVE PROCESSES	Quickwriting/ Know. Rating Scale	Semantic Feature Analysis	Questioning Strategies	Four-Step Summary
Develop Background Knowledge	✔			
Expand Vocabulary Knowledge		✔		
Use Text Structure				
Set a Purpose for Learning	✔		✔	
Infer/Select Information			✔	
Create Images			✔	
Relate/Connect Ideas			✔	
Clarify/Monitor Understanding			✔	
Analyze			✔	✔
Synthesize			✔	✔
Evaluate/Justify			✔	
Create/Invent			✔	
LANGUAGE PROCESSES				
Read			✔	
Write	✔			✔
Listen/View		✔	✔	
Communicate Orally		✔	✔	
COGNITIVE PROCESSES	Quickwriting/ Know. Rating Scale	Semantic Feature Analysis	Reciprocal Teaching	Learning Logs
Develop Background Knowledge	✔			
Expand Vocabulary Knowledge		✔		
Use Text Structure				
Set a Purpose for Learning	✔		✔	
Infer/Select Information			✔	
Create Images			✔	
Relate/Connect Ideas			✔	
Clarify/Monitor Understanding			✔	
Analyze				✔
Synthesize				✔
Evaluate/Justify				✔
Create/Invent				
LANGUAGE PROCESSES				
Read				
Write	✔			✔
Listen/View		✔	✔	
Communicate Orally		✔	✔	

CHAPTER 8

Assessment of ThinkingWorks Strategies

In Chapters 2 through 7, we provide brief descriptions of assessment options for the strategies in the ThinkingWorks lessons. In this chapter we discuss how to apply the performance-based assessment measures of rubrics, checklists, and observation notes to ThinkingWorks strategies for both narrative and expository text. In addition, we provide a brief overview of how to use portfolios.

Performance-Based Assessment of Reading and Writing

One area in which there has been significant educational reform in the last decade is assessment. The notion that standardized or classroom tests are sufficient for documenting student learning and achievement has been replaced with an emphasis on the cyclical and dynamic process of diagnosis (assessing, planning, teaching). By systematically and consistently using multiple authentic, performance-based measures of assessment, teachers can construct an accurate picture of their students' strengths and weaknesses to plan and implement appropriate instruction.

For example, a teacher can create a checklist of important concepts he wants students to learn in a social studies unit. As students demonstrate their understanding of a concept through their contributions to class discussion, their participation in group work, and their performance on writing assignments and quizzes, the teacher can check it off. At a glance, then, he can see who has mastered what content and which students need additional instruction in certain areas. Similarly, observation notes taken as students perform a science experiment can help a teacher evaluate content learned as well as students' abilities to make hypotheses and interpret data. The teacher can then use this information to determine the instructional focus of her next science lesson. Finally, a rubric applied to a RAFT letter in language arts class gives insight into a student's writing ability. Using the same rubric to evaluate several pieces during a grading period can demonstrate student progress. These three assessments, applied to various work products over time (e.g., a quarter), provide teachers with formative data to shape instruction and summative data to obtain grades.

Writing summaries is one essential task that allows teachers to assess students' comprehension. Once students have been taught how to compose a summary, and have had plenty of practice doing so (see page 194), you can use checklists and rubrics to assess written summaries. A checklist of the main ideas and key details in a text provides a guideline for teachers to examine content information in a summary. A number of graphic organizers (such as Story Grammar formats and About Point Notetaking) introduced in this book can be used as the basis of checklists for evaluating students' comprehension. Rubrics, on the other hand, are used to assess the mechanics of writing as well as students' content knowledge and ability to organize information. Checklists and rubrics can also be used to assess the comprehension of younger students, who may present their summaries orally or in writing. Summaries provide insight into students' understanding of vocabulary and sentence structure in addition to their comprehension. This insight can inform subsequent instruction. Student contributions to discussion are best evaluated with observation notes, discussed later in this chapter. (We have included several references on assessment in the reference section at the end of the book.)

THE ROLE OF CLASSROOM TESTS

How do classroom tests fit into performance-based assessment? Because of their practical nature, classroom tests will always be a part of assessment. In order to support performance-based assessment of reading and writing, however, Tierney (1998) suggests that tests should match instructional goals and give students the opportunity to construct meaning and think critically about the information. To accomplish this, test formats must allow students to develop their ideas in writing and to elaborate on their thinking. Untimed tests encourage students to think and respond fully to questions. As with the other types of performance-based assessments, tests should provide you with accurate information about student progress.

Young students may respond orally to "test questions" during individual reading conferences. Checklists and rubrics can also be adjusted to include a reduced number of items to evaluate the progress of young students. For example, a checklist for a younger student might include only a few statements related to the beginning, middle, and end of a reading. Similarly, a rubric might focus on only a few items to assess the mechanics of writing, such as capitalization and use of end punctuation.

Using rubrics, checklists, and observation notes in addition to classroom tests provides a well-rounded portrait of student achievement. These tools also give feedback on teaching practices, helping you select strategies to meet student needs in subsequent lessons. The next section discusses each of the performance-based assessment tools in more detail.

RUBRICS

A rubric is a point scale that represents the different levels of proficiency along a continuum. Rubrics can be used to evaluate any student work, from a summary to a poster to an oral presentation. An example of a rubric is the Holistic Scoring Rubric for Writing (Figure 8A). It shows the criteria for evaluating student work at five levels, from that of highest quality (Level 4) to that of minimal quality (Level 0). The scorer— either the teacher or the student—compares the work being evaluated to the descriptions in the rubric. The criteria serve as guidelines for helping students and teachers understand what is expected for high-quality work and what students need to be thinking about in order to improve their writing. In addition, rubrics help you to

Holistic Scoring Rubric for Writing

	CONTENT	ORGANIZATION	LANGUAGE USE	MECHANICS
LEVEL 4	Response clearly states and focuses on the topic, clearly addresses the purpose, and provides sufficient supporting details (well-developed writing).	Logical organizational pattern that displays a sense of flow and coherence; ideas relate to each other and the writing expresses a sense of completeness.	Uses vocabulary and writing style which is appropriate to the subject, purpose, and audience; uses complete sentences of varied length and structure.	Demonstrates correct usage, punctuation, capitalization, and spelling.
LEVEL 3	Response is related to the topic, generally addresses the purpose, and contains adequate supporting details.	Logical organizational patterns that display a sense of flow and completeness, although paragraphs may not be fully organized or there may be breaks in information.	Generally uses vocabulary and writing style which are appropriate to the subject, purpose, and audience. Sentences are somewhat varied in length and type. Complete sentences are used but some errors in sentence structure may occur but do not inhibit communication.	Demonstrates usage, punctuation, capitalization, and spelling. Errors may occur but do not interfere with communication.
LEVEL 2	Response indicates an awareness of the topic but may include loosely related or extraneous material. Writer attempts to address the purpose and includes some supporting details.	Attempts to use an organizational pattern but has little sense of flow or completeness.	Uses limited vocabulary, which may not be appropriate to the audience, purpose or subject. There is little attempt to vary writing style and errors in sentence structure and usage may affect communication.	Attempts to use punctuation, capitalization, and the correct spelling of common words.
LEVEL 1	Response is only slightly related to the topic and provides few supporting details. It may or may not address the purpose.	There is little evidence of an organizational pattern.	Uses limited or inappropriate vocabulary that reflects little awareness of audience, purpose, or subject. Communication of ideas is affected. There is little attempt to vary writing style according to purpose and there are errors in structure that impede readability.	Demonstrates little knowledge of usage, punctuation, capitalization, and spelling.
LEVEL 0	Used if there is no response or if the response is unreadable or off topic.			

monitor your students' growth in writing, to determine your students' strengths and weaknesses, and to guide students in performing self-evaluations.

Providing students with rubrics before beginning assignments gives them a focus for learning. They know what is expected of them before they begin their work. It is also a good idea to have students participate in the construction of rubrics. Developing rubrics with students helps them monitor their learning, value the activity, and accept responsibility for completing assignments carefully.

CHECKLISTS

Another form of assessment that can be used to evaluate students' growth is the checklist. Checklists can help you

1. assess student work;

2. record student attainment of grade-level competencies or state learning outcomes; and

3. evaluate your instruction.

Checklists differ from rubrics in that there are no levels of proficiency; the only criterion for assessment is the presence or absence of a competency or an element of a strategy.

Checklists are an effective way of judging whether a student has completed all the necessary parts of a specific work product appropriately. For example, a checklist for a Character Sketch would include all of the required parts, namely a title, topic sentence, three details, and a closing (see the checklist in Figure 8B). We recommend providing space for both the student and teacher to respond. Once students have evaluated their work, you can check it using the same checklist. You can give a point for each element completed, and the points are added up to provide a score, as seen in Figure 8B.

You can also use checklists to record student progress toward standards or benchmarks. For this type of checklist, enter national, state, or district standards in a column, putting your students' names in rows across the top. For each standard, record your assessment of the level of student achievement by using a coding system such as B (Beginning), D (Developing), and S (Secure). Base the level on your assessment of the work students have done during the grading period. Figure 8C shows a partial checklist of state standards in language arts that has been completed for five students.

You can also use checklists of standards as a way of documenting your instruction. Checklists of skills in the various content areas can be aligned with the ThinkingWorks strategies. For example, Figure 8D shows a checklist that matches fourth-grade state standards in language arts to the strategies in a four-part

ThinkingWorks lesson consisting of an Anticipation Guide, Concept of a Definition, I-Chart, and Four-Step Summary. Note that the teacher has checked off the reading outcomes that the strategies help students accomplish. This is a powerful way of showing that what you are teaching is promoting students' achievement of outcomes specified by your state or district. Each time you teach a ThinkingWorks lesson, check the skills that the strategies promote and, in that way, you will be recording the number and variety of ways an outcome has been taught. You can then share with other teachers or administrators how state learning outcomes are addressed in your daily lessons.

Finally, you can use the ThinkingWorks Lesson Planning Guide as a checklist to determine the types of cognitive processes that you have taught in a lesson with the four strategy components. Two examples of Lesson Planning Guides are included at the end of Chapters 2–7, one of which shows how substituting alternative strategies encourages the use of some different cognitive and language processes.

FIGURE 8B

Character Sketch and Checklist

STUDENT OUTLINE FOR CHARACTER SKETCH

Topic Sentence: Natasha was naughty because she wanted her grandmother to do everything for her when she was busy.

Babushka was washing the clothes but Natasha wanted to swing.

Babushka was feeding the goats. Natasha was hungry and wanted to each lunch.

Babushka was hanging up clothes but Natasha wanted a ride.

Closing: Natasha was not thoughtful.

STUDENT CHARACTER SKETCH

Natasha was naughty because she wanted her grandmother to do everything for her when she was busy. Babushka was washing the clothes but Natasha wanted to swing. Babushka was hanging up clothes but Natasha wanted a ride. Babushka was feeding the goats. Natasha was hungry and wanted to each lunch. Natasha was not thoughtful.

COMPREHENSION CHECKLIST

	STUDENT	TEACHER
1. Title	____	____
2. Topic Sentence (About Point)	✔	✔
3. Three Supporting Details	✔	✔
4. Closing	✔	✔

Total Points: 3/4

A=   B=3/4   C=   D=   E=

Comments: A very nice job. Remember to include the title.

Student and teacher evaluated the Character Sketch with the teacher-created Comprehension Checklist.

Checklist Showing Student Progress on Fourth-Grade Academic Content Standards in Language Arts

	David	Tanya	Cody	Jenny	Carla
READING PROCESS: Concepts of Print, Comprehension Strategies, and Self-Monitoring Strategies					
Establish a purpose for reading, including to find out, to understand, to interpret, to enjoy and to solve problems.	B	D	D	D	S
Predict and support predictions using an awareness of new vocabulary, text structures and familiar plot patterns.	B	D	D	D	S
Compare and contrast information on a single topic or theme across different text and non-text resources.	B	D	D	D	D
Summarize important information in texts to demonstrate comprehension.	B	D	D	D	S
Make inferences or draw conclusions about what has been read and support those conclusions with textual evidence.	B	D	D	D	D
Select, create and use graphic organizers to interpret textual information.	B	D	D	D	D
Answer literal, inferential and evaluative questions to demonstrate comprehension of grade-appropriate print texts and electronic and visual media.	B	S	S	S	S
Monitor own comprehension by adjusting speed to fit the purpose, or by skimming, scanning, reading on or looking back.	D	D	D	S	S
List questions and search for answers within the text to construct meaning.	B	S	S	S	S
Use criteria to choose independent reading materials (e.g., personal interest, knowledge of authors and genres or recommendations from others).	B	S	D	S	S
Independently read books for various purposes (e.g., for enjoyment, for literary experience, to gain information or to perform a task).	B	S	S	S	S
READING APPLICATIONS: Informational, Technical, and Persuasive Text					
Make inferences about informational text from the title page, table of contents and chapter headings.	B	D	D	D	D
Summarize main ideas in informational text, using supporting details as appropriate.	B	D	D	D	S
Locate important details about a topic, using different sources of information, including books, magazines, newspapers and online resources.	B	D	D	D	D
Identify examples of cause and effect used in informational text.	B	D	D	D	D
Draw conclusions from information in maps, charts, graphs and diagrams.	B	D	D	D	D
Clarify steps in a set of instructions or procedures for completeness.	D	S	S	S	S
Distinguish fact from opinion.	D	S	S	S	S

Checklist Showing Student Progress on Fourth-Grade Academic Content Standards in Language Arts

	David	Tanya	Cody	Jenny	Carla
RESEARCH					
Identify a topic and questions for research and develop a plan for gathering information.	B	D	D	D	D
Locate sources and collect relevant information from multiple sources (e.g., school library catalogs, online databases, electronic resources and Internet-based resources).	B	S	S	S	S
Identify important information found in the sources and summarize important findings.	B	D	D	D	S
Create categories to sort and organize relevant information charts, tables or graphic organizers.	B	D	D	D	D
Discuss the meaning of plagiarism and create a list of sources.	D	D	S	S	S
Use a variety of communication techniques, including oral, visual, written or multimedia reports, to present information gathered.	D	S	S	S	S
WRITING APPLICATIONS					
Write narratives that sequence events, including descriptive details and vivid language to develop plot, characters and setting and to establish a point of view.	D	D	D	S	S
Write responses to novels, stories and poems that include a simple interpretation of a literary work and support judgments with specific references to the original text and to prior knowledge.	D	D	S	D	S
Write formal and informal letters (e.g., thank you notes, letters of request) that follow letter format (e.g., date, proper salutation, body, closing and signature), include important information and demonstrate a sense of closure.	D	S	S	S	S
Write informational reports that include facts and examples and present important details in a logical order.	D	D	D	D	S
Produce informal writings (e.g., messages, journals, notes and poems) for various purposes.	D	S	S	S	S

Checklist Showing ThinkingWorks Lesson Matched to Fourth-Grade Academic Content Standards in Language Arts

	Background Knowledge	Vocabulary	Comprehension	Application/ Extension
	Anticipation Guide	Concept of a Definition	I-Chart	Four-Step Summary
READING PROCESS: Concepts of Print, Comprehension Strategies, and Self-Monitoring Strategies				
Establish a purpose for reading, including to find out, to understand, to interpret, to enjoy and to solve problems.	✔		✔	
Predict and support predictions using an awareness of new vocabulary, text structures and familiar plot patterns.	✔	✔		
Compare and contrast information on a single topic or theme across different text and non-text resources.			✔	
Summarize important information in texts to demonstrate comprehension.			✔	✔
Make inferences or draw conclusions about what has been read and support those conclusions with textual evidence.	✔		✔	
Select, create and use graphic organizers to interpret textual information.			✔	
Answer literal, inferential and evaluative questions to demonstrate comprehension of grade-appropriate print texts and electronic and visual media.			✔	
Monitor own comprehension by adjusting speed to fit the purpose, or by skimming, scanning, reading on or looking back.			✔	
List questions and search for answers within the text to construct meaning.			✔	
Use criteria to choose independent reading materials (e.g., personal interest, knowledge of authors and genres or recommendations from others).			✔	
Independently read books for various purposes (e.g., for enjoyment, for literary experience, to gain information or to perform a task).			✔	
READING APPLICATIONS: Informational, Technical, and Persuasive Text				
Make inferences about informational text from the title page, table of contents and chapter headings.			✔	
Summarize main ideas in informational text, using supporting details as appropriate.			✔	✔
Locate important details about a topic, using different sources of information, including books, magazines, newspapers and online resources.			✔	
Identify examples of cause and effect used in informational text.				
Draw conclusions from information in maps, charts, graphs and diagrams.				
Clarify steps in a set of instructions or procedures for completeness.				
Distinguish fact from opinion.			✔	

Checklist Showing ThinkingWorks Lesson Matched to Fourth Grade Academic Content Standards in Language Arts

	Background Knowledge	Vocabulary	Comprehension	Application/ Extension
	Anticipation Guide	Concept of a Definition	I-Chart	Four-Step Summary
RESEARCH				
Identify a topic and questions for research and develop a plan for gathering information.			✔	
Locate sources and collect relevant information from multiple sources (e.g., school library catalogs, online databases, electronic resources and Internet-based resources).			✔	
Identify important information found in the sources and summarize important findings.			✔	✔
Create categories to sort and organize relevant information charts, tables or graphic organizers			✔	
Discuss the meaning of plagiarism and create a list of sources.				
Use a variety of communication techniques, including oral, visual, written or multimedia reports, to present information gathered.			✔	✔
WRITING APPLICATIONS				
Write narratives that sequence events, including descriptive details and vivid language to develop to develop plot, characters and setting and to establish a point of view.				
Write responses to novels, stories and poems that include a simple interpretation of a literary work and support judgments with specific references to the original text and to prior knowledge.				
Write formal and informal letters (e.g., thank you notes, letters of request) that follow letter format (e.g., date, proper salutation, body, closing and signature), include important information and demonstrate a sense of closure.				
Write informational reports that include facts and examples and present important details in a logical order.			✔	✔
Produce informal writings (e.g., messages, journals, notes and poems) for various purposes.				

OBSERVATION NOTES

Observation notes can informally document students' performance as they work individually, in small groups, or as part of the class. This form of assessment is particularly useful for discussion or group work. Taken regularly during the year, the notes can give insight about a student's progress, helping you determine whether that student has attained a certain skill, such as making inferences or activating background knowledge. Figure 8E shows a chart of a teacher's observation notes made for four students as they participated in a ThinkingWorks narrative lesson. Observation notes may also be made for only a portion of a lesson—for example, the comprehension section.

FIGURE 8E

Observation Notes for a Narrative Lesson

LESSON

B Background Knowledge: Semantic Map
V Vocabulary: Concept Circles
C Comprehension: Story Grammar/Summary
A Application/Extension: Literary Report Card/Character Sketch

Date: January 10   Class: Reading

Carlos

B did not contribute

V understood antonyms, synonyms — did not use

C partial understanding of Story Grammar

A Enjoyed Literary Report Card — justified response
no topic sentence or closing in Character Sketch

Maya

B gave examples of naughty

V contributed synonym

C related story sequentially

A gave appropriate grades with justification complete Character Sketch

Latisha

B contributed examples

V low vocabulary, did not use vocabulary in oral or written language

C gave major events in order

A partial support of grades
copied list of responsibilities
no paragraph

Terri

B gave example of naughty

V understood naughty — knew no antonyms or synonyms

C couldn't identify the problem

A had difficulty with grading and support
wrote one example of responsibility

In making observation notes, you need to consider the practical issues of how to record notes while teaching. You may decide to observe only one or a few students during any particular lesson. Then in subsequent lessons you can observe others. We suggest that you record and organize your observations on a chart that you've prepared for one student or several students, as seen in Figure 8E. You can then use information on the chart to help you determine students' progress in achieving standards or benchmarks in language arts and various content areas (see Figure 8C). Your notes will help you decide what skills students need to develop or refine and what corresponding strategies will provide them with skill-building opportunities.

Using Checklists and Rubrics to Evaluate Comprehension and Writing

Checklists, rubrics, and observation notes are invaluable tools for assessing student achievement in reading and writing. However, they do not always translate easily into traditional grades (Tierney, 1998). This next section discusses how to use the data gained through performance-based assessments to assign students grades as required by most schools. In addition, we present the idea of using a portfolio to collect and showcase student work.

EVALUATING COMPREHENSION OF NARRATIVE TEXT: AN EXAMPLE

You can use rubrics and checklists to evaluate students' comprehension with any of the strategies described in this book (e.g., Circle Story, Story Pyramid, or Plot Relationships Chart). For demonstration purposes, we have chosen the Story Grammar (see page 45) for our example.

Comprehension

The following procedure is designed especially for older students. To adapt it for younger students, simply complete the steps with them. You could also have them complete a simple Story Grammar or do an oral summary from a Circle Story.

EVALUATING THE STRATEGY

- After students have read the story, have them complete their own Story Grammar, as described on page 45.

- Have students write a summary of the story using their Story Grammar.

- Construct a Story Grammar of your own, which you can use whenever you teach that particular story.

- Using your Story Grammar as a checklist, check off the parts of the Story Grammar that students have included in their summaries.

- Assign each student a comprehension score—for example, 6 out of 8, or 75%. You can then record this score as a grade for the assignment.

Figure 8F shows how a teacher-constructed Story Grammar and a comprehension checklist have been used to obtain a score for a first-grade student's summary of *Babushka's Doll*. The teacher indicated with an "X" that the story element or event from her Story Grammar is present in the student's summary. This same assessment procedure—creating a checklist based on your own version of the graphic organizer—will work with any other strategy. You can also evaluate a student's comprehension by applying these checklists to a written summary or an oral retelling of a story.

FIGURE 8F

Story Grammar Outline, Student Summary, and Checklist for *Babushka's Doll*

TEACHER-CONSTRUCTED STORY GRAMMAR

CHARACTERS: Babushka, Natasha, Babushka's doll

SETTING: Babushka's house and yard

PROBLEM: Natasha thinks only of what she wants and demands Babushka's attention

EVENTS:

1. Natasha demanded that Babushka play with her and make her lunch even though Babushka had work to do.
2. After lunch, Babushka gave Natasha a doll to play with while she went out.
3. The doll came alive and demanded that Natasha play with her and make her lunch even though she was tired.
4. While eating, the doll made a mess so Natasha had to wash and iron her dress.
5. The doll complained and Natasha cried.
6. Babushka returned home and told Natasha she probably had a bad dream.
7. Natasha decided not to play with the doll again and Babushka returned it to the shelf.

ENDING: Natasha turned out to be a nice girl.

COMPREHENSION CHECKLIST

Characters: **X**

Setting:

Events:

1. **X**
2. **X**
3. **X**
4.
5.
6.
7.

Ending: **X**

Score: 5/10

STUDENT SUMMARY

Gramdma was doing wrok and Natasha whats to play. Gramdma said wait. Natasha said now. Then Gramdma went to the stor and Natasha waned to play with the doll. The doll rushed Natasha. At the End Natasha lured not to rush peopol. The End.

The Comprehension Checklist was created from the teacher-written Story Grammar; the student summary on the bottom was evaluated and scored with the checklist.

Evaluating Writing

To derive a writing score from summaries written for the comprehension assessment, encourage students to revise their summaries based on the feedback you gave them from your checklist. In addition, remind them to edit and proofread their work to get it ready for publication. "Publishing" a story can include sharing a final draft with the teacher or class or displaying it in a portfolio. Students will then have a polished piece for which you can assign a writing score by using the Holistic Scoring Rubric for Writing (Figure 8A). Because students have had a chance to revise their writing, it would be appropriate to assign a grade based upon the score (e.g., Level 3 = B).

You can also separate the writing assessment from the comprehension assessment by implementing the following procedure.

• Give students a copy of the Holistic Scoring Rubric for Writing and review the levels with them, discussing each area (Content, Organization, Language Use, and Mechanics). If they have had no experience evaluating a piece of writing with a rubric, have them practice on writing samples that you've prepared. Direct students to determine how the piece ranks in each of the four categories; have them discuss their decisions and how the writer could have improved the piece. Students can also volunteer to revise their work for the class on an overhead, modeling how to make changes and corrections to meet the criteria in the rubric.

• Have the students apply the Holistic Scoring Rubric to their summaries to ensure they have included appropriate content, organized their ideas, varied their language use and sentence construction, and applied all conventions of writing. If you wish, you can check the students' summaries and their scores and assign a grade for their writing product.

Figure 8G is an example of a holistic score for a first grader's summary of *Babushka's Doll*. It is important to remember that holistic scoring emphasizes the

---

Holistic Writing Assessment for Summary of *Babushka's Doll*

SUMMARY

Gramdma was doing wrok and Natasha whats to play. Gramdma said wait. Natasha said now. Then Gramdma went to the stor and Natasha waned to play with the doll. The doll rushed Natasha. At the End Natasha lured not to rush peopol. The End.

HOLISTIC WRITING ASSESSMENT

	Writing
Content	2
Organization	3
Language Use	3
Mechanics	2
	10/4 = 2.5 = 3

---

overall impression of the writing and not the parts. Tell students—and then keep reminding them—that their writing may contain mistakes in any of the four areas, but their mistakes do not limit the overall effect of their message. The areas, or levels, of the rubric are not meant to be rigid criteria but simply to be guidelines that remind students what they need to do in order to write well. You can simplify the writing requirements for young students by using the rubric shown in Figure 8H (Schaefer, 2001).

FIGURE 8H

Early Literacy Writing Assessment

	EXCELLENT	GOOD	NEEDS WORK
MEANING	Reader or listener can understand all of the writing.	Reader or listener can understand some of the writing.	Reader or listener is confused and cannot understand the writing.
FOCUS	All writing stays on one topic.	Some of the writing stays on one topic.	Reader or listener cannot find the one topic of the writing.
VOCABULARY	Writing has three GREAT words.	Writing has two GREAT words.	Writing has one GREAT word.

A simple rubric appropriate for using with young students

EVALUATING COMPREHENSION OF EXPOSITORY TEXT: AN EXAMPLE

As is the case with narrative text, we have chosen to use certain strategies—About Point Notetaking and Frames—to demonstrate the application of rubrics and checklists for evaluating students' comprehension and writing in conjunction with expository text.

Comprehension

To evaluate students' comprehension of expository text, apply the same procedure as outlined for narrative text, but use a strategy outline appropriate for expository text.

- Complete a frame (e.g., descriptive, sequence, compare/contrast, cause/effect, or problem/solution; see pages 146–154) with the students after they have read the material.

- Have your students use the frame to write a summary of the information.

- Construct an About Point Notetaking outline which you can use whenever you teach that particular piece of text (see page 134).

FIGURE 81

About Point Notetaking Outline, Student Summary and Checklist for The Oregon Trail

TEACHER-CONSTRUCTED ABOUT POINT NOTE-TAKING OUTLINE

About Point: The Oregon Trail was the highway to the West.

1. The 2,000 mile trail began in Missouri and ended in Oregon or California.
2. It takes four to five months moving 15 to 20 miles a day to travel through Colorado, Utah, Wyoming, and Idaho to complete the journey.
3. The trail is rough and grassy and often surrounded by trees.
4. Steep mountain passes running along the Platte River make the trail difficult to follow.

About Point: Crossing the Oregon Trail caused many hardships for the pioneers.

1. Rough river crossings, fires, and mountains caused problems.
2. Robbers, animals, and Indians attacked the travelers.
3. Difficult weather conditions also caused problems.

4. Cholera spread easily.
5. One in 17 died on the journey.

About Point: Pioneers brought mostly necessities on their journey.

1. Limited space dictated essentials for travel: cooking supplies, water, tools, animals
2. Some heirlooms were carried.
3. Wagons were full of supplies for travel and life out West.

About Point: Pioneers had a variety of tasks to ensure a successful trip.

1. People traveled in a group or train for safety.
2. The captain of the train made decisions that all were required to follow or leave the train.
3. At their destination, men and boys made camp until they built a home.
4. Men provided food by hunting and planting crops.
5. Everyone worked to take care of the animals.

COMPREHENSION CHECKLIST FROM OUTLINE

About Point	✔	
Details	1.	✔
	2.	✔
	3.	✔
	4.	✔
About Point	✔	
Details	1.	✔
	2.	
	3.	✔
	4.	✔
	5.	✔
About Point	✔	
Details	1.	✔
	2.	✔
	3.	✔
About Point	✔	
Details	1.	✔
	2.	✔
	3.	✔
	4.	✔
	5.	✔

About Points 4/4
Details: 16/17

STUDENT SUMMARY

Most people traveled the Oregon Trail out West. Many people said it starts in Missouri. It is two thousand miles long. It ended in Oregon or California. There are four different states the trail goes through Colorado, Utah, Wyoming, and Idaho. It usually takes four to five months. They always travel fifteen to twenty miles a day. Sometimes on flat areas the trail would be twenty miles wide. Most of the trail is really rough and grassy. One of the rivers that runs a long way is the Platte River. Very often there are trees. They had to go through very steep mountain passes. That is what the Oregon Trail looks like.

Many people had many hardships. Pioneers say it is really hard crossing rivers. There were really bad fires long the trail. Weather was often bad. If they left to early there wagon would get stuck. They would have to push the wagons up the mountains. If there was one little mistake the wagon ran away down the hill. One out of seventeen died. Many

people died of the disease cholera. Abandoned wagons meant dead people.

Many people brought there heirlooms. Pioneers had to bring their needs. Coal, sleeping stuff, and cooking supplies were needed for the trip. Wash items, water and tools were also needed. Two horses, one cow and flour was needed. Cornmeal and sugar were used for cooking. When they left the wagon would be full.

Pioneers did a lot of things. They have to travel in groups which is called a train. There was a captain who had to make decisions, and if someone did not agree they would have to split up. When they got to where they wanted to settle they would have to make camp. Then they would have to build their home. Now the boys and the men would have to plant crops. Men hunted a lot. Everybody needs to help take care of the farm animals. Men also had to deliver baby animals and humans. That is all about the Oregon Trail.

- Using your About Point Notetaking outline as a checklist, check off the information the students included in their summaries.

- Assign each student a comprehension score which can also be used as a grade for that work product.

Figure 8I is an example of how an About Point Notetaking outline and a comprehension checklist have been used to obtain a score for a student summary about the Oregon Trail. This assessment procedure can be implemented with any of the frames used to help students understand expository text.

Evaluating Writing

As is the case with students' narrative summaries, you can obtain a writing score for summaries of expository text by having students revise their work. They will then have a polished piece that you can score using the Holistic Scoring Rubric for Writing. You can assign students a grade for their revised summary (see Figure 8J).

If you would like a writing score separate from the comprehension score, you can implement the following procedure:

- Give students a copy of the Holistic Scoring Rubric for Writing and review the levels with them, discussing each area (Content, Organization, Language Use, and Mechanics). If they have had no experience evaluating a piece of writing with a rubric, have them practice on writing samples that you've prepared. Direct students to determine how the piece ranks in each of the four categories; have them discuss their decisions and how the writer could have improved the piece. Students can also volunteer to revise their work for the class on an overhead, modeling how to make changes and corrections to meet the criteria in the rubric.

- Have the students apply the Holistic Scoring Rubric to their summaries to ensure they have included appropriate content, organized their ideas, varied their language use and sentence construction, and applied all conventions of writing. If you wish, you can check the students' summaries and their scores and assign a grade for their writing product.

FIGURE 8J

Holistic Writing Assessment for Summary About The Oregon Trail

	WRITING
CONTENT	4
ORGANIZATION	5
LANGUAGE USE	3
MECHANICS	4

$$10/4 = 2.5 = 3$$

This figure shows how the Oregon Trail Summary from Figure 8I was scored with the Holistic Scoring Rubric (see page 206). With younger children, you will have to complete the frame with them and help them apply an easier form of the writing rubric.

PORTFOLIOS

Portfolios are collections of student work, selected by students and teacher to demonstrate student growth and progress. Reviewing the portfolio is an excellent opportunity for student self-evaluation and teacher assessment. Portfolios are also useful for discussing students' work and progress with parents and administrators. Farr (1992) notes three qualities that make using portfolios successful:

1. the portfolio belongs to the individual students—they should have some choice in deciding what goes into the portfolio;

2. the teacher's role in portfolio development is that of a facilitator who helps the student select work for inclusion; and

3. the portfolio should contain numerous and varied pieces written and revised in response to reading.

Examples of work samples are written responses to questions, learning logs, journals, summaries, creative writing, graphic organizers, study guides, and the results of a variety of comprehension and vocabulary activities. Portfolios represent work collected over time, so they demonstrate a student's growth in particular areas and provide direction for instruction. Work may be kept in folders or binders or even transferred to computer discs to show progress over time.

We do not recommend grading portfolios. Because of the unique and diverse nature of the work gathered, the value of portfolios can be easily diminished if they are graded or graded inappropriately, either without any student input or without consideration for diversity and richness (Tierney, 1998). Portfolios and self-evaluations provide valuable information about students that, used along with test grades and informal comprehension and writing grades, will result in a complete picture of students' performance and progress.

The assessment methods described in this chapter will help you evaluate the effectiveness of your instruction and identify students' needs and strengths. The next chapter shows how teachers put it all together—develop four-part lesson plans and use assessments to evaluate the lessons and inform their instruction.

CHAPTER 9

Putting It All Together

The ThinkingWorks framework allows teachers to plan a lesson consisting of a variety of strategies for helping students comprehend text and apply what they have learned. Students will benefit most from a lesson that includes each of the four components of the ThinkingWorks framework: background knowledge, vocabulary, comprehension, and application/extension. In addition, students should always have an opportunity to write during a lesson. But there is virtually no limit on the combination of strategies you can use; the framework is a flexible tool that helps you address the particular needs of your students.

This chapter presents lessons created by teachers learning to use the ThinkingWorks framework over the course of a school year. As they taught the lessons, the teachers reflected upon why they chose to combine certain strategies, how the strategies and the lesson worked in their classroom, and what aspects of the strategies needed to be adapted for their particular situation. We share their stories here to show how the pieces of the ThinkingWorks framework come together in powerful lessons for all grade levels and across content areas.

A Kindergarten Science Lesson

Primary grade teachers will most likely adapt the ThinkingWorks strategies so their students can perform successfully. Doing a lot of modeling, group work, and having students talk through the strategies are all effective ways of helping young students begin to think critically. This section presents a science lesson on dinosaurs that implements the strategies in an appropriate way for kindergartners.

Holly Glassford was planning a lesson on dinosaurs, with a particular emphasis on Tyrannosaurus Rex. To accomplish the goals of her lesson, she selected the following strategies from the ThinkingWorks framework:

BACKGROUND KNOWLEDGE: . . . . .Anticipation Guide

VOCABULARY: . . . . .Concept Circles

COMPREHENSION: . . . . .I-Chart

APPLICATION/EXTENSION: . . . . .RAFT and Friendly Letter

At first glance, these strategies might appear too difficult for kindergartners. However, Holly adapted the strategies so that her students were learning both content and ways of thinking successfully.

ANTICIPATION GUIDE

Holly began the lesson with an Anticipation Guide because she wanted to engage students in the topic and determine any preconceptions they may have had about Tyrannosaurus Rex. In addition, she wanted to revisit the guide later in the lesson to change students' misconceptions and provide a visual reminder of what they had learned.

Figure 9A shows how she adapted the Anticipation Guide strategy for her kindergartners. She used a computer to make separate pages for each statement she wanted students to consider. The key adaptation she made was to include pictures or drawings of a few words in each statement. She read each statement to the class and asked everyone to agree or disagree. Holly recorded how many agreed and how many disagreed and circled the majority opinion. Students were actively involved in reading since the statements consisted of pictures and drawings as well as words. After the lesson, students revisited the statements in the Anticipation Guide. They discussed what they had learned that related to them and voted whether to change them or not (see the *Yes* and *No* below the statements). Holly wrote the corrections on each of the pages, reinforcing important information for her students.

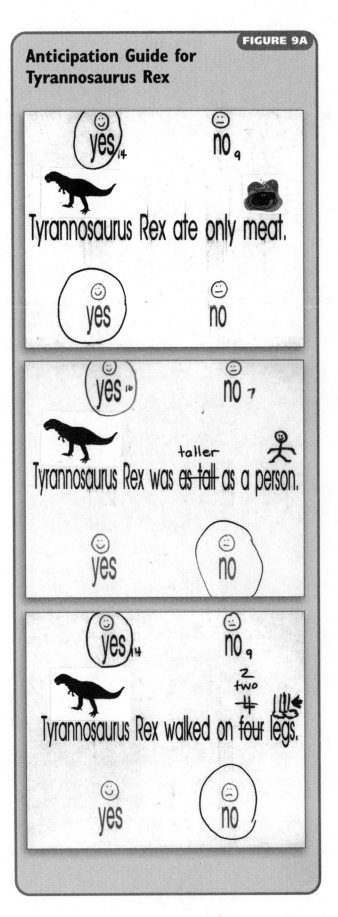

FIGURE 9A

Anticipation Guide for Tyrannosaurus Rex

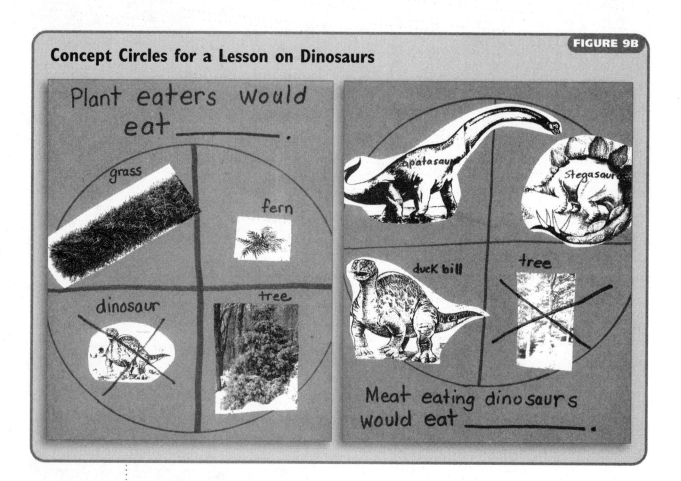

Concept Circles for a Lesson on Dinosaurs

Plant eaters would eat _____.

grass

fern

dinosaur

tree

apatasaur

Stegasaur

duck bill

tree

Meat eating dinosaurs would eat _____.

CONCEPT CIRCLES

To reinforce two key concepts in the lesson, *plant eater* and *meat eater*, Holly next used the vocabulary strategy Concept Circles. Figure 9B shows how she adapted it for her kindergartners. She labeled each circle with a sentence: *Plant eaters would eat _____. Meat eating dinosaurs would eat _____.* She then divided each circle into four sections. In each quadrant, she wrote a different food source and illustrated it with a picture from a magazine so students could read it easily. One of the words in each circle was incorrect. Holly asked students which food source did not belong in each circle. She crossed out the word. Holly reflected that, by using pictures in the circles, she ensured that her students would be able to participate in completing the strategy even if they had word recognition problems. The students were comfortable with the Concept Circle strategy and Holly could see ways to build on it throughout the year.

I-CHART WITH A CLASS BOOK

Holly used an I-Chart to teach her students how to organize and record the information that she read aloud to them from two books about dinosaurs (see the sources in the I-Chart in Figure 9C). Holly introduced the strategy to her class by displaying an

I-Chart on chart paper and writing the topic, Tyrannosaurus Rex, on it. She and the class developed questions that they wanted to answer about the dinosaur. Holly recorded the questions on the I-Chart. Then the class brainstormed information that they already knew about each question and Holly wrote that information on the chart. After listening to Holly read aloud from the two texts, students responded orally to the questions and Holly wrote their responses on the I-Chart. A major adaptation that Holly made was to have students contribute to a class book on what

I-Chart for Tyrannosaurus Rex

Topic: Tyrannosaurus Rex	Question #1 Can we go see one alive today?	Question #2 What did he eat?	Question #3 How did he walk?	Question #4 How tall was he?
What We Know:	No. The dinosaurs all died. (hot, meteoroid, cold)	He eats other animals.	He walks on legs.	He was big.
Source: A Picture Book of Dinosaurs by Claire Nemes	No. Tyrannosaurus died.	He ate only meat. Other dinosaurs.	He walked on two legs. He had very short arms.	He was as tall as a school bus is long.
Source: Tyrannosaurus by Janet Riehecky		Tyrannosaurus ate other dinosaurs.		

Pages From a Class Book About Tyrannosaurus Rex

Tyrannosaurs Rex walked on two feet.

A big rock came down out of the sky and made lots of clouds. It got cold. The dinosaurs didn't like cold. They died

they learned rather than write summaries. In this way, students summarized and synthesized information orally. Figure 9C shows the I-Chart that the class completed. Figure 9D shows one page from the class book called *Things We Learned about Tyrannosaurus Rex*. The children drew pictures of something they had learned during the lesson and dictated sentences to Holly, who added them to their drawing. Holly determined that the I-Chart helped students focus on what to look for in the books that they were reading about dinosaurs. The Class Book was an effective way of encouraging her students to share important information and begin summarizing.

RAFT AND FRIENDLY LETTER

RAFT was used to help students sum up the lesson on dinosaurs and ask some new questions that were raised after they had completed the I-Chart. This was the second time that Holly had asked students to use the RAFT technique. She noted that the first time, the students did not understand to whom they were writing. However, this time, the strategy worked better. As a group, students completed the four parts of the

---

RAFT and Friendly Letter
FIGURE 9E

R: Kindergarten Class
A: Paleontologist
F: Letter
T: Dinosaurs that lived in Toledo

Dear Paleontologist,

We read a lot of books about dinosaurs. We couldn't find a book about dinosaurs in Toledo. Do you know which dinosaurs lived in Toledo? We would like to see some dinosaur bones.

(Children's signatures)

Observation Notes for a Lesson on Dinosaurs
FIGURE 9F

Observation Notes for Anticipation Guide (two children)

B — Cody added information about another dinosaur that ate plants.
B — Kenesha was able to correct misinformation about the size and number of legs of the T Rex.

Observation Notes for the Complete Lesson (one child)

B — Anticipation Guide

Joshua was able to correct misinformation about the size and number of legs of the T Rex.

V — Concept Circles

He understood the distinction between meat and plant eaters.

C — I-Chart/Class Book

He listened attentively to informational text and completed his section of the Class Book. His sentence was clearly stated.

A — RAFT/Letter

He added ideas to the letter and remembered to capitalize the beginning of a sentence.

RAFT outline and dictated their letter to Holly. They were writing to a paleontologist to ask about the types of dinosaurs that once lived in their area; they had not discovered that information in any of the books they read. (See their outline and letter in Figure 9E.)

ASSESSMENT AND ACCOUNTABILITY

Holly made observation notes on several students throughout the lesson to gauge their ability to participate in class discussions. Holly noted that all three students she observed contributed to the class discussions. She concluded that the Anticipation Guide was particularly effective in stimulating discussion among her young students. (See samples of her notes in Figure 9F.) Figure 9G is a ThinkingWorks Lesson Planning Guide on which she recorded the cognitive and language processes that were covered in the lesson.

FIGURE 9G

ThinkingWorks Lesson Planning Guide —Kindergarten Science

	STRATEGIES			
	Background Knowledge	Vocabulary	Comprehension	Application/ Extension
COGNITIVE PROCESSES	Anticipation Guide	Concept Circles	I-Chart/ Class Book	RAFT/ Friendly Letter
Develop Background Knowledge	✔		✔	
Expand Vocabulary Knowledge		✔		
Use Text Structure				
Set a Purpose for Learning	✔		✔	
Infer/Select Information			✔	
Create Images			/✔	
Relate/Connect Ideas			✔	
Clarify/Monitor Understanding			✔	
Analyze			✔	✔
Synthesize				
Evaluate/Justify			✔	
Create/Invent				
LANGUAGE PROCESSES				
Read			✔	
Write			/✔	/✔
Listen/View	✔	✔	✔	✔
Communicate Orally	✔	✔	✔	✔

A First-Grade Science Lesson

In this lesson, students compared and contrasted mammals and reptiles. The lesson was planned to help students accomplish the following state standards in science:

- Use categories to organize a set of objects, organisms, or phenomena.

- Make observations and organize observations of an event, object, or organism.

- Understand the basic needs of living things.

- Classify living things.

First-grade teacher Verdell Battle selected the following strategies for her lesson:

BACKGROUND KNOWLEDGE: . . . . .Structured Overview

VOCABULARY: . . . . .Concept of a Definition

COMPREHENSION: . . . . .Descriptive Frame and Summary with Drawing

APPLICATION/EXTENSION: . . . . .Compare/Contrast Venn Diagram and Summary

She prepared a Structured Overview to build students' background knowledge about both types of animals. She then used the Concept of a Definition vocabulary strategy to reinforce students' understanding of the concepts *mammal* and *reptile*. To deepen their understanding of the characteristics of mammals and reptiles, Verdell used the descriptive frame with summary strategy. Half the class described mammals and half described reptiles. To extend students' learning, she had them complete a Venn Diagram about the animals and then write a compare/contrast summary.

STRUCTURED OVERVIEW

Verdell began the lesson by displaying a Structured Overview that showed the two habitats in which mammals and reptiles are found (see Figure 9H). She listed the types of animals under study at the top, with the two main habitats for each branching out beneath them. Finally, she listed examples of animals found in each habitat. This graphic representation helped students see that both mammals and reptiles are found on land and in water, an important concept she wanted students to grasp from this lesson. The overview was also used for review throughout and after the lesson.

Structured Overview on Mammals and Reptiles

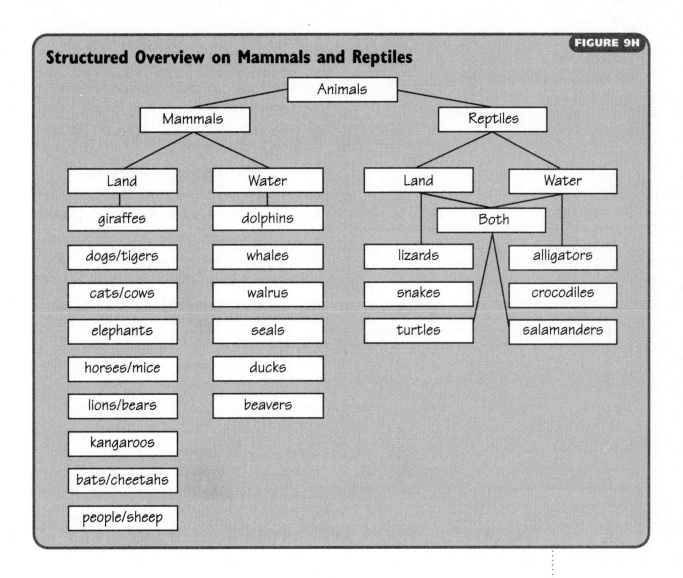

FIGURE 9I

Concept of a Definition for Mammals and Reptiles

Concept of a Definition

What is it? — mammal — What is it like?
an animal
warm blooded
has hair
or fur
backbone

What are examples?
dog cats
monkeys
tigers
cows
bats
dolphin
cheetahs

What is it? — reptile — What is it like?
an
animal
scaly skin
cold blooded

What are examples?
lizards
snakes
alligators
turtle
crocodiles

CONCEPT OF A DEFINITION

Verdell then used the Concept of a Definition strategy to help her students develop a complete definition of two key words in the lesson, *mammal* and *reptile*. Two of the three questions (*What is it?* and *What are some examples?*) were answered by having students refer to the Structured Overview, from which they could determine that each is a kind of animal. They also found examples on the Overview. Students were able to answer the third question (*What is it like?*) through a discussion Verdell led about the different characteristics of mammals and reptiles. For example, Verdell asked, "What do mammals such as cats, dogs, and monkeys have in common?" Students indicated that mammals have fur or hair. Verdell then explained additional characteristics such as "warm-blooded" and "have a backbone." Students completed Concept of a Definition during the discussion. Figure 9I shows how one student in the class completed the strategy.

DESCRIPTIVE FRAME AND SUMMARY WITH DRAWING

Verdell demonstrated how to create a descriptive frame by putting the topic in a circle in the center of a page and drawing lines radiating from it. She explained that students could write information that described the topic on the lines. She then told students that some of them were going to complete a frame on mammals and others were going to complete one on reptiles. To review the characteristics of mammals and reptiles, Verdell showed examples of animals in each category using sand pets, a type of small stuffed animal. Each time Verdell showed an animal, students explained what distinguished it as a mammal or a reptile. Verdell observed that students were excited and engaged during that part of the lesson.

Verdell then divided the class into groups, assigning each to focus on either mammals or reptiles. Students in each group discussed the information that they were going to include in their frame, and each student completed a descriptive frame for the type of animal his or her group discussed. Students also wrote a summary based on the information in their frame and included a drawing that illustrated their summary. Figure 9J shows one student's descriptive frame and summary for mammals. Her summary consists of text accompanied by an illustration of one mammal, a whale, in its habitat, the ocean.

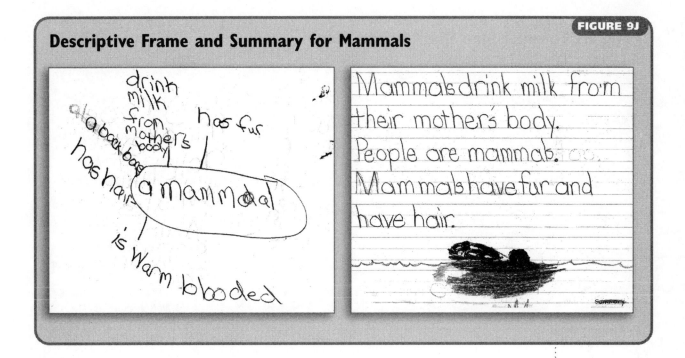

FIGURE 9J

Descriptive Frame and Summary for Mammals

drink milk from mothers body

has fur

a backbone

has hair

a mammal

is warm blooded

Mammals drink milk from their mother's body. People are mammals too. Mammals have fur and have hair.

COMPARE/CONTRAST VENN DIAGRAM AND SUMMARY

On a third day, Verdell asked students to apply what they had learned about reptiles and mammals by comparing and contrasting the two types of animals. She drew a Venn Diagram on chart paper and asked the class to contribute information for the different sections of the diagram. She wrote their responses on the chart and asked students to record the information on their charts. Then she asked students to write a summary of the similarities and differences between the two types of animals. She reminded them to write about the particular characteristics of mammals first, then about the characteristics of reptiles, and finally about the similarities between them. Figure 9K is another student's Venn diagram showing the similarities and differences between mammals and reptiles; it includes the summary the student wrote based on the information in her frame.

Verdell reflected that her first-grade students attained a high level of comprehension because they could follow the visual organization provided by the strategies used in the lesson—Structured Overview, Concept of a Definition, the Descriptive Frame, and the Venn Diagram. That structure helped them understand information, see relationships among concepts, and write about them.

Compare/Contrast Venn Diagram and Summary on Mammals and Reptiles

Mammals ①

warm blooded
have hair or fur
drink mother's milk
have backbones

living things
animals
live in water
live on land
need food
love

Reptiles ②

cold blooded
scaly skin
don't drink
mother's milk

③

Summary

Mammals are warm blooded. They have backbones and hair or fur. They drink their mother's milk. Reptiles are cold blood and have scaly skin. Mammals and reptiles are living things. They are animals that live on land and in water.

Obtaining a Grade for a Descriptive Summary of Mammals

STUDENT SUMMARY

Mammals drink milk from their mother's body. People are mammals. Mammals have fur and have hair.

WRITING SCORE

	Writing
Content	3
Organization	4
Language Use	4
Mechanics	4
	15/4 = 3.75 = Level 4

TEACHER-CREATED OUTLINE AND CHECKLIST

About Point: Mammals
are warm blooded animals. _____

1. nurse their young   ✔ _____

2. have backbones   _____

3. have hair or fur   ✔ _____

4. people are mammals   ✔ _____

Score: 3/5 = B

ASSESSMENT AND ACCOUNTABILITY

From this lesson, you could derive a writing score and/or a comprehension score from either the descriptive summary (see Figure 9J) or the compare/contrast summary (see Figure 9K). Verdell created an About Point Notetaking outline and comprehension checklist to evaluate students' descriptive summaries. To assess the writing, she used the Holistic Scoring Rubric for Writing (see page 206); that evaluation is also shown in Figure 9L. After reflecting on her evaluation of the student summaries, Verdell decided to discuss with her students the importance of including all important details in their writing. In Figure 9M, the ThinkingWorks Lesson Planning Guide shows the cognitive and language processes that were addressed in the lesson.

ThinkingWorks Lesson Planning Guide
—First-Grade Science

	STRATEGIES			
	Background Knowledge	Vocabulary	Comprehension	Application/ Extension
COGNITIVE PROCESSES	Structured Overview	Concept of a Definition	Descriptive Frame /Summary	C/C Venn Diag. /Summary
Develop Background Knowledge	✔			
Expand Vocabulary Knowledge	✔	✔		
Use Text Structure			✔	
Set a Purpose for Learning	✔		✔	
Infer/Select Information			✔	
Create Images			✔	
Relate/Connect Ideas			✔	
Clarify/Monitor Understanding			✔	
Analyze				✔
Synthesize				✔
Evaluate/Justify				
Create/Invent				
LANGUAGE PROCESSES				
Read			✔	
Write			I✔	I✔
Listen/View	✔	✔	✔	
Communicate Orally	✔	✔	✔	

A Second-Grade Lesson on The Bossy Gallito

In this lesson, students read a folk tale entitled *The Bossy Gallito* (Gonzales, 1999). The story is about a rooster, Gallito, who is bossy to everyone except his friend, the sun. In planning the lesson, Carolyn Nusbaum wanted her students to accomplish the following objectives:

• Understand vocabulary critical to the meaning of the text

• Analyze the text and determine sequence of events

• Demonstrate an understanding of the story by writing a retelling that stays on topic and includes supporting details

• Analyze the traits and actions of characters

She integrated the following ThinkingWorks strategies to meet the objectives.

BACKGROUND KNOWLEDGE: . . . . Semantic Map

VOCABULARY: . . . . Possible Sentences

COMPREHENSION: . . . . Story Grammar and Retelling

APPLICATION/EXTENSION: . . . . Literary Report Card

Carolyn first used a Semantic Map to activate students' background knowledge about roosters. Next, she introduced a vocabulary strategy, Possible Sentences, to involve students in defining and writing about words critical to understanding the story. Students then read *The Bossy Gallito* and, as a continuation of Possible Sentences, they looked for how the vocabulary words appeared in the context of the story. After reading, students completed the comprehension strategy, Story Grammar, as a class and revisited the vocabulary words by writing new sentences with them that reflected the content of the story. Finally, students analyzed the traits of the main character, Gallito, by doing the application/extension strategy, Literary Report Card.

SEMANTIC MAP

Carolyn believed that her students needed to know about roosters and their typical behaviors to understand the story. To determine how much they knew about roosters, she decided to complete a Semantic Map with her students. Together, they generated ideas about roosters, which she recorded on the map. Figure 9N shows the Semantic Map completed by the class as a group.

Based on the students' contributions to the Semantic Map, Carolyn realized that they had some knowledge about roosters. However, they did not understand that

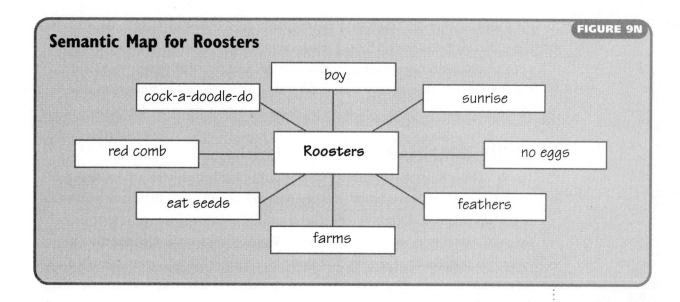

Semantic Map for Roosters

FIGURE 9N

- boy
- cock-a-doodle-do
- sunrise
- red comb
- **Roosters**
- no eggs
- eat seeds
- feathers
- farms

roosters are considered bossy, a character trait that is important in the story. Carolyn knew that her students were going to discuss the meaning of the word *bossy* as part of the vocabulary strategy, Possible Sentences, that she was teaching next. She decided that she would bring up the link between bossy and roosters just before students began reading the story. She also would explain that *Gallito* means *little rooster* in Spanish.

POSSIBLE SENTENCES

Carolyn selected six key vocabulary words she felt students needed to know to understand the text. She asked students to write Possible Sentences containing the words after she had introduced them and discussed their meanings. The activity demonstrated that students not only understood the gist of each word, but also were able to use them in sentences correctly (see Figure 9O). The activity also challenged students to incorporate the words into their personal vocabulary.

FIGURE 9O

Possible Sentences for
The Bossy Gallito

Vocabulary Words: bossy, pardon, scolded, elegant, demanded, quenched

Prereading Sentences:
1. My mom is bossy because she tells me what to do.
2. Pardon me for kicking you.
3. My dad scolded me for not cleaning my room.
4. Your dress is elegant because it is white.
5. I demanded my mom to get me candy.
6. I quenched because I was thirsty.

Postreading Sentences:
1. The bossy gallito demanded the grass to clean his beak.
2. The grass said pardon me I will clean your beak.
3. The gallito scold the stick for not hitting the goat.
4. The gallito looked elegant in his tuxedo.
5. The gallito demanded the fire to burn the stick.
6. The gallito told the water to quench the fire.

Carolyn reminded students to observe how the words were used in the story. Once they had read the story and completed the Story Grammar, she asked them to write another set of sentences with the words that reflected the story content. Carolyn felt that this strategy was useful because it encouraged students to show their understanding of the words by using them twice in original sentences.

STORY GRAMMAR AND RETELLING

Carolyn chose Story Grammar as a means of helping her students understand the story. She had used this strategy with previous stories and found that it was well-suited to her second graders' abilities. She also felt that this strategy was an effective one for a sequential story such as *The Bossy Gallito*. Her students completed the Story Grammar together after reading and then wrote their retellings independently. Figure 9P presents the Story Grammar completed by the whole class followed by one student's retelling. Note that the story outline contains only kernels of information since Carolyn wanted students to use their own words when writing their retellings.

Story Grammar and Retelling of *The Bossy Gallito*

STORY GRAMMAR

Characters: Rooster

Setting: city street before wedding

Events:

Rooster's beak dirty

Rooster tells grass clean beak

Rooster orders goat eat grass

Rooster scolded stick, hit goat

Rooster demanded fire burn stick

Rooster commanded water quench fire

Rooster ask politely sun dry water

Ending: All change mind, will do what Rooster wants—clean, late

RETELLING

There once was a rooster named Gallito. He was walking to his uncle's wedding. Gallito saw two kernels of corn in the mud. Gallito ate the corn and his beak got dirty. Gallito told the grass to clean his beak but the grass said no. Gallito ordered goat to eat the grass but the goat said no. Gallito scolded the stick to hit the goat but the stick said no. Gallito demanded the fire to burn the stick but the fire said no. Gallito commanded water to quench the fire but the water said no. Gallito asked the sun politely to dry up the water. The water said pardon me I will quench the fire. The fire said pardon me I will burn the stick. The stick said I will hit the goat. The goat said I will eat the grass. The grass said I will clean your beak. And so they did. Gallito was late for his uncle's wedding.

LITERARY REPORT CARD

For an application/extension activity, Carolyn chose Literary Report Card. She considered this a perfect strategy for her students to complete independently because the story focused on the rooster's traits and actions; character traits was a topic the class had discussed often. The strategy encouraged students to make judgments about the rooster and to support their decisions with evidence from the text. While students could easily identify traits and make judgments about the rooster, they had difficulty presenting evidence to support their opinions. Carolyn concluded that her students had not had enough practice validating their opinions and decided to work on the strategy in the future as a whole class, or in small groups, to provide more support for students so they would learn the skill.

Figure 9Q shows one student's completed Literary Report Card. For her second graders, Carolyn adapted the strategy, putting each character trait on a separate page so students had plenty of room to write their justification of the grade. She noted that for the trait "selfish" the student may have misunderstood the use of the report card and given Gallito a D+ because "selfish" is a negative trait. If indeed he was sometimes selfish, the grade may have been a C+ or a B-. Carolyn remarked that next time she would explain that even a negative trait such as selfishness requires a high grade if there is evidence that it is part of the character.

FIGURE 9Q

Literary Report Card for *The Bossy Gallito*

Literary Report Card

Character: Gallito

Subject: bossy   Grade: A-

Comments: Gallito got an A- because he is bossy and one time wasn't bossy. He asked the sun politely and didn't scold him.

Literary Report Card

Character: Gallito

Subject: clever   Grade: C+

Comments: Gallito got a C+ because he's a trekster. He treked or scared all the things.

Literary Report Card

Character: Gallito

Subject: selfish   Grade: D+

Comments: Gallito's sometimes selfish because he asked one after the other to help.

Literary Report Card

Character: Gallito

Subject: wise   Grade: D+

Comments: Only 2 times was Gallito wise. When he was going to his uncle's wedding and when he asked the sun politely.

Holistic Writing Assessment for a Retelling of *The Bossy Gallito*

	Writing
Content	4
Organization	4
Language Use	3
Mechanics	3

14/4 = 3.5 = Level 4

ASSESSMENT AND ACCOUNTABILITY

Carolyn assessed students' retellings to obtain a writing score since the students completed them independently and had a chance to revise them for publication. She then assigned them grades using the Holistic Scoring Rubric for Writing. Reflecting on her students' work, Carolyn noted that she would focus more on language use and mechanics during writing lessons. Figure 9R shows the rubric used to assess the writing in Figure 9P. Carolyn also completed a ThinkingWorks Lesson Planning Guide (see Figure 9S) that shows the cognitive and language processes that her particular selection of strategies required students to use.

ThinkingWorks Lesson Planning Guide for *The Bossy Gallito*

	STRATEGIES			
	Background Knowledge	Vocabulary	Comprehension	Application/ Extension
COGNITIVE PROCESSES	Semantic Map	Possible Sentences	Story Grammar/ Retelling	Literary Report Card
Develop Background Knowledge	✔			
Expand Vocabulary Knowledge		✔		
Use Text Structure			✔	
Set a Purpose for Learning	✔			
Infer/Select Information			✔	
Create Images			✔	
Relate/Connect Ideas		✔	✔	
Clarify/Monitor Understanding		✔	✔	
Analyze				✔
Synthesize				
Evaluate/Justify				✔
Create/Invent				
LANGUAGE PROCESSES				
Read		✔	✔	
Write			I✔	
Listen/View	✔	✔		✔
Communicate Orally	✔	✔	✔	✔

A Second-Grade, Title I, Science Lesson

This lesson was taught by two second-grade teachers, Julie Wallace and Pat Daniel, with the support of a science consultant, Karen Mitchell. The lesson was part of a thematic unit on life cycles. The lessons in the unit used both narrative and expository material. We include here one of the lessons from that unit, an expository lesson on mammals. The entire lesson was planned around a trip to the Toledo Zoo and strategy instruction took place before, during, and after the visit.

From their zoo visit and other sources, students learned about several concepts related to mammals, including how animals change and how habitats change. The teachers divided their class into six groups with each group studying a different type of animal. They focused their visit and lesson on six mammals: a giraffe, tiger, monkey, gorilla, snow leopard, and hippopotamus.

Before the zoo visit, the teachers guided students to select a topic, develop research questions, and complete the What We Know or background knowledge portion of the comprehension strategy for the lesson, the I-Chart. Students then learned new vocabulary by doing the Personal Clues strategy. During and after the zoo visit, students completed the comprehension portions of the I-Chart. To conclude the lesson, the students completed compare/contrast Venn diagrams and paragraphs.

BACKGROUND KNOWLEDGE: . . . . .I-Chart (What We Know part only)

VOCABULARY: . . . . .Personal Clues

COMPREHENSION: . . . . .I-Chart

APPLICATION/EXTENSION: . . . . .Compare/Contrast Venn Diagram
and Paragraphs

I-CHART (WHAT WE KNOW)

The teachers used the I-Chart as both a background knowledge and comprehension strategy. They began the lesson by focusing students' attention on the topic they would be studying and students wrote that in the top left corner of the I-Chart. In this case, the members of each of the six groups wrote down the name of the animal the group was going to study. Next, as a class, the teachers and students developed four general questions that each of the groups would investigate for their particular animal: Where do they live?, What do they look like?, What do they eat?, and Are males and females different? (see Figure 9T). The questions came from students' interests and the objectives for the lesson. After the questions were developed, students then completed the background knowledge or "What We Know" part of the I-Chart.

I-Chart and Report on Snow Leopard

Topic: Snow leopard	Q1: where do they live?	Q2: What do they look like?	Q3: Whot do they eat?	Q4: Are mole and femal different?	Other Interesting Facts	New Questions
What We Know:	cage	meat	white			
Source: zoo	Rocky terrain and Alpine medows Asia	It is whit and they hoyk to of soot	deer meat goaty		it had srop tits	
Source: books	Aifteen Asia	white and spots	they eat Deer	they hav different spots	does not roar	they are hunted by hrcanas
Source: videos computer	they live in the wode	they are whit and black	they eat fih		they ranpose Tomoys por owrei	winhis tayhe is a late happy
Summaries:	Aifteen 4sia	3to63ft long,tar tail is 3ft long	They eat mice fruit baboons	the femal have backs	Same Asia carnivas	wite winh blcak spot

Snowleopard

I gathered information about snow leopard. Snowleopard live in Asia. They are wite wiht blcak spots. Snowleopard are carnvores. The mate and female look the same. I learned all this from the zoo, books, videos and the internet.

They discussed in groups and wrote down on their I-Charts what they knew about their animal that was pertinent to each of the questions. Julie, Pat, and Karen liked this way of activating students' background knowledge because students had to relate their knowledge to the research questions rather than just listing whatever they knew about the animal.

Personal Clues for Zoo Visit

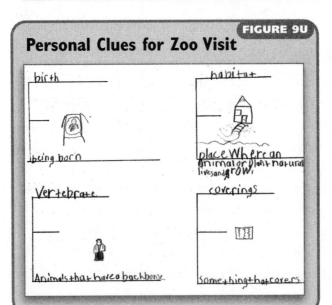

birth — being born

habitat — place where an animal or plant natural lives and grow

vertebrate — Animals that have a backbone

coverings — something that covers

PERSONAL CLUES

Students completed the Personal Clues strategy for six vocabulary words that they would encounter in the zoo exhibits. Figure 9U shows how one student completed the strategy for four of the six words: *birth*, *habitat*, *vertebrate*, and *coverings*. Note that the student drew images for his clues.

I-CHART

The teachers used the I-Chart as their comprehension strategy for several reasons. First, their students would be learning about mammals, not only by visiting the zoo, but also through books, videos, and the Internet. The I-Chart helped the students organize information from different sources. Second, completing the questions on their I-Chart gave students a clear purpose when they went on their trip and encouraged them to see that important information can be obtained from sources other than books. When the class arrived at the zoo, all students had their own I-Chart with the same questions. Their work was to answer the questions for the mammal that they had been assigned. They wrote their answers in the "Zoo" row of the I-Chart. The children loved having this work to do during their zoo visit. Upon their return to the classroom, students wrote a report on their mammal using information they had obtained from the zoo exhibits, books, videos, and the Internet. Figure 9T shows how one student completed his I-Chart and report on the snow leopard.

COMPARE/CONTRAST VENN DIAGRAM AND PARAGRAPHS

Julie, Pat, and Karen wanted students to extend their learning by comparing the animal they had studied with a new animal. They chose to read aloud a book about a koala growing up. Using the questions from the I-Chart as a guide, students listened for information during the Read Aloud that would help them answer those questions for the koala. After the Read Aloud, they listed information they learned about the

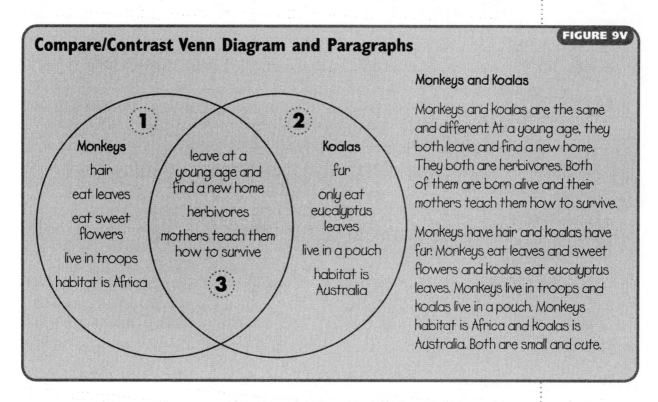

FIGURE 9V

Compare/Contrast Venn Diagram and Paragraphs

1

Monkeys

hair

eat leaves

eat sweet flowers

live in troops

habitat is Africa

leave at a young age and find a new home

herbivores

mothers teach them how to survive

3

2

Koalas

fur

only eat eucalyptus leaves

live in a pouch

habitat is Australia

Monkeys and Koalas

Monkeys and koalas are the same and different. At a young age, they both leave and find a new home. They both are herbivores. Both of them are born alive and their mothers teach them how to survive.

Monkeys have hair and koalas have fur. Monkeys eat leaves and sweet flowers and koalas eat eucalyptus leaves. Monkeys live in troops and koalas live in a pouch. Monkeys habitat is Africa and koalas is Australia. Both are small and cute.

FIGURE 9W

Observation Note for Personal Clues

V — Nico understood the concept of Personal Clues and chose good ones to match the definitions. He was able to explain why he chose the clues and recalled the definitions easily.

koala on one section of the compare/contrast chart. They used what they had learned about the animal they researched in another section of the chart. They then noted similarities between the two animals. To write compare/contrast paragraphs, students used information from their charts. Figure 9V is an example of one student's work.

FIGURE 9X

ThinkingWorks Lesson Planning Guide for Second-Grade, Title I Science

	STRATEGIES			
	Background Knowledge	Vocabulary	Comprehension	Application/ Extension
COGNITIVE PROCESSES	I-Chart (What We Know)	Personal Clues	I-Chart/ Report	C/C Venn Diag./ Paragraphs
Develop Background Knowledge	✔			
Expand Vocabulary Knowledge		✔		
Use Text Structure				
Set a Purpose for Learning			✔	
Infer/Select Information			✔	✔
Create Images		✔		
Relate/Connect Ideas			✔	✔
Clarify/Monitor Understanding			✔	✔
Analyze				✔
Synthesize				✔
Evaluate/Justify				
Create/Invent				
LANGUAGE PROCESSES				
Read			✔	
Write			/✔	/✔
Listen/View	✔	✔	✔	✔
Communicate Orally	✔	✔	✔	✔

ASSESSMENT AND ACCOUNTABILITY

There are many opportunities for assessment in this lesson. Julie and Pat made observation notes assessing how the students completed the Personal Clues strategy and for how they completed portions of their I-Chart before, during, and after their visit to the Toledo Zoo. They also used comprehension checklists to evaluate reports based on information in the I-Charts and the compare/contrast paragraphs. Figure 9W is an observation note on one student's work with the vocabulary strategy Personal Clues. Figure 9X is a ThinkingWorks Lesson Planning Guide showing the cognitive and language processes that this lesson addressed.

A Sixth-Grade Narrative Lesson

In this lesson, sixth-grade students read *The Watsons Go to Birmingham—1963* (Curtis, 1995), a novel about the Civil Rights movement. Cheryl Wozniak wanted her students to accomplish the following objectives:

- Build background knowledge

- Learn vocabulary

- Recall main events from the reading passage

- Identify literary elements such as problem, characters, setting

- Make judgments about characters

- Write a summary

She designed a ThinkingWorks lesson with the following components:

BACKGROUND KNOWLEDGE: . . . . .Semantic Map

VOCABULARY: . . . . .Concept Circles

COMPREHENSION: . . . . .Story Pyramid

APPLICATION/EXTENSION: . . . . .Character Rating Scale and
Character Sketch

SEMANTIC MAP

Since the class was beginning a new novel, Cheryl chose the Semantic Map strategy to help students activate their background knowledge about the historical period in which the novel was set, the 1960s. She had students write "the Civil Rights Movement" in the middle of their Semantic Map graphic organizer. Working in small groups, they completed the map by writing events or ideas that represented what they knew about that concept. The small-group setting encouraged students to tap into each other's background knowledge about the 1960s. Figure 9Y is a Semantic Map completed by one of the groups.

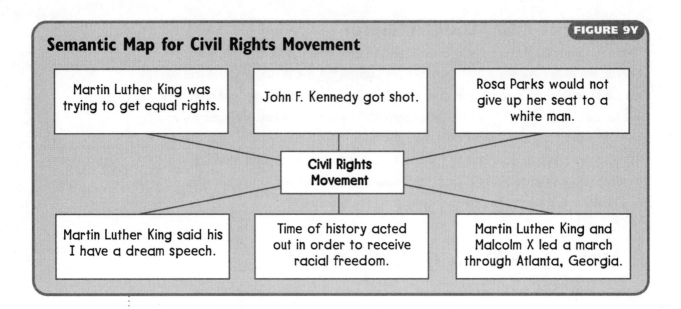

Semantic Map for Civil Rights Movement

Martin Luther King was trying to get equal rights.	John F. Kennedy got shot.	Rosa Parks would not give up her seat to a white man.

Civil Rights Movement

Martin Luther King said his I have a dream speech.	Time of history acted out in order to receive racial freedom.	Martin Luther King and Malcolm X led a march through Atlanta, Georgia.

The students' work with the Semantic Map showed that they had some familiarity with events in the Civil Rights movement that touched on important issues such as segregation and discrimination. Cheryl then knew that she had a foundation on which to build and refine her students' knowledge of the period. The concepts that she was going to teach would not be totally new to them.

CONCEPT CIRCLES

Cheryl used Concept Circles because she felt that her students would understand the novel better if they had a full understanding of certain essential concepts rather than specific vocabulary words used in the text. Although the students had some understanding of these concepts as shown on their Semantic Maps, Cheryl wanted to refine and build their understanding. She gave each group of students four concept circles to complete. In the first three circles, students were given two words or phrases related to the concept named beneath the circle. They were asked to discuss the meanings of the words and their relationship to the concept. Two sections of the first three circles were blank and students had to identify two more words or phrases related to the concept. The last circle contained four words. Three words were related to the concept named beneath the circle, liberation, and one word was not related to the other words or the concept. Students were asked to discuss the meanings of the words and identify the one that did not belong. They crossed out the antonym or unrelated word. Figure 9Z is one group's completed set of Concept Circles.

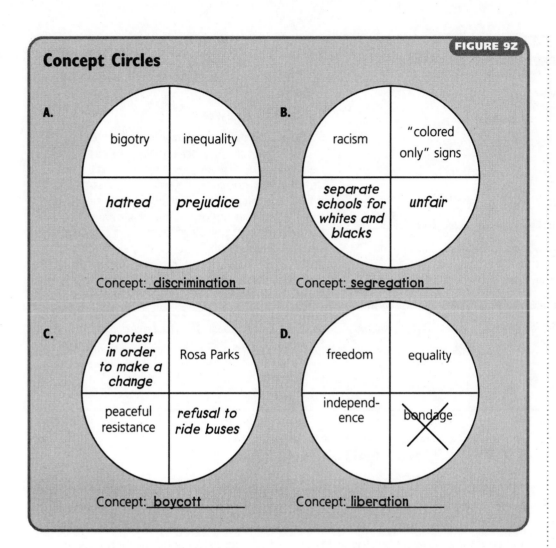

Concept Circles

A.

bigotry	inequality
hatred	*prejudice*

Concept: __discrimination__

B.

racism	"colored only" signs
separate schools for whites and blacks	*unfair*

Concept: __segregation__

C.

protest in order to make a change	Rosa Parks
peaceful resistance	*refusal to ride buses*

Concept: __boycott__

D.

freedom	equality
independ-ence	~~bondage~~

Concept: __liberation__

Story Pyramid and Summary

STORY PYRAMID

1. Byron
2. daring troublesome
3. Watson's livingroom bathroom
4. Byron plays with matches
5. Byron flushes Nazi toys down toilet
6. Byron's mom found him with matches
7. Byron's mom tried to burn his fingers
8. Joetta saved Byron by blowing out the matches

SUMMARY

Troublemaking Byron

Byron is causing trouble again. Let me explain. In this chapter the only characters are Byron, Kenny, Mama, Joetta. Byron is the main character in this chapter. He's daring, disobedient and a troublemaker. It takes place mostly in the Watson's livingroom., but it starts in the bathroom. The problem is Byron is playing with matches again. The first thing that happened was Byron catching little Nazi toys on fire and then flushing them down the toilet. Soon after Byron's mom caught him with those matches. His mom was so mad she was going to burn his fingers. Joetta saved Byron by blowing out the matches. Finally Byron's mom is going to let the dad deal with him. After all this did Byron learn his lesson or not?

STORY PYRAMID AND SUMMARY

After students read Chapter 5 of *The Watsons Go to Birmingham—1963,* they were asked to complete a Story Pyramid to help them understand the focus of that particular chapter (see Figure 9AA for a sample). Students were familiar with the strategy and completed their Story Pyramids in small groups. Each student then wrote a summary of the chapter using a comprehension checklist (see Figure 9DD) Cheryl had given them as a guide to make sure that all the key parts were included. Figure 9AA shows a student's completed Story Pyramid and summary. In reflecting on the quality of the summaries, Cheryl decided that she needed to teach a mini-lesson on writing a good introductory sentence for a summary so that students would not just begin by writing: "This summary is about . . . ."

CHARACTER RATING SCALE AND CHARACTER SKETCH

Students then completed a Character Rating Scale and Character Sketch for one of the characters in the novel. Students evaluated the character Byron Watson, based on two traits Cheryl suggested and one trait they selected themselves. Figure 9BB shows a Character Rating Scale completed by one student who added *polite/rude* to the traits provided by Cheryl, *well-behaved/troublemaker* and *caring/selfish*. Note that Cheryl is encouraging her sixth-grade students to complete part of the strategy independently. She is also fostering deeper comprehension because in order to come up with their own traits, students must analyze the text a bit further. Figure 9CC shows the Character Sketch written by the student who completed the Character Rating Scale in Figure 9BB.

FIGURE 9BB

Character Rating Scale for Byron Watson

well-behaved __ __ __ ✔ __ trouble maker

Supporting ideas:
1. Byron causes trouble like beating up kids.
2. Although he tries to do what he is told.
3. Byron didn't listen to his mama about matches.

caring __ ✔ __ __ __ selfish

Supporting ideas:
1. He cares about his family
2. Byron is sometimes mean to his family like Kenny.
3. Byron cares because he dug a little grave for the bird.

polite __ __ ✔ __ __ rude

Supporting ideas:
1. Byron is rude to other kids and his brother.
2. Although he tries to be polite to adults.
3. It was polite of him to bury the bird he injured.

FIGURE 9CC

Character Sketch of Byron Watson

The Special Traits of Byron Watson

Byron Watson is an interesting character. I hope as you read this you'll find him interesting too.

Byron Watson is more a trouble maker than someone who is well-behaved. Byron causes trouble by beating up other kids. He caused trouble when he played with matches. Even though he causes trouble he tries to do what his mom and dad want him to do.

He may not seem like it but Byron is caring in his own way. He cares about what happens to his family. Byron could be a little mean to family members like Kenny. It was also very caring when he dug a grave for the bird he hit.

Byron is between polite and rude. It was a polite thing to do to bury the little bird he injured. He tries to be polite to adults. He may be polite to some people but he is rude to his brother and to the kids at Clark School.

Now that you know a little about Byron you can see he is special in his own way. He is a person of many traits and that is what makes him special.

Comprehension Checklist for Narrative Text

COMPREHENSION CHECKLIST

I will earn my best reading score if my summary includes the following:

	student check	agree	disagree
1. Title of the selection	✔	✔	___
2. Introductory sentence	✔	✔	___
3. Characters	✔	✔	___
4. Description	✔	✔	___
5. Setting	✔	✔	___
6. Problem	✔	✔	___
7. First Event	✔	✔	___
8. Second Event	✔	✔	___
9. Third Event	✔	✔	___
10. Conclusion	✔	✔	___

Comments: Good summary! Total points earned 10/10 A

A = 10   B = 9   C = 8   D = 7

ASSESSMENT AND ACCOUNTABILITY

In this lesson, both the summaries and the Character Sketches provided good opportunities for analyzing student progress and scoring and obtaining grades for student work. Cheryl encouraged students to evaluate their own work in both cases. The students completed a comprehension checklist to score their summaries. Then Cheryl checked their work and their scores and assigned them a grade. (Figure 9DD shows a completed comprehension checklist for the student summary presented in Figure 9AA.) The students also scored their Character Sketches using a comprehension checklist and the Holistic Scoring Rubric for Writing (see page 206). Cheryl again checked their work and their scores and assigned them a grade for comprehension and a competency level for writing.

Cheryl completed a ThinkingWorks Lesson Planning Guide (Figure 9EE) that shows the cognitive and language processes used by students throughout the lesson. Note that, with the summary and the Character Sketch, students had two major opportunities to write. They also worked in small groups and independently during the various activities. Once students became familiar with the strategies used in this lesson, they could do all of them independently. Cheryl noted that the particular combination of strategies in this lesson allowed students to interact more with the print as they read the novel. The variety of activities engaged student interest. In the end, the students all realized a feeling of success.

ThinkingWorks Lesson Planning Guide for
The Watsons Go to Birmingham—1963

	STRATEGIES			
	Background Knowledge	Vocabulary	Comprehension	Application/ Extension
COGNITIVE PROCESSES	Semantic Map	Concept Circles	Story Pyramid/ Summary	Char. Rating Scale/ Char. Sketch
Develop Background Knowledge	✔	✔		
Expand Vocabulary Knowledge		✔		
Use Text Structure			✔	
Set a Purpose for Learning	✔		✔	
Infer/Select Information			✔	
Create Images			✔	
Relate/Connect Ideas			✔	
Clarify/Monitor Understanding				
Analyze				✔
Synthesize				✔
Evaluate/Justify				✔
Create/Invent				✔
LANGUAGE PROCESSES				
Read			✔	✔
Write			/✔	/✔
Listen/View	✔	✔		
Communicate Orally	✔	✔		

A Sixth-Grade Social Studies Lesson

In Claudia Trombla's sixth-grade class, students were learning about ancient cultures, specifically, ancient Egypt. For this particular lesson, students were reading a text called *Into the Mummy's Tomb* (Reeves, 1992). The specific objectives for the lesson were as follows:

- Understand text information and construct answers to different types of questions about the text, including literal, inferential, and scriptal.

- Use a business letter format to describe a historical event, the revealing of King Tutankhamen's mummy.

- Describe the event in terms of time ordered activities.

- Write in the first person.

Claudia designed a ThinkingWorks lesson with the following components:

BACKGROUND KNOWLEDGE:	Quickwriting
VOCABULARY:	Knowledge Rating Scale and Possible Sentences (adapted)
COMPREHENSION:	Question Answer Relationship (QAR)
APPLICATION/EXTENSION:	RAFT and Business Letter

In her lesson, Claudia used Quickwriting and a Knowledge Rating Scale to determine her students' knowledge of ancient Egypt and of words critical to an understanding of the text they were going to be reading. For her comprehension strategy, QAR, she developed a variety of questions and asked students to construct answers to them in writing. With RAFT, students had to use what they had learned from the text to write a letter in which they took on the role of an archaeologist present when King Tut's tomb was opened.

QUICKWRITING WITH KNOWLEDGE RATING SCALE AND POSSIBLE SENTENCES (ADAPTED)

Before students read the text selection, Claudia asked them to do the Quickwriting strategy, combined with a strategy to determine their knowledge of key vocabulary, the Knowledge Rating Scale. Students rated their knowledge of six words that were critical to their understanding of the text selection on the finding of King Tutankhamen's mummy and wrote as many sentences as they could using those words (see Figure 9FF).

In looking at the students' responses, Claudia realized that most had little or no knowledge of the topic. She decided to have students do another Quickwriting about a related topic that might be more familiar to them, mummies. Students had ten

Quickwriting with Knowledge Rating Scale on Ancient Egypt

FIGURE 9FF

Write what you know about the following words:

	Have No Idea	Have Seen	Can Define	Can Use it in a sentence
Tutankhamen				✔
shroud	✔			
amulets				✔
embalming		✔		
linen bandages	✔			
scalpel	✔			

STUDENT RESPONSE

1. My mom bought an amulet for my sister.
2. Tutankhamen stayed in the pyramid all day.

Quickwriting for Mummies

FIGURE 9GG

I know that Egyptian mummies are very old and you can get a mummy by letting a dead body sit out in the sun and it will harden. And you can even have an animal mummy also. And mummies sometimes fall apart if they are not handled right.

Postreading Sentences Using Vocabulary Words

FIGURE 9HH

Tutankhamen was an Egyptian boy king who died at an early age.

There was a shroud on King Tutankhamen.

My mom had an amulet to keep her safe.

The doctors were embalming a patient.

King Tut was wrapped in linen bandages.

The doctors need a scalpel to work on the patient.

minutes to write what they could about mummies (see Figure 9GG). Their responses gave her a good idea of the extent of their background knowledge, and she used that information to plan her instruction.

After they read the text selection, Claudia asked her students to write sentences using the six vocabulary words that had been on the Knowledge Rating Scale. She noted that their understanding of the vocabulary words had improved greatly. For example, before reading the text, one student in the class indicated that he had no knowledge of three of the six vocabulary words, and he could only write two sentences using any of the vocabulary (see Figure 9FF). However, the sentences written by the same student (see Figure 9HH) show that after reading he had a better understanding of the meaning of the words. By asking students to write sentences with the vocabulary words after reading the text, Claudia was using a portion of another vocabulary strategy, Possible Sentences. In this lesson, she supplemented the Knowledge Rating Scale, which only allows students to indicate their knowledge of words before they read, with a strategy that encourages students to write sentences after reading that use vocabulary words and that reflect the content of the text.

QUESTION ANSWER RELATIONSHIP (QAR)

To encourage student comprehension of *Into the Mummy's Tomb*, Claudia used the questioning strategy QAR after students had finished reading the text. On the first day that she used the strategy, she explained to her students the three different types of questions, literal (right there), inferential (think and search), and scriptal (on my own). She then modeled the use of the strategy by asking students to answer orally QAR questions that she had developed for a previously read text selection. The next day, she gave the students a series of QAR questions related to content from *Into the Mummy's Tomb* which they answered in writing. Figure 9II shows the questions, labeled according to type, and one student's responses.

Claudia noted that it was hard for her to write the QAR questions, as she was used to using questions provided in teacher guides. She felt that she needed to do more writing of questions herself.

FIGURE 9.11

QAR for *Into the Mummy's Tomb*

1. How did Carter feel about returning to open and examine King Tut's mummy? (inferential)
Carter felt scared because he was having dreams about people going to the tomb and dropping, breaking, and handling artifacts. And he was nervous because his stomach was churning.

2. How many coffins enclosed Tut's mummy? (literal)
There were 3 coffins that enclosed Tut's mummy.

3. Why were pulleys used? (inferential)
Pulleys were used because the Egyptians did not leave much "elbow room" when putting the coffins together.

4. What made coffin two so heavy? (inferential)
The second coffin was made out of beaten gold and inlaid with glass. That's what made it so heavy.

5. Why did Carter's heart almost stop beating? (literal)
Carter's heart almost stopped beating because when he saw the third coffin it was made of solid gold!

6. Why were there amulets in the layers of the linen bandages of the mummy? (literal)
Amulets were there to protect the king from the dangers of the underworld.

7. Why was there a large golden bird on the chest of King Tut's mummy? (literal)
The bird represented a sacred image of the king's spirit.

8. Why did Egyptians mummify bodies? (inferential)
Egyptians mummified bodies because the body had to be so preserved that the spirit could recognize it when it came back.

9. What was the condition of King Tut's body? (literal)
King Tut's body was brittle. The limbs were shrunken and thin.

10. What did the doctor conclude about the cause of King Tut's death? (literal)
The doctor concluded that he didn't die of a disease but could only have died of an accident or...murder.

11. Why does Carter puzzle about the death of King Tut? (scriptal)
Carter puzzles about the death of King Tut because all the things (for example: the second tomb found, the face that didn't look like any other face. It was not made for King Tut) were not in place.

12. What do you think caused the death of King Tut? (scriptal)
I personally think the death of the boy King was murder. Why would he die at the age of 18 and not because of disease? Murder is what I think (strongly).

RAFT AND BUSINESS LETTER

For the application/extension activity, Claudia prepared a writing prompt and asked students to use the RAFT format as the basis for composing a business letter (see the directions in Figure 9JJ). The students worked with a partner, taking on the role of a famous archaeologist present at the opening of the tomb of King Tutankhamen (role). In that role, they were to write a business letter (format) to the Archaeological Society of America (audience) for the purpose of informing its members of what took place at this event (topic).

Claudia reviewed the format of a business letter before sending students off to write. As a large group, the class made up possible addresses and discussed various experiences of Howard Carter, a main character in the book. The blackboard was covered with ideas. To help students with writing the body of the letter, Claudia encouraged them to act as if they were writing an essay using the About Point Writing Response strategy. Students were asked to write a letter of four to six paragraphs, with each paragraph containing an About Point, or topic sentence, and supporting details. Claudia noted that, the next time students wrote letters, she would teach them how to write a closing paragraph.

Students wrote their letters over a two-day period and the results were very successful. Claudia found that students enjoyed imagining that they were present at the exhumation of King Tutankhamen's mummy. Her students were indeed applying the knowledge they had gained by reading the text. They were also refining their knowledge. Claudia noted that the writing of the letter required each student to clarify what the coffins looked like, how they were arranged, and what sequence the exhumation followed. The RAFT and letter-writing assignment cleared up some of the errors that appeared in students' answers to the QAR questions in the comprehension part of the lesson. Figure 9JJ shows one student's completed RAFT and his letter.

RAFT and Business Letter

Directions:

Pretend you are a great archaeologist present at the opening of the gilded coffin of King Tutankhamen. You will also observe the examination of King Tut's mummy. You will need to write a business letter to the Archaeological Society of America in Washington, DC explaining your observations of the event. Be sure your letter contains the six letter parts: heading, inside address, greeting, body, closing, and signature. When writing the letter, use the information that you read about in Into the Mummy's Tomb to inform the society.

R = Morris Jordan, archaeologist

A = Director of the Archaeological Society of America

F = business letter

T = informing the society about the opening of King Tut's tomb

---

Morris Jordan
Harvard College
Cambridge, Mass.
December 19, 1925

Frederick Holmes
American Archaeological Society
Washington, D.C.

Dear Mr. Holmes:

My reason for writing this letter is to inform the society that I have been invited by Howard Carter to observe the revealing of the mummy, on November 11, 1925.

There are three coffins placed together with a tight fit like Russian dolls. The first coffin was made of wood, covered with a thin layer of skinny beaten gold. The second one was also covered with brilliantly colored glass. The second coffin had to be hoisted up with pulleys because the third coffin was made of solid gold and it was heavy. They all seemed to have a tight fit. Finally, they got to a small coffin with the king in it.

The reason that mummifying was so important to Egyptians was because they thought that the body had to be perfectly preserved so the spirit would recognize it when it would return to the tomb. King Tut's mummy was neatly wrapped in linen bandages. The bandages were held together by decorated gold bands. They were covered with the exact same oils that were found on the outside of the coffin. In the bandages they found a hundred jewels and amulets. These were charms whose magical powers would protect the king from the dangers of the underworld.

When they examined the body they removed the brittle bandages from the mummy's body. Around the mummy's neck were layers of collars and pendants. His arms were encircled by bracelets inlaid with semiprecious stones. On his fingers were two rings. King Tut's feet were encased in gold sandals and a set of gold sheaths which protected his toes. On his waist was a gold-handle dagger with a blade made of iron.

King Tut may have died from an accident or by murder.

I hope to come home with more information from King Tut's tomb.
Sincerely,

Morris Jordan

ASSESSMENT AND ACCOUNTABILITY

Since the students based their RAFT and business letter on information they had learned from reading and answering questions about the text, Claudia used the Holistic Scoring Rubric for Writing to score their letters. Figure 9KK shows the writing rubric applied to the letter in Figure 9JJ. After assessing all of the letters written by her students, Claudia decided to focus on language use and mechanics in future lessons.

Claudia completed a ThinkingWorks Lesson Planning Guide (Figure 9LL) that indicated the cognitive and language processes addressed in her lesson. For this final lesson, we also have included a chart that aligns the lesson with sixth-grade standards in reading (Figure 9MM), writing (Figure 9NN), and Social Studies (Figure 9OO). Both the completed Lesson Planning Guide and the alignment with standards are valid indications of the content that students were taught and the competencies that were developed in this lesson.

The examples in this chapter clearly demonstrate the benefits of using the ThinkingWorks framework to plan instruction. The ThinkingWorks framework allows teachers to use a variety of strategies to engage students and teach content across the curriculum. In the course of the lessons, students used cognitive and language processes critical to comprehension of text. In addition, teachers demonstrated an "executive command" of the strategies by deciding which ones to use in a given lesson and which ones needed modification for their particular teaching situation.

Finally, the framework provides many opportunities for both teachers and students to assess and document student progress and for teachers to plan instruction based on a variety of types of assessment data. Teachers can also document what they teach by aligning their lessons with the cognitive and language processes listed in the ThinkingWorks Lesson Planning Guide and/or standards in various content areas. In fact, several of the teachers used their ThinkingWorks lessons as documentation when applying for National Board Certification.

FIGURE 9KK

Holistic Scoring Assessment for a Business Letter

	Writing
Content	4
Organization	4
Language Use	3
Mechanics	3

14/4 = 3.5 = Level 4

ThinkingWorks Lesson Planning Guide
for *Into the Mummy's Tomb*

	STRATEGIES			
	Background Knowledge	Vocabulary	Comprehension	Application/ Extension
COGNITIVE PROCESSES	Quickwriting	Know. Rating Scale/ Poss. Sentences	QAR	RAFT/ Business Letter
Develop Background Knowledge	✔			
Expand Vocabulary Knowledge		✔		
Use Text Structure				
Set a Purpose for Learning	✔		✔	
Infer/Select Information			✔	
Create Images			✔	
Relate/Connect Ideas			✔	
Clarify/Monitor Understanding			✔	
Analyze			✔	✔
Synthesize				✔
Evaluate/Justify				
Create/Invent				✔
LANGUAGE PROCESSES				
Read			✔	
Write	✔			/✔
Listen/View		✔	✔	✔
Communicate Orally		✔	✔	✔

Sixth-Grade Academic Content Standards in Reading

	STRATEGIES			
	Background Knowledge	Vocabulary	Comprehension	Application/ Extension
	Quickwriting	Know. Rating Scale/Poss. Sentences	QAR	RAFT/ Business Letter
READING PROCESS: Concepts of Print, Comprehension Strategies and Self-Monitoring Strategies				
Establish and adjust purposes for reading, including to find out, to understand, to interpret, to enjoy and to solve problems.	✔	✔		
Predict or hypothesize as appropriate from information in the text, substantiating with specific references to textual examples that may be in widely separated sections of text.				
Make critical comparisons across texts, noting author's style as well as literal and implied content of text.			✔	✔
Summarize the information in texts, recognizing important ideas and supporting details, and noting gaps or contradictions.			✔	✔
Select, create and use graphic organizers to interpret textual information.				
Answer literal, inferential, evaluative and synthesizing questions to demonstrate comprehension of grade-appropriate print texts, electronic and visual media.			✔	
Monitor own comprehension by adjusting speed to fit the purpose, or by skimming, scanning, reading on, looking back, note taking or summarizing what has been read so far in text.			✔	
List questions and search for answers within the text to construct meaning.			✔	
Use criteria to choose independent reading materials (e.g., personal interest, knowledge of authors and genres or recommendations from others).				
Independently read books for various purposes (e.g., for enjoyment, for literary experience, to gain information or to perform a task).				
READING APPLICATIONS: Informational, Technical and Persuasive Text				
Use text features, such as chapter titles, headings and subheadings; parts of books, including the index, appendix, table of contents and online tools (search engines) to locate information.			✔	
Analyze examples of cause and effect and fact and opinion.			✔	✔
Compare and contrast important details about a topic, using different sources of information including books, magazines, newspapers and online resources.				
Compare original text to a summary to determine the extent to which the summary adequately reflects the main ideas and critical details of the original text.				
Analyze information found in maps, charts, tables, graphs, diagrams and cutaways.				
Identify an author's argument or viewpoint and assess the adequacy and accuracy of details used.				
Identify and understand an author's purpose for writing, including to explain, entertain, persuade or inform.				
Summarize information from information text, identifying the treatment, scope and organization of ideas.				

Sixth-Grade Academic Content Standards in Writing

	STRATEGIES			
	Background Knowledge	Vocabulary	Comprehension	Application/ Extension
	Quickwriting	Know. Rating Scale/Poss. Sentences	QAR	RAFT/ Business Letter
WRITING PROCESSES				
Generate writing ideas through discussions with others and from printed material, and keep a list of writing ideas.				✔
Conduct background reading, interviews or surveys when appropriate.				
Establish a thesis statement for informational writing or a plan for narrative writing.				
Determine a purpose and audience.				✔
Use organizational strategies (e.g., rough outlines, diagrams, maps, webs and Venn diagrams) to plan writing.				✔
Organize writing, beginning with an introduction, body and a resolution of plot, followed by a closing statement or a summary of important ideas and details.				
Vary simple, compound and complex sentence structure.				✔
Group related ideas into paragraphs, including topic sentences following paragraph form, and maintain a consistent focus across paragraphs.				✔
Vary language and style as appropriate to audience and purpose.				✔
Use available technology to compose text.				
Reread and analyze clarity of writing.				✔
Add and delete information and details to better elaborate on a stated central idea and to more effectively accomplish purpose.				✔
Rearrange words, sentences and paragraphs, and add transitional words and phrases to clarify meaning.				✔
Use resources and reference materials (e.g., dictionaries and thesauruses) to select more effective vocabulary.				
Proofread writing, edit to improve conventions (e.g., grammar, spelling, punctuation and capitalization) and identify and correct fragments and run-ons.				✔
Apply tools (e.g., rubric, checklist and feedback) to judge the quality of writing.				✔
Prepare for publication (e.g., for display or for sharing with others) writing that follows a format appropriate to the purpose, using techniques such as electronic resources and graphics to enhance the final product.				✔
WRITING APPLICATIONS				
Write narratives that maintain a clear focus and point of view and use sensory details and dialogue to develop plot, characters, and a specific setting.				
Write responses to novels, stories and poems and plays that provide an interpretation, critique or reflection and support judgments with specific reference to the text.				
Write letters that state the purpose, make requests or give compliments and use business letter format.				✔
Write informational essays or reports, including research, that present a literal understanding of the topic, include specific facts, details and examples from multiple sources and create an organizing structure appropriate to the purpose, audience and context.				
Produce informal writings (e.g., journals, notes and poems) for various purposes.				

Sixth-Grade Academic Content Standards in Social Studies

FIGURE 900

	STRATEGIES			
	Background Knowledge	Vocabulary	Comprehension	Application/ Extension
	Quickwriting	Know. Rating Scale/Poss. Sentences	QAR	RAFT/ Business Letter
HISTORY: EARLY CIVILIZATIONS				
Describe the early development of humankind from prehistoric times including: Hunting and gathering; Tool making; Use of fire; Domestication of plants and animals; Organizing societies; Government.				
Compare the river civilizations in the Tigris and Euphrates, Nile, Huang Ho and Indus valleys before 1000 B.C. including location, government, religion, agriculture and cultural and scientific contributions.			✔	✔
HISTORY: THE FIRST GLOBAL AGE				
Describe the characteristics of the Maya, Inca, Aztec and Mississippian civilizations including location, government, religion, agriculture and cultural and scientific contributions.				
Compare the daily life of people in the societies studied including class structure, gender roles, beliefs, and customs and traditions.				
Compare religions and belief systems focusing on geographic origins, founding leaders and teaching including Buddhism, Christianity, Judaism, Hinduism and Islam.				
PEOPLE IN SOCIETIES: INTERACTION				
Explain factors that foster conflict or cooperation among countries, such as language, religion, types of government, historic relationships and economic interests.				
SOCIAL STUDIES SKILLS AND METHODS: OBTAINING INFORMATION		✔	✔	✔
Use multiple sources to define essential vocabulary and obtain information for a research project including: Almanacs, Gazetteers, Trade Books, Periodicals, Videotapes, Electronic Sources.				
SOCIAL STUDIES SKILLS AND METHODS: THINKING AND ORGANIZING				
Analyze information from primary and secondary sources in order to summarize, make generalizations and draw conclusions.			✔	✔
Organize information using outlines and graphic organizers.				✔
Read and interpret pictographs, bar graphs, line graphs, circle graphs, tables and flow charts.				

Closing Thoughts

We said at the beginning of this book that our goal is to provide you with a framework for planning and implementing comprehension strategies instruction to help your students understand text and apply what they have learned. We assured you that by using this book, you would not only revisit some familiar strategies but also learn many more, emerging with a repertoire of strategies for your lesson plans, based on your students' needs and curriculum content. We hope that our goal has been achieved and that you now have a clear vision of the view of effective comprehension strategies instruction that we embrace today: instruction that has at its center a reflective, knowledgeable teacher making important decisions regarding which strategies should be taught to meet student needs and accomplish lesson objectives. By using the strategies presented in this book and the ThinkingWorks framework to develop lessons, you can plan and implement effective comprehension strategies instruction. Furthermore, as you and your colleagues increase your commitment to strategies instruction and continue to use a repertoire of strategies, we hope that you will discuss what strategies worked well at different grade levels and in different content areas. If you continue this collaboration within and across grade levels, you and your colleagues will eventually develop a cohesive, flexible program of comprehension strategies instruction that will become an essential part of the curriculum.

Appendix A—Alignment of ThinkingWorks Strategies With Cognitive Processes

Develop Background Knowledge

NARRATIVE TEXT STRATEGIES	EXPOSITORY TEXT STRATEGIES
Problem/Solution Guide	Problem/Solution Guide
Experience Text Relationship	Experience Text Relationship
Quickwriting	Quickwriting
Semantic Map	Semantic Map
Anticipation Guide	Structured Overview
	Anticipation Guide
	KWL (part of strategy)
	KWL Plus (part of strategy)
	I-Chart (part of strategy)

Expand Vocabulary Knowledge

NARRATIVE TEXT STRATEGIES	EXPOSITORY TEXT STRATEGIES
Possible Sentences	Possible Sentences
Concept Circles	Concept Circles
Personal Clues	Personal Clues
Concept of a Definition	Concept of a Definition
Concept of a Definition (Technical)	Concept of a Definition (Technical)
Semantic Map	Semantic Map
Semantic Feature Analysis	Semantic Feature Analysis
	Structured Overview

Use Text Structure

NARRATIVE TEXT STRATEGIES	EXPOSITORY TEXT STRATEGIES
Story Grammar	Frames
Circle Story	Structured Overview
Story Pyramid	
Story Map from Characters' Perspectives	
Probable Passage	
Plot Relationships Chart	

Set a Purpose for Learning

NARRATIVE TEXT STRATEGIES

Problem/Solution Guide
Experience Text Relationship
Quickwriting
Semantic Map
Anticipation Guide
Structured Overview
Personal Response/Literary Analysis
Prediction/Prediction Chart
Action Belief Chart
Story Grammar
Circle Story
Story Pyramid
Story Map from Characters' Perspectives
Probable Passage
Plot Relationship Chart

EXPOSITORY TEXT STRATEGIES

Problem/Solution Guide
Experience Text Relationship
Quickwriting
Semantic Map
Anticipation Guide
About Point
About Point Notetaking
Question Answer Relationship (QAR)
Questions for Quality Thinking
Thinking Minds
Question, Clues, Response
Reciprocal Teaching
KWL (part of strategy)
KWL Plus (part of strategy
I-Chart (part of strategy)
Frames

Infer/Select Information

NARRATIVE TEXT STRATEGIES

Prediction/Prediction Chart
Story Grammar
Circle Story
Story Pyramid
Story Map from Characters' Perspectives
Personal Response / Literary Analysis
Action Belief Chart

EXPOSITORY TEXT STRATEGIES

Question Answer Relationship (QAR)
Question, Clues, Response
Thinking Minds
Questions for Quality Thinking
About Point
About Point Notetaking
KWL
KWL Plus
I-Chart
Frames
Exploration Frame/Science

Relate/Connect Ideas

NARRATIVE TEXT STRATEGIES	EXPOSITORY TEXT STRATEGIES
Concept Circles	Concept Circles
Semantic Map	Semantic Map
Personal Response/Literary Analysis	Structured Overview
Prediction/Prediction Chart	About Point
Action Belief Chart	About Point Notetaking
Story Grammar	Question Answer Relationship (QAR)
Circle Story	Questions for Quality Thinking
Story Pyramid	Thinking Minds
Story Map from Characters' Perspectives	Question, Clues, Response
Probable Passage	Reciprocal Teaching
Plot Relationships Chart	KWL
	KWL Plus
	I-Chart
	Frames

Clarify/Monitor Understanding

NARRATIVE TEXT STRATEGIES	EXPOSITORY TEXT STRATEGIES
Anticipation Guide	Anticipation Guide
Semantic Map	Semantic Map
Personal Response/Literary Analysis	About Point
Prediction/Prediction Chart	About Point Notetaking
Action Belief Chart	Question Answer Relationship (QAR)
Story Grammar	Questions for Quality Thinking
Circle Story	Thinking Minds
Story Pyramid	Question, Clues, Response
Story Map from Characters' Perspectives	Reciprocal Teaching
Probable Passage	KWL
Plot Relationships Chart	KWL Plus
	I-Chart
	Frames

Analysis

NARRATIVE TEXT STRATEGIES	EXPOSITORY TEXT STRATEGIES
Story Grammar	Frames
Circle Story	Question Answer Relationship (QAR)
Story Pyramid	Question, Clues, Response
Plot Relationships Chart	Questions for Quality Thinking
Story Map from Characters' Perspectives	Thinking Minds
Probable Passage	Reciprocal Teaching
Action Belief Chart	
Personal Response/Literary Analysis	
Prediction/Prediction Chart	

Create Images

NARRATIVE TEXT STRATEGIES

Compare/Contrast Venn Diagram
Compare/Contrast Paragraphs
Emotions Chart
Editorial
Literary Report Card
Character Sketch
Character Rating Scale
SCAMPER
Literary Poster
Pictorial Outline
Journal Responses

EXPOSITORY TEXT STRATEGIES

Learning Logs
Four-Step Summary
Editorial
Discussion Web
Proposition/Support Outline
RAFT/Letters, Reports
SCAMPER (Expository)
Question, Clues, Response

Synthesis

NARRATIVE TEXT STRATEGIES

Character Sketch
Editorial
SCAMPER

EXPOSITORY TEXT STRATEGIES

Discussion Web
Editorial
Proposition Support Outline
Question, Clues, Response

Evaluate/Justify

NARRATIVE TEXT STRATEGIES

Character Rating Scale
Literary Report Card
Journal Response
Editorial

EXPOSITORY TEXT STRATEGIES

Discussion Web
Proposition Support Outline
Editorial

Create/Invent

NARRATIVE TEXT STRATEGIES

SCAMPER
Literary Poster
Pictorial Outline

EXPOSITORY TEXT STRATEGIES

RAFT/Letters, Reports
SCAMPER (Expository)

Appendix B—ThinkingWorks Strategies Aligned to Standards

Strategies Aligned to Language Arts Standards for Comprehending Expository Text (Informational, Technical, and Persuasive Text)

READING PROCESS

STANDARD: ACQUIRE VOCABULARY

Strategies to Acquire Vocabulary

Semantic Map
Concept Circles
Concept of a Definition
Concept of a Definition (Technical)
Personal Clues
Semantic Feature Analysis
Possible Sentences

STANDARD: SET A PURPOSE

Strategies to Set a Purpose

Problem/Solution Guide
Experience Text Relationship (ETR)
Quickwriting
Semantic Map
Anticipation Guide
Structured Overview
About Point Notetaking
Question Answer Relationship (QAR)
Questions for Quality Thinking
Thinking Minds
Question, Clues, Response
Reciprocal Teaching
KWL
KWL Plus
I-Chart
Frames

STANDARD: PREDICT

Strategies to Predict

Prediction/Prediction Chart
Exploration Frame/Science

STANDARD: INFER

Strategies to Infer

About Point
About Point Notetaking
Anticipation Guide
Exploration Frame/Science
Frames
I-Chart
KWL
KWL Plus
Question Answer Relationship (QAR)
Question, Clues, Response
Questions for Quality Thinking
Reciprocal Teaching
Thinking Minds

STANDARD: CONSTRUCT MAIN IDEAS AND DETAILS

Strategies to Construct Main Ideas and Details

About Point
About Point Notetaking
Four-Step Summary
Frames
KWL
KWL Plus
Reciprocal Teaching
I-Chart

STANDARD: QUESTION

Strategies to Question

I-Chart
KWL
KWL Plus
Question Answer Relationship (QAR)
Question, Clues, Response
Questions for Quality Thinking
Reciprocal Teaching
Thinking Minds

STANDARD: CLARIFY/MONITOR UNDERSTANDING

Strategies to Clarify/Monitor Understanding

About Point
About Point Notetaking
Frames
I-Chart
KWL
KWL Plus
Question Answer Relationship (QAR)
Question, Clues, Response
Questions for Quality Thinking
Reciprocal Teaching
Thinking Minds

STANDARD: USE TEXT FEATURES

Strategies to Use Text Features

I-Chart
KWL
KWL Plus
Structured Overview
Frames

STANDARD: DETERMINE CAUSE/EFFECT

Strategies to Determine Cause/Effect

Frames
Discussion Web
Proposition/Support Outline
Editorial

STANDARD: COMPARE/CONTRAST

Strategies to Compare/Contrast

Exploration Frame/Science
Frames
Question Answer Relationship (QAR)
Question, Clues, Response
Questions for Quality Thinking
SCAMPER
Compare/Contrast Venn Diagram

STANDARD: DETERMINE FACT/OPINION

Strategies to Determine Fact/Opinion

About Point
About Point Notetaking
Discussion Web
Frames
I-Chart
KWL
KWL Plus
Proposition/Support Outline
Question Answer Relationship (QAR)
Questions for Quality Thinking
Thinking Minds

STANDARD: CREATE AND USE GRAPHIC ORGANIZERS

Strategies to Create and Use Graphic Organizers

Frames
I-Chart
KWL
KWL Plus
Question, Clues, Response

STANDARD: SUMMARIZE

Strategies to Summarize

About Point
About Point Notetaking
Four-Step Summary
Frames
I-Chart
KWL Plus
Reciprocal Teaching

READING APPLICATIONS

STANDARD: ANALYZE TEXT

Strategies to Analyze Text

Discussion Web
Exploration Frame/Science
Frames
Proposition/Support Outline
Question Answer Relationship (QAR)
Question, Clues, Response
Questions for Quality Thinking
Thinking Minds
Reciprocal Teaching
Learning Logs
Editorial
RAFT/Letters, Reports
SCAMPER

STANDARD: CRITIQUE/EVALUATE TEXT

Strategies to Critique/Evaluate Text

Editorial
Question Answer Relationship (QAR)
Question, Clues, Response
Questions for Quality Thinking
Thinking Minds

STANDARD: ANALYZE AUTHOR'S PURPOSE/PERSPECTIVE

Strategies to Analyze Author's Purpose/Perspective

Discussion Web
Frames
Proposition/Support Outline
Question Answer Relationship (QAR)
Question, Clues, Response
Questions for Quality Thinking
Thinking Minds

STANDARD: RESPOND TO TEXT

Strategies to Respond to Text

About Point Writing Response
Discussion Web
Editorial
Journal Response
Learning Log
Proposition/Support Outline
Question, Clues, Response
RAFT/Letters, Reports
Thinking Minds

STANDARD: CONDUCT RESEARCH

Strategies to Conduct Research

Exploration Frame/Science
I-Chart
KWL
KWL Plus

STANDARD: SELECT MATERIALS/READ INDEPENDENTLY

Strategies to Select Materials and Read Independently

Discussion Web
Exploration Frame/Science
Frames
I-Chart
KWL
KWL Plus
Proposition/Support Outline
Question, Clues, Response
Questions for Quality Thinking

STANDARD: RECOMMEND TEXT TO OTHERS

Strategies to Recommend Text to Others

Discussion Web
Editorial
Proposition/Support Outline
RAFT/Letters, Reports

Strategies Aligned to Language Arts Standards for Comprehending Fictional Text

READING PROCESS

STANDARD: ACQUIRE VOCABULARY

Strategies to Acquire Vocabulary

Semantic Map
Concept Circles
Concept of a Definition
Personal Clues
Semantic Feature Analysis
Possible Sentences

STANDARD: SET A PURPOSE

Strategies to Set a Purpose

Problem Solution Guide
Experience Text Relationship
Quickwriting
Semantic Map
Anticipation Guide
Structured Overview
Personal Response/Literary Analysis
Prediction/Prediction Chart
Action Belief Chart
Story Grammar
Circle Story
Story Pyramid
Story Map from Characters' Perspectives
Plot Relationships Chart

STANDARD: PREDICT

Strategies to Predict

Prediction/Prediction Chart

STANDARD: INFER

Strategies to Infer

Prediction/Prediction Chart
Story Grammar
Circle Story
Story Pyramid
Plot Relationships Chart
Story Map from Characters' Perspective
Personal Response/Literary Analysis
Action Belief Chart

STANDARD: CONSTRUCT MAIN IDEAS/DETAILS

Strategies to Construct Main Ideas/Details

Prediction/Prediction Chart
Story Grammar
Circle Story
Story Pyramid
Plot Relationships Chart
Story Map from Characters' Perspectives
Personal Response/Literary Analysis
Action Belief Chart

STANDARD: QUESTION

Strategies to Question

Journal Response
Personal Response/Literary Analysis
Question Answer Relationship (QAR)
Question, Clues, Response
Questions for Quality Thinking
Thinking Minds

STANDARD: CLARIFY/MONITOR UNDERSTANDING

Strategies to Clarify/Monitor Understanding

Semantic Map
Personal Response/Literary Analysis
Prediction/Prediction Chart
Action Belief Chart
Story Grammar
Circle Story
Story Pyramid
Story Map from Characters' Perspectives
Probable Passage
Plot Relationships Chart

STANDARD: USE TEXT FEATURES

Strategies to Use Text Features

Circle Story
Plot Relationships Chart
Four-Step Summary/Chapter Books
Story Grammar
Story Map from Characters' Perspectives
Story Pyramid

STANDARD: COMPARE/CONTRAST TEXT ASPECTS

Strategies to Compare/Contrast Text Aspects

Compare/Contrast/Venn Diagram
Emotions Chart
Literary Report Card
Probable Passage
Personal Response/Literary Analysis
SCAMPER
Story Map from Characters' Perspectives

STANDARD: CREATE/USE GRAPHIC ORGANIZERS

Strategies to Create/Use Graphic Organizers

Action Belief Chart
Character Rating Scale
Compare/Contrast Venn Diagram
Editorial
Emotions Chart
Literary Report Card
Prediction Chart
RAFT/Letters, Reports
Story Grammar
Circle Story
Story Pyramid
Plot Relationships Chart
Story Map from Characters' Perspectives
Probable Passage

STANDARD: SUMMARIZE

Strategies to Summarize

Circle Story
Four-Step Summary/Chapter Books
Plot Relationships Chart
Probable Passage
Story Grammar
Story Map from Characters' Perspectives
Story Pyramid

READING APPLICATIONS

STANDARD: ANALYZE TEXT/LITERARY TECHNIQUES AND FEATURES

Strategies to Analyze Text

Action Belief Chart
Circle Story
Personal Response/Literary Analysis
Plot Relationships Chart

Story Grammar
Story Map from Characters' Perspectives
Story Pyramid
Emotions Chart
Literary Report Card
Character Rating Scale

STANDARD: CRITIQUE/EVALUATE TEXT

Strategies to Critique/Evaluate Text

Editorial
Personal Response/Literary Analysis

STANDARD: RESPOND TO TEXT

Strategies to Respond to Text

Editorial
Journal Response
Literary Poster
Pictorial Outline
RAFT/Letters, Reports

STANDARD: SELECT MATERIALS/READ INDEPENDENTLY

Strategies to Select Materials/Read Independently

Personal Response/Literary Analysis
Story Grammar
Circle Story
Story Pyramid
Story Map from Characters' Perspectives
Plot Relationships Chart

STANDARD: RECOMMEND TEXT TO OTHERS

Strategies to Recommend Text to Others

Editorial
Personal Response/Literary Analysis
RAFT/Letters, Reports

STANDARD: ANALYZE AUTHOR'S PURPOSE/PERSPECTIVE

Strategies to Analyze Author's Purpose/Perspective

Action Belief Chart
Character Rating Scale
Emotions Chart
Literary Report Card
Personal Response/Literary Analysis

Strategies Aligned to Language Arts Standards for Writing Expository Text

WRITING PROCESS

STANDARD: USE A PROCESS APPROACH TO WRITING

Strategies to Use a Process Approach to Writing

About Point Writing Response
Question, Clues, Response
KWL Plus
Frames/Summary
I-Chart
About Point Notetaking
Editorial
RAFT/Letters, Reports

STANDARD: USE TECHNOLOGICAL RESOURCES

Strategies to Use Technological Resources

Semantic Map
Quickwriting
KWL Plus
About Point
About Point Notetaking
I-Chart
Question, Clues, Response
Editorial
RAFT/Letters, Reports

WRITING APPLICATIONS

STANDARD: USE VARIOUS MODES OF WRITING

Strategies to Use Various Modes of Writing

Summary

KWL Plus
About Point/Summary
Frames/Summary
I-Chart
Four-Step Summary

Persuasive

Editorial
About Point Writing Response
Proposition/Support Outline
Discussion Web

Informational (Research, Reports, Essays)

KWL Plus
I-Chart
About Point Notetaking
Frames/Summary

Communication

RAFT/Letters, Reports
Editorial
Sequence Frame (applied to directions)
Journals (informal writing)

WRITING CONVENTIONS

STANDARD: USE WRITING CONVENTIONS

Strategies to Use Writing Conventions

About Point
Question, Clues, Response
Editorial
RAFT/Letters, Reports
KWL Plus
About Point Notetaking
Frames/Summary

EVALUATION

STANDARD: USE EVALUATIVE TOOLS

Strategies to Use Evaluative Tools

For evaluating use of strategies:
Rubrics
Checklists
Observation Notes

Strategies Aligned to Language Arts Standards for Writing Fictional Text

WRITING PROCESS

STANDARD: USE A PROCESS APPROACH TO WRITING

Strategies to Use a Process Approach to Writing

Semantic Map
Story Grammar/Summary
Circle Story/Summary
Story Pyramid/Summary
Story Map from Characters' Perspectives/Summary
Probable Passage
Plot Relationships Chart/Summary

STANDARD: USE TECHNOLOGICAL RESOURCES

Strategies to Use Technological Resources

Semantic Map
Story Grammar/Summary
Circle Story/Summary
Story Pyramid/Summary
Story Map from Characters' Perspectives/Summary
Probable Passage
Plot Relationships Chart/Summary

WRITING CONVENTIONS

STANDARD: USE WRITING CONVENTIONS

Strategies to Use Writing Conventions

Story Grammar/Summary
Circle Story/Summary
Story Pyramid/Summary
Story Map from Characters' Perspectives/Summary
Probable Passage
Plot Relationships Chart/Summary

WRITING APPLICATIONS

STANDARD: USE VARIOUS MODES OF WRITING

Strategies to Use Various Modes of Writing

Summary

Story Grammar
Story Pyramid
Plot Relationships Chart
Four-Step Summary/Chapter Books

Fictional Narrative

Probable Passage
SCAMPER
Story Grammar
Circle Story
Plot Relationships Chart
Story Pyramid
Story Map from Characters' Perspectives
Probable Passage

Personal Response Narrative

Character Sketch
Personal Response/Literary Analysis
SCAMPER
Journal Response
Literary Poster
Pictorial Outline
RAFT/Letters, Reports

Persuasive

Editorial
RAFT/Letters, Reports

Communication

RAFT/Letters
Editorial
Journals (Informal Writing)

EVALUATION

STANDARD: USE EVALUATIVE TOOLS

Strategies to Use Evaluative Tools

For evaluating use of strategies:
Rubrics
Checklists
Observation Notes

Strategies Aligned to Language Arts Standards for Discussing Expository Text (Informational, Technical, and Persuasive Text)

ORAL COMMUNICATION

STANDARD: INTERPRET IDEAS AND DRAW CONCLUSIONS

Strategies to Interpret Ideas and Draw Conclusions

KWL
KWL Plus
I-Chart
Question Answer Relationship (QAR)
Questions for Quality Thinking
Thinking Minds
Reciprocal Teaching
SCAMPER
Discussion Web

STANDARD: DEMONSTRATE ACTIVE LISTENING STRATEGIES

Strategies to Demonstrate Active Listening Strategies

Semantic Map
Problem Solution Guide
Experience Text Relationship
Knowledge Rating Scale
Anticipation Guide
Concept Circles
KWL
KWL Plus
I-Chart
Frames
Questions Answer Relationship (QAR)
Question, Clues, Response
Questions for Quality Thinking
Thinking Minds
Reciprocal Teaching
SCAMPER
Discussion Web
Compare/Contrast Venn Diagram

STANDARD: USE APPROPRIATE MODES OF PRESENTATION FOR AUDIENCES

Strategies to Use Appropriate Modes of Presentation for Audiences

Informational Presentations (research, expository)

KWL
KWL Plus
I-Chart
Frames/Summaries
Question, Clues, Response

Persuasive Presentations

Discussion Web

Strategies Aligned to Language Arts Standards for Discussing Fictional Texts

ORAL COMMUNICATION

STANDARD: DEMONSTRATE ACTIVE LISTENING STRATEGIES

Strategies to Demonstrate Active Listening Strategies

Semantic Map
Problem Solution Guide
Experience Text Relationship
Knowledge Rating Scale
Concept Circles
Story Grammar
Circle Story
Story Pyramid
Story Map from Characters' Perspectives
Plot Relationships Chart
Probable Passage
Action Belief Chart
Question Answer Relationship (QAR)
Question, Clues, Response
Questions for Quality Thinking
Thinking Minds
Literary Report Card
Character Rating Scale
Emotions Chart
Compare/Contrast Venn Diagram
Personal Response/Literary Analysis
Prediction/Prediction Chart
SCAMPER

STANDARD: USE APPROPRIATE MODES OF PRESENTATION FOR AUDIENCES

Strategies to Use Appropriate Modes of Presentation for Audiences

<u>Descriptive Presentations</u>

RAFT/Letters, Reports
Literary Poster
Character Sketch
Retelling/Summary
Probable Passage
SCAMPER
Pictorial Outline

<u>Persuasive Presentations</u>

Discussion Web

References

Alvermann, D.E. (1991). The discussion web: A graphic aid for learning across the curriculum. *The Reading Teacher, 45,* 92-99.

Alvermann, D.E., & Phelps, S.F. (1994). *Content reading and literacy.* Needham Heights, MA: Allyn and Bacon.

Anderson, R.C., & Pearson, P.D. (1984). A schema-thematic view of reading. In P.D. Pearson (Ed.), *Handbook of reading research* (pp. 295-291). New York: Longman.

Au, K. (1979). Using the experience-text-relationship method with minority children. *The Reading Teacher, 32,* 677-679.

Beach, R.W., & Marshall, J. (1991). *Teaching literature in the secondary school.* Orlando, FL: Harcourt, Brace, Jovanovich.

Beck, I., McKeown, M., Hamilton, R., & Kucan, L. (1997). *Questioning the author: An approach for enhancing student engagement with text.* Newark, DE: International Reading Association.

Beck, I., Perfetti, C., & McKeown, M. (1982). The effect of long-term vocabulary instruction on lexical access and reading comprehension. *Journal of Educational Psychology, 74,* 506-521.

Biemiller, A. (2001). Teaching vocabulary: Early, direct and sequential. *American Education, 25,* 25-28.

Blachowicz, C. (1986). Making connections: Alternatives to the vocabulary notebook. *Journal of Reading, 29,* 643-649.

Block, C.C. (2000). The case for exemplary instruction, especially for students who come to school without the precursors for literary success. *National Reading Conference Yearbook, 49,* 155-167.

Block, C.C., & Pressley, M. (2002). Introduction. In C.C. Block & M. Pressley (Eds.), *Comprehension instruction: Research based best practices* (pp. 1-7). New York: Guilford Press.

Bloom, B. (1956). *Taxonomy of educational objectives.* New York: David McKay.

Carr, E. (1985). The vocabulary overview guide: A metacognitive strategy to improve vocabulary comprehension and retention. *Journal of Reading, 21,* 684-689.

Carr, E. (January, 2000). Personal communication.

Carr, E. (March, 2000). Personal communication.

Carr. E., & Aldinger, L. (1994). *Thinking Works: Using cognitive processes in the language arts classroom.* Ann Arbor, MI: Exceptional Innovations.

Carr, E., Aldinger, L., & Patberg, J. (2000). *Thinking Works for early and middle childhood teachers.* Toledo, Ohio: ThinkingWorks.

Carr, E., Dewitz, P., & Ogle, D. (1988). A strategy to improve comprehension and summarization. Paper presented at the National Reading Conference, St. Petersburg, FL.

Carr, E., Dewitz, P., & Patberg, J. (1989). Using cloze for inference training with expository text. *The Reading Teacher, 42,* 380-385.

Carr, E., & Ogle, D. (1987). K-W-L Plus: A strategy for comprehension and summarization. *Journal of Reading, 30,* 626-631.

Carr, E., & Wixson, K. (1986). Guidelines for evaluating vocabulary instruction. *Journal of Reading, 29,* 588-595.

Costa, A., & Kallick, B. (2000). Changing perspectives about intelligence. In A. Costa & B. Kallick (Eds.), *Discovering and exploring habits of mind* (pp. 1-20). Alexandria, VA: Association for Supervision and Curriculum Development.

de Bono, E. (1985). *Six thinking hats.* Boston: Little, Brown.

de Bono, E. (1991). The CORT thinking program. In A. Costa (Ed.), *Developing minds: Programs for teaching thinking* (Rev. ed., Vol. 2, pp. 27-32). Alexandria, VA: Association for Supervision and Curriculum Development.

Duffy, G.G., & Roehler, L.R. (1982). Improving reading instruction through responsive elaboration. *The Reading Teacher, 40*, 514-520.

Duke, N.K., & Pearson, P.D. (2002). Effective practices for developing reading comprehension. In A.E. Farstrup & S.J. Samuels (Eds.), *What research has to say about reading instruction* (pp. 205-242). Newark, DE: International Reading Association.

Elbow, P. (1973). *Writing without teachers.* New York: Oxford University Press.

Ennis, R. (1985). Critical thinking: A definition. In A. Costa (Ed.), *Developing minds: A resource book for teaching thinking.* Alexandria, VA: Association for Supervision and Curriculum Development.

Farr, R. (1992). Putting it all together: Solving the reading assessment puzzle. *The Reading Teacher, 46*, 26-37.

Fitzgerald, J. (1983). Helping readers gain self-control over reading comprehension. *The Reading Teacher, 37*, 249-253.

Frager, A.M., & Thompson, L.C. (1985). Conflict: The key to critical reading instruction. *Journal of Reading, 28*, 676-683.

Freebody, P., & Anderson, R.C. (1983). Effects of vocabulary difficulty, text cohesion and schema availability on lexical access and reading comprehension. *Reading Research Quarterly, 18*, 277-299.

Fulweiler, T. (1982). Writing: An act of cognition. In C.W. Griffin (Ed.), Teaching writing in all disciplines. *New directions for teaching and learning* No.12 (pp. 15-26). San Francisco: Jossey-Bass.

Gambrell, L.B., & Bales, R.J. (1986). Mental imagery and the comprehension-monitoring performance of fourth and fifth grade poor readers. *Reading Research Quarterly, 21*, 454-464.

Graves, M., Juel. C., & Graves, B. (1998). *Teaching reading in the 21st century.* Boston: Allyn and Bacon.

Graves, M., & Watts-Taffe, S. (2002). The place of word consciousness in a research-based vocabulary program. In A.E. Farstrup & S.J. Samuels (Eds.), *What research has to say about reading instruction* (pp. 140-165). Newark, DE: International Reading Association.

Hammond, D. (1991). Prediction chart. In J. Macon, D. Bewell, & M.E. Vogt (Eds.), *Responses to literature* (pp. 11-12). Newark, DE: International Reading Association.

Heller, M. (1991). *Reading-writing connections from theory to practice.* White Plains, NY: Longman.

Hoffman, J. (1992). Critical reading/thinking across the curriculum: Using I-Charts to support learning. *Language Arts, 69*, 120-127.

Jett-Simpson, M. (1981). Writing stories using model structures: The circle story. *Language Arts, 58*, 293-300.

Johnson, T., & Louis, D. (1987). *Literacy through literature.* Portsmouth, NH: Heinemann.

Johnson, D.D., & Pearson, P.D. (1984). *Teaching reading vocabulary.* New York: Holt, Rinehart & Winston.

Jones, B.F., Pierce, J., & Hunter, B. (1988-89). Teaching students to construct graphic representations. *Educational Leadership, 46* (4), 20-25.

Lynch-Brown, C., & Tomlinson, C.M. (1993). *Essentials of children's literature.* Boston: Allyn and Bacon.

Macon, J., Bewell, D., & Vogt, M.E. (1991). *Responses to literature.* Newark, DE: International Reading Association.

Mandler, J., & Johnson, N. (1977). Remembrance of things parsed: Story structure and recall. *Cognitive Psychology*, 9, 115-151.

Manzo, A., & Manzo, U. (1990). *Content area reading: A heuristic approach.* Columbus, OH: Merrill.

Marshall, N. (1983). Using story grammar to assess reading comprehension. *The Reading Teacher*, 36, 176-179.

Martin, D.C., Lorton, M., Blanc, R.A., & Evans, C. (1977). *The learning center: A comprehensive model for colleges and universities.* Grand Rapids, MI: Central Trade Plant.

McTigue J., & Lyman, F. (1988). Cueing thinking in the classroom: The promise of theory-embedded tools. *Educational Leadership*, 45 (April), 18-24.

Moore, S.A., & Moore, D.W. (1992). Possible sentences. In E.K. Dishner, T.W. Bean, & J.E. Readence (Eds.), *Reading in the content areas: Improving classroom instruction* (3rd ed., pp. 196-201). Dubuque, IA: Kendall Hunt.

Ogle, D. (1986). The KWL: A teaching model that develops active reading of expository text. *The Reading Teacher*, 39, 564-570.

Ogle, D., & Blachowicz, C. (2002). Beyond literature circles: Helping students comprehend informational texts. In C.C. Block & M. Pressley (Eds.), *Comprehension Instruction: Research based best practices* (pp. 259-274). New York: Guilford Press.

Palincsar, A.M., & Brown, A.L. (1984). Reciprocal teaching of comprehension-fostering and comprehension-monitoring activities. *Cognition and Instruction*, 1, 117-175.

Palmatier, R.A. (1973). A notetaking system for learning. *Journal of Reading*, 17, 36-39.

Pappas, C., Keiffer, B., & Levstick, L. (1990). *An integrated language perspective in the elementary school.* New York: Longman.

Paris, S.C., Lipson, M.Y., & Wixson, K.K. (1983). Becoming a strategic reader. *Contemporary Educational Psychology*, 8, 293-316.

Pearson, P.D., & Duke, N. (2002). Comprehension instruction in the primary grades. In C.C. Block & M. Pressley (Eds.), *Comprehension instruction: Research based best practices* (pp. 247-258). New York: Guilford Press.

Pearson, P.D., & Gallagher, M.C. (1983). The instruction of reading comprehension. *Contemporary Educational Psychology*, 8, 317-344.

Pearson, P.D., & Johnson, D. (1984). *Teaching reading vocabulary.* New York: Holt, Rinehart & Winston.

Perkins, D. (1990). The nature and nurture of creativity. In B.F. Jones & Idol, L. (Eds.), *Dimensions of thinking and cognitive instruction* (pp. 415-443). Hillsdale, NJ: Lawrence Erlbaum.

Perkins, D. (1991). What creative thinking is. In A. Costa (Ed.), *Developing minds: Programs for teaching thinking* (pp. 85-88). Alexandria, VA: Association for Supervision and Curriculum Development.

Pressley, M. (2002). Comprehension strategies instruction: A turn-of-the-century status report. In C.C. Block & M. Pressley (Eds.), *Comprehension instruction: Research based best practices* (pp. 11-27). New York: Guilford Press.

Pressley, M., & Block, C.C. (2002). Summing up: What comprehension instruction could be. In C.C. Block & M. Pressley (Eds.), *Comprehension instruction: Research-based best practices* (pp. 383-392). New York: Guilford Press.

Pressley, M., Schuder, T., SAIL Faculty and Administration, Bergman, J.L., & Dinary, P.B. (1992). A researcher-educator collaborative interview study of transactional comprehension strategies instruction. *Journal of Educational Psychology*, 84, 231-246.

Prichert, J.A., & Anderson, R.C. (1977). Taking perspectives on a story. *Journal of Educational Psychology*, 69, 309-315.

Rosenblatt, L.M. (1989). Writing and reading: The transactional theory. In J.M. Mason (Ed.), *Reading and writing connections* (pp. 153-176). Boston: Allyn and Bacon.

Raphael, T.E. (1982). Question-answering strategies for children. *The Reading Teacher*, 36, 186-191.

Santa, C.M. (1988). *Content reading including study systems*. Dubuque, IA: Kendall Hunt.

Schaefer, L.M. (2001). *Teaching young writers: Strategies that work*. New York: Scholastic.

Schmidt, B., & Buckley, M. (1991). Plot Relationships Chart. In J. Macon, D. Bewell, & M.E. Vogt (Eds.), *Responses to literature* (pp. 7-8). Newark, DE: International Reading Association.

Shanahan, T., & Shanahan, S. (1997). Character perspective charting: Helping children to develop a more complete conception of a story. *The Reading Teacher*, 50, 668-677.

Smith, R.J., & Dauer, V.L. (1984). A comprehension monitoring strategy for reading content area materials. *Journal of Reading*, 28, 144-147.

Stanfill, S. (1978). The great American one-sentence summary. In A. Berger, O. Clapp, J. Golub, N. Nathan, R. Rodrigues, S. Seale, G. Stanford, & S. Yesner (Eds.), *Classroom practices in teaching classroom English* (pp. 47-49). Urbana, IL: National Council of Teachers of English.

Schwartz, R.M., & Raphael, T.E. (1985). Concept of a definition: A key to improving students' vocabulary. *The Reading Teacher*, 39, 198-204.

Taba, H. (1967). *Teachers' handbook for elementary social studies*. Reading, MA: Addison-Wesley.

Tharpe, R., & Gallimore, R. (1989). *Rousing minds to life: Teaching learning and schooling in social context*. Cambridge: Cambridge University Press.

Tierney, R.J. (1998). Literacy assessment reform: Shifting beliefs, principles, possibilities, and emerging practices. *The Reading Teacher*, 51, 374-390.

Trabasso, T., & Bouchard, E. (2002) Teaching readers how to comprehend text strategically. In C.C. Block & M. Pressley (Eds.), *Comprehension instruction: Research-based best practices* (pp. 176-200). New York: Guilford Press.

Vacca, R.T., & Vacca, J.L. (1999). *Content area reading: Literacy and learning across the curriculum* (6th ed.). New York: Longman.

Watts, S.M. (1995). Vocabulary instruction during reading lessons in six classrooms. *Journal of Reading Behavior*, 27, 399-424.

Williams, J. P. (2002). Using the theme scheme to improve story comprehension. In C.C. Block & M. Pressley (Eds.), *Comprehension instruction: Research-based best practices* (pp. 126-139). New York: Guilford Press.

Wolf, K. (1993). From informal to informed assessment: Recognizing the role of the classroom teacher. *Journal of Reading*, 36, 518-523.

Wood, K.D. (1984). Probable passages: A writing strategy. *The Reading Teacher*, 37, 496-499.

Zull, J. (2002). *The art of changing the brain*. Sterling, VA: Stylus Publishing.

LITERATURE-BASED CURRICULUM RESOURCES

Campbell Hill, B., Jackson, N.J., & Schlick Noe, K.L., Eds. (1995). *Literature circles and response*. Norwood, MA: Christopher-Gordon.

Daniels, H. (1994). *Literature circles: Voice and choice in the student-centered classroom.* York, ME: Stenhouse.

Hancock, M.R. (2000). *A celebration of literature and response: Children, books, and teachers in K-8 classrooms.* Upper Saddle River, NJ: Prentice-Hall.

McMahon, S., & Raphael, T., Eds. (1997). *The book club connection: Literacy learning and classroom talk.* New York: Teachers College Press.

Peterson, R., & Eeds, M. (1990). *Grand conversation: Literature groups in action.* New York: Scholastic.

Roser, N.L., & Martinez, M.G., Eds. (1995). *Book talk and beyond: Children and teachers respond to literature.* Newark, DE: International Reading Association.

Samway, K.D., & Whang, G. (1996). *Literature study circles in a multicultural classroom.* York, ME: Stenhouse.

ASSESSMENT RESOURCES

Bratcher, S. (1994). *Evaluating children's writing.* New York: St. Martin's Press.

Cohen, J.H., & Wiener, R.B. (2003). *Literary portfolio: Improving assessment, teaching, and learning.* Upper Saddle River, NJ: Pearson Education Inc.

Farris, P.J. (1997). *Language arts: Process, product, and assessment* (2nd Ed.). Madison, WI: Brown and Benchmark.

CHILDREN'S LITERATURE

Allard, H., & Marshall, J. (1977). *Miss Nelson is missing.* New York: Scholastic.

Armstong, W. (1969). *Sounder.* New York: Harper Collins.

Babbitt, N. (1970). *Knee-knock rise.* New York: Avon Books.

Babbitt, N. (1970). *The something.* New York: Dell Publications.

Babbitt, N. (1975). *Tuck everlasting.* New York: Farrar, Straus, & Giroux.

Brittain, B. (1982). *All the money in the world.* San Francisco: Harper Collins.

Brown, M. (1986). *Arthur's eyes.* New York: Little, Brown & Co.

Cannon, J. (1993). *Stellaluna.* San Diego: Harcourt Brace.

Cannon, J. (1997). *Verdi.* San Diego: Harcourt Brace.

Carle, E. (1985). *The very busy spider.* New York: Putnam.

Compton, J. (1994). *Ashpet.* New York: Holliday House.

Curtis, C. (1995). *The Watsons go to Birmingham – 1963.* New York: Bantam Doubleday-Dell Books for Young Readers.

dePaola, T. (1975). *Strega Nona.* New York: Simon & Schuster.

Drucker, M. (1993). *Jacob's rescue: A holocaust story.* New York: Bantam Doubleday.

Gardiner, J.R. (1980). *Stone Fox.* New York: Harper Collins.

Gonzales, L. (1999). *The bossy Gallito.* New York: Scholastic.

Hillert, M. (1963). *The three little pigs.* Columbus: Modern Curriculum.

Hutchins, P. (1986). *The doorbell rang.* New York: Scholastic.

Kasza, K. (1993). *The rat and the tiger.* New York: Putnam.

Keats, E.J. (1964). *Whistle for Willie.* New York: Puffin Books (Penguin Group).

Konigsburg, E.L. (1967). *From the mixed-up files of Mrs. Basil E. Frankweiler.* New York: Atheneum.

London, J. (1996). *Froggy goes to school.* New York: Viking Penguin.

Luenn, N. (1997). *Nessa's fish.* Old Tappan, NJ: Simon & Schuster.

Mayer, G. (1992). *Rosie's mouse.* Golden Book.

Mayhar, A. (1997). *The secret among the stones.* In Literature Works: A Collection of Readings-Collection 5 (pp. 240-251). Needham Heights, MA: Silver Burdett Ginn.

McCloskey, R. (1941). *Make way for ducklings.* New York: Viking Press.

O'Dell, S. (1970). *Sing down the moon.* New York: Bantam Doubleday.

Paulsen, G. (1987). *Hatchet.* New York: Penguin Books.

Polacco, P. (1990). *Babushka's doll.* New York: Simon & Schuster.

Reeves, N. (1992). *Into the mummy's tomb: The real-life discovery of Tutankhamen's treasures.* New York: Scholastic/Madison Press.

San Souci, R.D. (1989). *The talking eggs.* New York: Dell.

Scieszka, J. (1996). *The true story of the three little pigs.* New York: Viking Penguin.

Sendak, M. (1963). *Where the wild things are.* New York: Harper & Row.

Shulevitz, U. (1967). *One Monday morning.* New York: Macmillan.

Steig, W. (1983). *The amazing bone.* New York: Farrar, Straus, & Giroux.

Steptoe, J. (1992). *Mufaro's beautiful daughters.* New York: Lothrop, Lee, & Shepard.

Thaler, M. (1997). *Librarian from the Black Lagoon.* New York: Scholastic.

Van Allsburg, C. (1988). *Two bad ants.* Indianapolis: Houghton Mifflin.

White, E.B. (1952). *Charlotte's web.* New York: Harper Collins.

Wyeth, S. (1995). *Always my dad.* New York: Krops.

Wood, A. (1985). *King Bidgood's in the bathtub.* New York: Harcourt Brace Jovanovich.

Wordsworth, W. (1956). *I wandered lonely as a cloud.* In H.F. Foster & W. Thorp (Eds.), An Oxford Anthology of English Poetry (2nd Ed.), (p. 648). New York: Oxford University Press, (Original work published in 1807).

Zeinert, K. (1997). *The Amistad slave revolt.* North Haven, CT: Shoestring Press.

Directory of Graphic Organizers and Explanation Sheets on the CD

The CD attached to the inside back cover of *Teaching Comprehension* contains graphic organizers that go along with the strategies discussed in the book. On the CD, the strategies are grouped into four categories:

- Background Knowledge

- Vocabulary

- Comprehension

- Application/Extension

There is a folder for each category, and within each, the strategies appear alphabetically. For each strategy, there is an explanation page, which has _Exp.pdf at the end of its file name. If a strategy has a graphic organizer (and most do), the explanation page and the graphic organizer(s) are grouped in a subfolder labeled by the strategy. For example, in the Background Knowledge folder, the first strategy is the Anticipation Guide. The explanation page (Anticipation_Exp.pdf) and the graphic organizer (AnticipationGuide.pdf) appear in the subfolder labeled "Anticipation Guide." In addition to the strategy folders, there is an assessment folder that contains rubrics, checklists, a lesson plan template, and other forms. The directory below shows thumbnails of the graphic organizers for your convenience.

The files are in PDF format. You can use Acrobat Reader to open the files. If you do not have Acrobat Reader, you can download it for free from http://www.adobe.com; click on the "Get Adobe Acrobat" button.

Printing the Graphic Organizers

You may have to adjust your printer settings for the graphic organizers to print completely. All printers are different, but if you find the bottom of the page to be cut off, follow this procedure:

1. In Adobe Acrobat, go to the "File" menu and open "Page Setup."

2. Adjust the scale. Try printing at 97%, and continue adjusting until the page prints correctly.

3. Close the "Page Setup" window and print as usual.

BACKGROUND KNOWLEDGE STRATEGIES

ANTICIPATION GUIDE
(see page 115 for a description of this strategy)
- Anticipation_Exp.pdf
- Anticipation.pdf

EXPERIENCE TEXT RELATIONSHIP *(see page 91 for a description of this strategy)*
- ETR_Exp.pdf

PROBLEM/SOLUTION GUIDE *(see page 153 for a description of this strategy)*
- ProbSolution_Exp.pdf
- ProbSolution.pdf

QUICKWRITING
(see page 177 for a description of this strategy)
- Quickwriting_Exp.pdf
- Quick+Know.pdf

SEMANTIC MAP *(see page 39 for a description of this strategy)*
- Semantic_Exp.pdf
- Semantic.pdf

- Semantic2.pdf

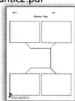

STRUCTURED OVERVIEW
(see page 141 for a description of this strategy)
- StructuredOverview_Exp.pdf

VOCABULARY STRATEGIES

CONCEPT CIRCLES
(see page 41 for a description of this strategy)
- ConceptCircle_Exp.pdf
- ConceptCircle1.pdf

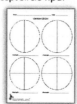

- ConceptCircle2.pdf

- ConceptCircle4.pdf

- ConceptCircle6.pdf

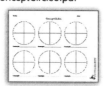

CONCEPT OF A DEFINITION *(see page 70 for a description of this strategy)*
- ConceptDef_Exp.pdf
- ConceptDef.pdf

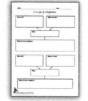

- ConceptDefTechnical_Exp.pdf
- ConceptDefTechnical.pdf

PERSONAL CLUES
(see page 144 for a description of this strategy)
- PersonalClue_Exp.pdf
- PersonalClue.pdf

POSSIBLE SENTENCES
(see page 94 for a description of this strategy)
- PossibleSentences_Exp.pdf
- PossibleSentences.pdf

SEMANTIC ANALYSIS
(see page 179 for a description of this strategy)
- SemanticAnalysis_Exp.pdf
- SemanticAnalysis1.pdf

- SemanticAnalysis2.pdf

COMPREHENSION STRATEGIES

ABOUT POINT *(see page 21 for a description of this strategy)*
- AboutPoint_Exp.pdf
- AboutPoint.pdf

- AboutPointNote.pdf

ACTION BELIEF
(see page 82 for a description of this strategy)
- ActionBelief_Exp.pdf
- ActionBelief.pdf

CAUSE/EFFECT FRAME
(see page 151 for a description of this strategy)
- CauseEffectFrame_Exp.pdf
- CauseEffectFrame1.pdf

- CauseEffectFrame2.pdf

- CauseEffectFrame3.pdf

- CauseEffectFrame4.pdf

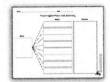

CIRCLE STORY (see page 54 for a description of this strategy)
- CircleStory_Exp.pdf
- CircleStory1.pdf

- CircleStory2.pdf

- CircleStory3.pdf

- CircleStory4.pdf

- CircleStory5.pdf

COMPARE/CONTRAST FRAME (see page 150 for a description of this strategy)
- CompareContrastFrame_Exp.pdf
- CompareContrastFrame1.pdf

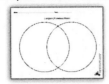

- CompareContrastFrame2.pdf

- CompareContrastFrame3.pdf

- CompareContrastFrame4.pdf

- CompareContrastFrame5.pdf

DESCRIPTION FRAME (see page 230 for a description of this strategy)
- DescFrame_Exp.pdf
- DescFrame1.pdf

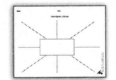

- DescFrame2.pdf

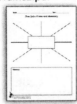

- SimpleList.pdf

- SimpleList+Sum.pdf

EXPLORATION FRAME (see page 156 for a description of this strategy)
- ExplorationFrame_Exp.pdf
- ExplorationFrame.pdf

I-CHART (see page 131 for a description of this strategy)
- I-Chart_Exp.pdf
- I-Chart1.pdf

- I-Chart2.pdf

- I-Chart3.pdf

KWL AND KWL PLUS (see page 120 for a description of this strategy)
- KWL_Exp.pdf
- KWL.pdf

- KWL+Map.pdf

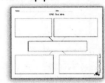

LITERARY ANALYSIS (see page 121 for a description of this strategy)
- LiteraryAnalysis_Exp.pdf
- LiteraryAnalysis.pdf

PERSONAL RESPONSE (see page 95 for a description of this strategy)
- PersonalResponse_Exp.pdf
- PersonalResponse.pdf

PLOT RELATIONSHIP (see page 59 for a description of this strategy)
- PlotRel_Exp.pdf
- PlotRelChart.pdf

- PlotRelSum.pdf

PREDICTION CHART
(see page 106 for a description of this strategy)
- PredictionChart_Exp.pdf
- PredictionChart.pdf

PROBABLE PASSAGES
(see page 81 for a description of this strategy)
- ProbPassage_Exp.pdf
- ProbPassage.pdf

PROBLEM/SOLUTION FRAME *(see page 153 for a description of this strategy)*
- ProblemSolution_Exp.pdf
- ProblemSolution1.pdf

- ProblemSolution2.pdf

- ProblemSolution3.pdf

QUESTION ANSWER RELATIONSHIP
(see page 182 for a description of this strategy)
- QAR_Exp.pdf

QUESTION, CLUES, RESPONSE *(see page 184 for a description of this strategy)*
- QuesCluesRes_Exp.pdf
- QuesCluesRes1.pdf

- QuesCluesRes2.pdf

QUESTIONS FOR QUALITY THINKING
(see page 187 for a description of this strategy)
- QuesQualThinking_Exp.pdf
- QuesQualThinking.pdf

RECIPROCAL TEACHING
(see page 196 for a description of this strategy)
- ReciprocalTeaching_Exp.pdf

SEQUENCE FRAME
(see page 149 for a description of this strategy)
- SequenceFrame_Exp.pdf
- SequenceFrame.pdf

STORY CHART
(see page 48 for a description of this strategy)
- StoryChart_Exp.pdf
- StoryChart1.pdf

- StoryChart2.pdf

STORY GRAMMAR
(see page 45 for a description of this strategy)
- StoryGram_Exp.pdf
- StoryGram1.pdf

- StoryGram2.pdf

- StoryGram3.pdf

- StoryGram4.pdf

STORY GRAMMAR (continued)

- StoryGramChptBk.pdf

STORY MAP *(see page 72 for a description of this strategy)*
- StoryMap_Exp.pdf
- StoryMap.pdf

STORY PYRAMID
(see page 57 for a description of this strategy)
- StoryPyramid_Exp.pdf
- StoryPyramid.pdf

THINKING MINDS
(see page 191 for a description of this strategy)
- ThinkingMinds_Exp.pdf
- ThinkingMinds.pdf

ABOUT POINT WRITING RESPONSE *(see page 119 for a description of this strategy)*
- AboutPointWtgRes_Exp.pdf
- AboutPointWtgRes1.pdf

- AboutPointWtgRes2.pdf

CHARACTER RATING
(see page 247 for a description of this strategy)

- CharacterRating_Exp.pdf
- CharacterRating1.pdf

- CharacterRating2.pdf

CHARACTER SKETCH
(see page 27 for a description of this strategy)

- CharacterSketch_Exp.pdf
- CharacterSketch1.pdf

- CharacterSketch2.pdf

COMPARE/CONTRAST VENN
(see page 76 for a description of this strategy)

- CompareContrastVenn_Exp.pdf
- CompareContrastVenn1.pdf

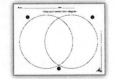

- CompareContrastVenn2.pdf

DISCUSSION WEB
(see page 159 for a description of this strategy)

- DiscussionWeb_Exp.pdf
- DiscussionWeb.pdf

EDITORIAL *(see page 164 for a description of this strategy)*

- Editorial_Exp.pdf
- Editorial.pdf

EMOTIONS CHART
(see page 63 for a description of this strategy)

- EmotionChart_Exp.pdf
- EmotionChart.pdf

FOUR-STEP SUMMARY
(see page 194 for a description of this strategy)

- FourStepSum_Exp.pdf
- FourStepSum1.pdf

- FourStepSum2.pdf

JOURNAL RESPONSE
(see page 102 for a description of this strategy)

- JournalResponse_Exp.pdf

LEARNING LOG
(see page 200 for a description of this strategy)

- LearningLog_Exp.pdf

LITERARY POSTER
(see page 109 for a description of this strategy)

- LiteraryPoster_Exp.pdf

LITERARY REPORT CARD
(see page 49 for a description of this strategy)

- LiteraryReportCard_Exp.pdf
- LiteraryReportCard1.pdf

- LiteraryReportCard2.pdf

- LiteraryReportCard3.pdf

- LiteraryReportCard4.pdf

PICTORAL OUTLINE
(see page 110 for a description of this strategy)

- PictoralOutline_Exp.pdf

PROPOSITION SUPPORT
(see page 162 for a description of this strategy)

- PropositionSupport_Exp.pdf
- PropositionSupport.pdf

RAFT *(see page 122 for a description of this strategy)*

- RAFT_EXP.pdf
- RAFT.pdf

SCAMPER
(see page 85 for a description of this strategy)

- SCAMPER_Narr_EXP.pdf
- SCAMPER_Exp_EXP.pdf
- SCAMPER.pdf

Index

Summary A 166